Engaging Crystallization in Qualitative Research

For Dr. Patrice M. Buzzanell and Dr. Carolyn Ellis
with admiration, gratitude, and love

Engaging Crystallization in Qualitative Research
An Introduction

Laura L. Ellingson
Santa Clara University

$SAGE

Los Angeles • London • New Delhi • Singapore

For information:

SAGE Publications, Inc.
2455 Teller Road
Thousand Oaks,
   California 91320
E-mail: order@sagepub.com

SAGE Publications Ltd.
1 Oliver's Yard
55 City Road
London EC1Y 1SP
United Kingdom

SAGE Publications India Pvt. Ltd.
B 1/I 1 Mohan Cooperative
   Industrial Area
Mathura Road, New Delhi 110 044
India

SAGE Publications
   Asia-Pacific Pte. Ltd.
33 Pekin Street #02-01
Far East Square
Singapore 048763

Printed in the United States of America

Library of Congress Cataloging-in-Publication Data

Ellingson, Laura L.
Engaging crystallization in qualitative research: An introduction/Laura L. Ellingson.
   p. cm.
Includes bibliographical references and index.
ISBN 978-1-4129-5906-3 (cloth)
ISBN 978-1-4129-5907-0 (pbk.)
   1. Qualitative research—Methodology. 2. Social sciences—Methodology.
I. Title.
H62.E493 2009
001.4—dc22   2008011097

Printed on acid-free paper

08   09   10   11   12   10   9   8   7   6   5   4   3   2   1

Acquiring Editor:	Todd R. Armstrong
Editorial Assistant:	Aja Baker
Production Editor:	Sarah K. Quesenberry
Copy Editor:	Teresa Wilson
Typesetter:	C&M Digitals (P) Ltd.
Proofreader:	Wendy Jo Dymond
Cover Designer:	Candice Harman
Cover Art:	Kathleen Peabody
Cover Designer:	Arup Giri
Marketing Manager:	Carmel Schrire

BRIEF CONTENTS

DETAILED CONTENTS

PREFACE

———◆·◆·◆———

WHY CRYSTALLIZATION?

I came to crystallization out of necessity. I needed a framework, a methodological path that I could follow that would enable me to construct and articulate multiple lived truths, rather than force me to choose among them. In 1999, having completed my master's thesis mentored by Dr. Patrice Buzzanell, an outstanding feminist organizational communication scholar, and working on my PhD with Dr. Carolyn Ellis, a leading proponent of autoethnography (i.e., personal narrative scholarship), I felt schizophrenic. I reveled in writing systematic, thorough, engaging grounded theory analyses with concrete pragmatic and theoretical applications, and I gloried in writing evocative narratives. Burke (1973) recommended that we "use all there is to use" (p. 23) in our work, and I wanted to do just that. While I never felt any internal conflict between my personal narrative work and my inductive qualitative analyses, others did, including my doctoral committee. "You can't have it all; pick something" was the initial consensus.

Depending upon the courses I took each term, I divided my ethnographic work up into autoethnography, narrative ethnography, feminist critique, and grounded theory analyses, all while conducting participant observation at a local cancer center. I felt confused, even angry for a while. Why did I have to choose? If the academic table has space for a wide variety of research approaches (e.g., Lindlof & Taylor, 2002), then I wanted to take up some room. When I found myself at this crossroads between social constructionist grounded theory informed by feminist (and postmodern) sensibilities on one side, and autoethnography and ethnographic narratives that privileged story over theory and evocative details over patterns on the other, I felt stuck. No one specifically forbade me to do both, but underlying tensions proved difficult to resolve, and a nagging sense of disloyalty to the different "camps" in the field of qualitative methods persisted. Scholars reading my grounded theory analysis of health communication contexts largely ignored my narrative work (although that has been changing; see Harter, Japp, & Beck, 2005), and no one interested in my embodied cancer survivor-qua-health care ethnographer autoethnographic narratives (Ellingson, 1998) appeared interested in (read: would publish) thematic analysis of communication in those health care contexts that I wrote in social science prose. Unsurprisingly, I turned to different publication outlets for the differing genres of ethnographic work I produced. I still felt no contradiction or sense of hypocrisy in showing *and* telling, but I encountered considerable resistance from mentors and colleagues who urged me to focus on one or the other.

I found a workable solution for my project and later my book, *Communicating in the Clinic* (Ellingson, 2005a) and other work (e.g., Ellingson, 2007), in the form of crystallization, a methodological framework I developed for bringing together not just different forms of data and analysis (as in multimethod research), but also different genres and forms of sense making within interpretive methodology. The framework is grounded in Richardson's (1994, 2000b) concept of qualitative *crystallization* as a postmodern reimagining of traditional, (post)positivist methodological triangulation (i.e., validating findings through mixed methods research design) as a messy, multigenre, paradigm-spanning approach to resisting the art/science dichotomy.

This book strikes a balance between establishing a theoretical, epistemological, and methodological foundation for understanding crystallization and providing hands-on strategies for practicing it. Crystallization continues to emerge for me and for others practicing boundary-spanning work; its parameters and processes are not fixed, and I wrote this book as an invitation to others to join me in further developing this framework. Also, while many researchers are practicing a wide variety of qualitative methods and mixed methodologies, relatively few currently produce multigenre work that reflects widely divergent forms of knowledge in a text or series of related texts focusing on a single topic. Hence, readers will notice a heavy reliance on my work and that of several others as core exemplars to illustrate strategies articulated here. I look forward to citing a proliferation of multigenre work in many disciplines in the future. Finally, although I endeavor to define terms as I invoke them, the book nonetheless presumes basic knowledge of qualitative methods and is intended to be used by scholars versed in such methods or by students accompanied by an introductory text (for good introductions to the field of qualitative methods, see Berg, 2007; Creswell & Clark, 2006; Lindlof & Taylor, 2002; Morse & Field, 1995; Morse & Richards, 2002).

ACKNOWLEDGMENTS

———•◦•———

T he support of a great number of people gave me the strength to finish this book. I offer my warmest thanks:

To my friends and colleagues at Santa Clara University (SCU), especially SunWolf who told me that it was time to write another book and kindly kept after me until I did. And to Leslie Gray, Linda Kamas, Betty Young, and Linda Garber who inspire me with a combination of their own impressive work and their enthusiastic cheering for mine across disciplinary divides. And to Hsin-I Cheng, my new and brilliant colleague who offers a wonderful perspective and lots of fun. To my outstanding research assistant, Kathleen Peabody, whose attention to detail, sharp editorial sense, and outstanding organizational skills made the completing of this book a much less stressful process. The nurturing of my "sabbatical support group" and of so many of the members of the SCU Women Faculty Group, Women's and Gender Studies Program, and Women's Reading Group keep me buoyant in the face of a hectic schedule, while Chris Changras, Helen Otero, and Vicky Arafa provide me friendship and administrative support in equal measure—my deepest gratitude.

To the Markula Center for Applied Ethics at SCU for awarding me a Hackworth Research Award and to the SCU Provost's office for the publication grant to support this work and for the research sabbatical that enabled me to complete it.

To the members of the Organization for the Study of Communication, Language, and Gender (www.osclg.org) who inspire, teach, and co-mentor with me, all while sharing chocolate and laughter—you are too many to list, and my gratitude for you is boundless. And to my colleague-friends without whom the communication discipline would be a lonely and passionless place for me, especially Patty Sotirin, Lainey Jenks, Lynn Harter, Kathy Propp, Deb Walker, Melanie Mills, Shirley Drew, and Patricia Geist-Martin. To the graduate students and recent PhDs who gifted me with the opportunity to pass on some of the wonderful feminist mentoring I have received over the years, especially Nicole, Jenn, Marie, and Maggie.

To Todd Armstrong at SAGE for his faith in my project, and to Aja Baker, Sarah Quesenberry, and Teresa Wilson for all their attention to detail throughout the production process. A special thanks to the reviewers who provided me with wonderfully constructive and encouraging feedback on an earlier draft of this work, including: Patrice M. Buzzanell (Purdue University), Patricia Geist-Martin (San Diego State University), Lynn M. Harter (Ohio University), Michelle Miller-Day (Pennsylvania State University), Robyn V. Remke (Copenhagen Business School), Patty Sotirin (Michigan Technological University), and Lynn H. Turner (Marquette University).

To so many of my family for their love and support of me: Jim, Brigitte, Zac, Jamie, Mark, Diane, Miette, my parents Jane and Larry, Eric, Elizabeth, Sam, Nina, Barbara, Janice, and Beloved Auntie Joan. And to my chosen family, Genni, Steve, Marissa, and Matt for the joy of being their sister and aunty.

To good friends who add so much to my life: Matt and Mary Bell, Lisa Osteraas, Geoffrey Mundon, Elizabeth Curry, Mary and Eric Kleppinger, and the indefatigable early morning crew: Connie, Kim, Pauline, Robin, and Sarah.

To Patrice Buzzanell and Carolyn Ellis, whose feminist mentoring made all my work at the intersections of qualitative research and communication possible, and whose belief in me makes all the difference.

And to my beloved life partner Glenn, whose love and faith in me proves unshakable, again and again—I am grateful for you each and every day.

ONE

INTRODUCTION TO CRYSTALLIZATION

———•◆•◆•———

Truth is therefore not abstract and other-worldly, but concrete, particular and sensuous—while at the same time being open, *in an ongoing state of new creation by the actors, transcending the boundaries between the ordinary and the fabulous.*

—Alvesson and Sköldberg
(2000, p. 175, original emphasis)

Qualitative methods illuminate both the ordinary within the worlds of fabulous people and events and also the fabulous elements of ordinary, mundane lives. How to represent the truths we generate remains an open question. The interpretive turn in social sciences, education, and allied health fields inspired a wide variety of creative forms of representation of qualitative findings, including narratives, poetry, personal essays, performances, and mixed-genre/multimedia texts as alternatives to the hegemony of traditional social scientific research reporting strategies that pervaded the academy (e.g., Denzin, 1997). At the same time, scholars updated traditionally positivist or postpositivist approaches to grounded theory (inductive, constant comparative) analysis (Glaser & Strauss, 1967; Strauss & Corbin, 1990) by bringing them around the interpretive turn and situating them in social constructivist (Charmaz, 2000), postmodern (Clarke, 2005), and social justice/activist (Charmaz, 2005) frameworks. In both inductive analytic (e.g., grounded theory) and more artistic approaches to qualitative research, researchers abandoned claims of objectivity in favor of focusing on the situated researcher and the social construction of meaning.

However, the emphasis or focus of qualitative work differs markedly depending upon where researchers situated themselves along the continuum of qualitative methods. For some, the arrival of new artistic genres of representation—what Richardson (2000b) calls *creative analytic practices* that embody both rigorous data analysis and creative forms of representation—meant the end of the desire to utilize traditional research reporting strategies in their own work (e.g., Behar, 1996). Others rejected creative analytic work as merely experimental, or even possibly dangerous (e.g., Atkinson, 1997). Still others find new genres intriguing, but only as secondary representational strategies (Morse, 2004). Many researchers do not wish to abandon conventional forms of analysis as the primary outcomes of qualitative research because these analyses accomplish important goals: They highlight patterns in the data; privilege researchers' sense making by sublimating participants' voices in support of explicating themes or patterns in the data; and generate theoretical and conceptual insights, as well as pragmatic suggestions for improving practices and policy (e.g., Charmaz, 2000). My development of crystallization as a framework builds upon a rich tradition of diverse practices in ethnography and qualitative representation (see Clair's history of ethnography, 2003; Denzin & Lincoln's overview of the sociohistorical "moments" of qualitative methods, 2005). Now as always, wonderfully productive dissention—philosophical, practical, analytic, ethical—exists in the field of qualitative methodology (e.g., Potter, 1996), generating a myriad of opportunities for collecting, analyzing, and representing data and findings.

In the remainder of the chapter, I describe Richardson's (1994, 2000b) original conceptualization of crystallization, briefly overview the concept of genre and the continuum of qualitative methods, and offer a definition, principles, and types of crystallization as a framework for conducting qualitative research. Consideration of the benefits and limitations of crystallization follows, as well as an overview of two exemplars and a preview of the organization of this book. The chapter concludes with a "frequently asked questions" section and an interlude describing my authorial perspective.

CONSTRUCTING CRYSTALLIZATION

Sociologist Laurel Richardson (1994, 2000b; Richardson & St. Pierre, 2005) broadly introduced the concept of crystallization to qualitative methodologists in her now classic essay, "Writing as a Method of Inquiry." Richardson articulated crystallization in qualitative research as the capacity for writers to break out of traditional generic constraints:

> The scholar draws freely on his or her productions from literary, artistic, and scientific genres, often breaking the boundaries of each of those as well. In these productions, the scholar might have different "takes" on the same topic, what I think of as a postmodernist deconstruction of triangulation. . . . In postmodernist mixed-genre texts, we do not triangulate, we *crystallize*. . . . I propose that the central image for "validity" for postmodern texts is not the triangle—a rigid, fixed, two-dimensional object. Rather, the central imaginary is the crystal, which combines symmetry and substance with an infinite variety of shapes, substances, transmutations, multidimensionalities, and angles of approach. . . . Crystallization provides us with a deepened, complex, thoroughly partial, understanding of the topic. Paradoxically, we know more and doubt what we know. Ingeniously, we know there is always more to know. (Richardson, 2000b, p. 934, original emphasis)

Few outside of the community of those writing about ethnography and autoethnography use the term crystallization, but signs indicate that qualitative researchers are moving toward practices that reflect it, especially in their embracing of narrative representations and resistance to social scientific writing conventions, in communication (e.g., Defenbaugh, in press; Drew, 2001; Jago, 2006), sociology (Ronai, 1995), anthropology (Behar, 1996), nursing (Sandelowski, Trimble, Woodard, & Barroso, 2006), clinical social work (Carr, 2003), and aging studies/gerontology (Baker & Wang, 2006).

Feminist theorists and methodologists have long posited such disruption of conventional methodological practices as positive interventions into hegemonic (masculinist) disciplinary norms (Cook & Fonow, 1990; Fine, 1994; Harding, 1987; Mies, 1983; Nielsen, 1990; Spitzack & Carter, 1989). Eschewing the objectivity/subjectivity dichotomy, feminist researchers have often "combine[d] objective approaches with experiential strategies, balancing the empirical with the subjective, receptivity with authority, and the power of discourse with the irresistible evidence of women's lives" (Roof, 2007, p. 426). Crystallization's roots lie deep within the creative and courageous work of feminist methodologists who blasphemed the boundaries of art and science long before I did, irrevocably shaping my own thinking on methodology, and paving the way for the work of this book.

While Richardson (2000b) provided citations for others whose work she regarded as reflecting crystallization (e.g., Walkerdine, 1990), she did not explain crystallization as a methodological framework or process. Other researchers and methodologists detailed intriguing methodological processes (e.g., Thorp, 2006), but without connecting them to the concept of crystallization per se. I forged a path toward articulating crystallization as an emergent framework for qualitative research in order to accomplish my multigenre goals for ethnographic and other qualitative work. I do not promote a rigid, recipe-like, or formulaic approach to crystallization, but instead sought to provide a map of the terrain to guide those seeking to learn more, who could benefit from specificity and instructions. I have thus developed Richardson's original concept into a nuanced framework for qualitative research projects and a detailed set of recommended practices, defined as follows: Crystallization combines multiple forms of analysis and multiple genres of representation into a coherent text or series of related texts, building a rich and openly partial account of a phenomenon that problematizes its own construction, highlights researchers' vulnerabilities and positionality, makes claims about socially constructed meanings, and reveals the indeterminacy of knowledge claims even as it makes them.

Crystallization fits within social constructionist (e.g., Gergen, 1999; Holstein & Gubrium, 2008) and critical paradigms (e.g., feminism; Reinharz, 1992). Scholars who embrace a wide range of methods, practices, and perspectives can adapt crystallization to their needs and goals. The only position crystallization does not complement is positivism; researchers who truly believe in objectivity and the discovery of ahistorical, unbiased, universal truth will not find crystallization amenable. However, as Atkinson (2006) points out, very few researchers actually subscribe to such a perspective, with most acknowledging the impossibility of eliminating subjective influence from research processes. Virtually all qualitative researchers may benefit from understanding the principles of crystallization, even those who choose not to practice it. Awareness of these ideas serves to widen our methodological and epistemological horizons, enriching understanding of the breadth and depth of qualitative methodology (see Chapter 2 for a discussion of epistemology, or theories of knowledge). Crystallization does not depart radically from other recent developments in the wide field of qualitative methodology, but rather offers one valuable way of thinking through the links between grounded theory (and other systematic analyses) and creative genres of representation.

Crystallization necessitates seeing the field of methodology not as an art/science dichotomy but as existing along a continuum from positivism (i.e., scientific research that claims objectivity) through radical interpretivism (i.e., scholarship as art). Art and science do not oppose one another; they anchor ends of a continuum of methodology, and most of us situate ourselves somewhere in the vast middle ground (Ellis & Ellingson, 2000). When scholars argue that we cannot include narratives alongside analysis or poems within grounded theory, they operate under the assumption that art and science negate one another and hence are incompatible, rather than merely differ in some dimensions (see Krieger, 1991). Since my explanation of crystallization assumes a basic understanding of the complexities involved in combining methods and genres from across regions of the continuum, I will briefly discuss the meaning of genre and then outline a continuum of qualitative methods before continuing with my development of crystallization.

CONSIDERING GENRES

Crystallization involves multigenre representations; thus, we should consider what counts as a genre. Campbell and Jamieson (1995) define genres as

> groups of discourses which share substantive, stylistic, and situational characteristics. Or, put differently, in the discourses that form a genre, similar substantive and stylistic strategies are used to encompass situations perceived as similar by the responding rhetors. A genre is a group of acts unified by a constellation of forms that recurs in each of its members. These forms, *in isolation,* appear in other discourses. What is distinctive about the acts in a genre is the recurrence of the forms *together* in constellation. (p. 403, original emphasis)

Qualitative research traditionally appears in what might be termed the research report genre, grounded originally in positivist conventions, with some stylistic and substantive changes over time. Stylistically, this form favors technical language, explication of processes, making of defined claims supported by pieces of evidence from the data set, and a discussion of implications of the work. Other more artistic genres now in use to present qualitative research differ significantly from the report genre; the substantive and stylistic strategies used to present findings in creative genres such as performances, films, poetry, narratives, and so on, bear little resemblance to those of reports and vary considerably among themselves. Labeling discourse or artifacts as belonging to a particular genre involves not neutral description but an act of criticism: "As the critic conceives an object of criticism, so will he or she assess it" (W. R. Fisher, 1980, p. 290). Genres do not reflect natural categories but inductively derived generalizations based on existing discourse, and their value lies only in "the degree of illumination they provide in regard to the working and worth of an instance of discourse" (W. R. Fisher, 1980, p. 294). Determining a work to be of a particular genre may be helpful in understanding, constructing, critiquing, and/or applying it, yet there are no neutral choices of how to represent qualitative findings. Researchers need not constrain themselves with the traditional limits of genres in qualitative research, and crystallization provides a path toward pushing or even breaking the generic boundaries. Over time, genres do not remain pure; blending of generic elements may develop into what some call rhetorical hybrids, "a metaphor intended to emphasize the productive but transitory character of the combinations" (Jamieson & Campbell, 1982, p. 147). Hybrid representations of qualitative research continue to develop as researchers move outside the limitations of traditional research genres. Reports remain useful, however. There is no need to replace genres with which you are familiar or to view them as in competition with other genres; rather, I encourage you to be open to selecting genres that best represent the truths in your research. I discuss a wide range of genres in Chapter 3; for now, I turn to a discussion of the continuum of qualitative methods.

RESISTING DICHOTOMIES:
A CONTINUUM OF QUALITATIVE METHODS

A continuum approach to mapping the field of qualitative methodology constructs a nuanced range of possibilities to describe what many others have socially constructed as dichotomies (i.e., mutually exclusive, paired opposites) such as art/science, hard/soft, and qualitative/quantitative (Potter, 1996). Dichotomous thinking remains the default mode of the academy. "Language, and thus meaning, depends on a system of differences," explains Gergen

(1994). "These differences have been cast in terms of binaries. . . . All are distinguished by virtue of what they are not" (p. 9). Nowhere is this evidenced more strongly than in the quantitative/qualitative divide. Even within the qualitative field itself polarities mark the differences between interpretivists and realists (Anderson, 2006; Atkinson, Coffey, Delamont, Lofland, & Lofland, 2001; Ellis & Bochner, 2006).

Moving beyond defining art as "not science" and science as "not art" takes some creative thinking. Building upon Ellis's (2004) representation of the two ends of the qualitative continuum (i.e., art and science) and the analytic mapping of the continuum developed in Ellis and Ellingson (2000; see also Deetz's 2001 conceptualization of research as emerging along a "local/emergent—elite/a priori" axis), I envision the continuum as having three main areas, with infinite possibilities for blending and moving among them (see Figure 1.1).

As exemplified in Figure 1.1, the goals, questions posed, methods, writing styles, vocabularies, role(s) of researchers, and criteria for evaluation vary across the continuum as we move from a realist/positivist social science stance on the far right, through a social constructionist middle ground, to an artistic/interpretive paradigm on the left. Each of these general approaches offers advantages and disadvantages, and none of them is mutually exclusive. Moreover, no firm boundaries exist to delineate the precise scope of left/middle/right; these reflect ideal types only, and I do not intend to replace the art/science dichotomy with an equally rigid three-category system. Furthermore, terms of demarcation and description used throughout the continuum (e.g., interpretive, postpositivist) are suspect and contestable; use of key terminology in qualitative methods remains dramatically inconsistent across disciplines, paradigms, and methodological communities (Potter, 1996). K. I. Miller (2000) warns that too much emphasis on categorizing types of researchers or research orientations can serve to constrain researchers into thinking and acting in accordance with their perceptions of their researcher type rather than pursuing important research questions regardless of the categories they reflect. My goal is to move readers past dualistic partitioning of qualitative methods into art and science, and instead to encourage you to conceptualize productive blending of the two. Such middle-ground approaches need not represent a compromise or a lowering of artistic or scientific standards. Rather, they can signal innovative approaches to sense making and representation. The continuum holds heuristic value in its embodiment of a range of opportunities, a topic that will be more fully explored throughout this book, particularly in Chapters 2 and 3.

Figure 1.1 Qualitative Continuum

	Qualitative Continuum		
	Art/Impressionist	**Middle-Ground Approaches**	**Science/Realist**
Goals	To unravel accepted truths To construct personal truths To explore the specific To generate art	To construct situated knowledges To explore the typical To generate description and understanding To trouble the taken-for-granted To generate pragmatic implications for practitioners	To discover objective truth To generalize to larger population To explain reality "out there" To generate scientific knowledge To predict and control behavior
Questions	How do we/can we cope with life? What other ways can we imagine? What is unique about my or another's experience?	How do participants understand their world? How do the participants and author co-construct a world? What are the pragmatic implications of research?	What does it mean from the researcher's point of view? What is the relationship among factors? What behaviors can be predicted?
Methods	Autoethnography Interactive interviewing Particiticipant observation Performance Sociological interospection Visual arts	Semistructured interviewing Focus groups Participant observation/ethnography Thematic, metaphoric, and narrative analysis Grounded theory Case studies Participatory action research Historical/archival research	Coding textual data Random sampling Frequencies of behaviors Measurement Surveys Structured interviews

	Artistic/Interpretive	Social Constructionist/Postpositivist	Positivist
Writing	Use of first-person voice Literary techniques Stories Poetry/poetic transcription Multivocal, multigenre texts Layered accounts Experiential forms Personal reflections Open to multiple interpretations	Use of first-person voice Incorporation of brief narratives in research reports Use "snippets" of participants' words, with implied partiality and positionality Usually a single interpretation, Some consideration of researcher's standpoint(s)	Use of passive voice "View from nowhere" (Haraway, 1998) Claim single authoritative interpretation Meaning summarized in tables and charts Objectivity and minimization of bias highlighted
Researcher	Researcher as the main focus, or as much the focus of research as other participants	Participants are main focus, but researcher's positionality is key to forming findings	Researcher is presented as irrelevant to results
Vocabularies	Artistic/Interpretive: inductive, personal, ambiguity, change, adventure, improvisation, process, concrete details, evocative experience, creativity, aesthetics	Social Constructionist/Postpositivist: inductive, emergent, intersubjectivity, process, themes, categories; thick description, co-creation of meaning, social construction of meaning, standpoint, ideology (e.g., feminism, postmodernism, Marxism)	Positivist: deductive, tested, axioms, measurement, variables, manipulation of conditions, control, predication, generalizability, validity, reliability, theory driven
Criteria	Do stories ring true, resonate, engage, move? Are they coherent, plausible, interesting, aesthetically pleasing?	Flexible criteria Clarity and openness of processes Clear reasoning and use of support Evidence of researcher's reflexivity	Authoritative rules Specific criteria for data, similar to quantitative Proscribed methological processes

PRINCIPLES OF CRYSTALLIZATION

Crystallized projects span multiple points on the qualitative continuum in order to maximize the benefits of contrasting approaches to analysis and representation, while also being self-referential to their partiality. I propose that crystallization manifests in qualitative projects that

- Offer deep, thickly described, complexly rendered interpretations of meanings about a phenomenon or group.

- Represent ways of producing knowledge across multiple points of the qualitative continuum, generally including at least one middle-ground (constructivist or postpositivist) and one interpretive, artistic, performative, or otherwise creative analytic approach; often crystallized texts reflect several contrasting ways of knowing.

- Utilize more than one genre of writing (e.g., poetry, narrative, report) and/or other medium (e.g., video, painting, music).

- Include a significant degree of reflexive consideration of the researcher's self and roles in the process of research design, data collection, and representation.

- Eschew positivist claims to objectivity and a singular, discoverable Truth in favor of embracing knowledge as situated, partial, constructed, multiple, embodied, and enmeshed in power relations.

Crystallization involves each of these principles to greater or lesser degrees, as manifested in an infinite number of possible representational forms. I explore each of these principles in turn.

First, as with any qualitative approach, crystallization seeks to produce knowledge about a particular phenomenon through generating a deepened, complex interpretation (Richardson, 2000b). All good qualitative research should provide an in-depth understanding of a topic, since "thick description" forms the hallmark of our methods (Geertz, 1973). But crystallization provides another way of achieving depth, through the compilation not only of many details but also of different forms of representing, organizing, and analyzing those details. Strong themes or patterns supported by examples provide a wide-angle view of the setting or phenomenon; stories or poems highlight individual experiences, emotions, and expression; critiques shed light on relevant cultural assumptions and constructions; and so on. Brought together, the depth of understanding enlarges and also changes shape and form. Incorporating differing forms of analysis and genres enables researchers to cover more ground, incorporating the researchers' positionality, contrasting or conflicting points of view, patterns, and exceptions. The complexity of representation possible through crystallization is explored more thoroughly in Chapter 2. For now, I suggest that crystallization provides one effective approach to richly describing our findings and to marking both overt and subtle manifestations of power in analytic, narrative/artistic, critical genres.

Second, crystallization utilizes forms of analysis or ways of producing knowledge across multiple points of the qualitative continuum, generally including at least one middle-ground (constructivist) or middle-to-right (postpositivist) analytic method and one interpretive, artistic, performative, or otherwise creative analytic approach. That is, you must encounter and make sense of your data through more than one way of knowing. Multiple ways of knowing are analogous to viewing an object through a crystal: "Crystals are prisms that reflect externalities *and* refract within themselves, creating different colors, patterns, and arrays, casting off in different directions" (Richardson, 2000b, p. 934; see also Chapter 3 for an overview of possibilities across the continuum). I talk more about epistemology (i.e., ways of knowing) in Chapter 2; for now, suffice it to say that crystallization cannot involve several arts forms or several forms of social science; at least one from each general type must be included. Juxtaposing different ways of knowing through crystallization reveals subtleties in data that remain masked when researchers use only one genre to report findings. Thus, an emotionally evocative narrative points to the lack of human feeling captured in systematic data analysis, while analysis points to the larger social trends within which the unique, individual narrative must be situated to be understood. Constructing themes or patterns, searching for evocative moments to capture, and identifying invocations of power in discourse all constitute examples of good strategies, and crystallization requires engaging in at least two.

Third, crystallized texts include more than one genre of writing or representation. I do not dictate a precise minimum or maximum number of genres; undoubtedly others have or will develop wonderfully creative ways of combining only two or more than a dozen forms of analysis and representation to explore their topics, beyond anything I have conceived. However, crystallization depends upon including, interweaving, blending, or otherwise drawing upon *more than one* way of expressing data and/or the world. Of course, this raises the question of what "counts" as "other" genres; generic boundaries often blur (Ellis & Bochner, 2000). For example, grounded theory analysis discussion of themes could be considered to be in the same "report" genre as an ideological critique that draws upon feminist theory to deconstruct the taken-for-grantedness of a social phenomenon (Gergen, 1994); certainly we could label both as fairly conventional "academic writing." On the other hand, significant differences exist between the two: Ideological critique overtly draws on highly abstract and often jargon-laden philosophical treatises to deconstruct texts, while grounded theory researchers typically construct arguments bolstered with data excerpts that feature participants' voices and reflect a more concrete, data-based, inductive reasoning. Likewise, the lines between narrative ethnography and autoethnography shift continually. Ethnographic narratives always reflect and implicate the researcher's self even as they construct others' experiences, and autoethnographic stories of the self inevitably refer to social roles and interactions that imply relationships between the author and others (e.g., spouse, child, teacher; Ellis, 2004). Given the migrating boundaries among categories, often the label assigned by an author to a particular representation (e.g., autoethnography, narrative ethnography) reflects that researcher's preferences more than conformity to a specific set of criteria.

Furthermore, in all qualitative research methods, analysis and writing intrinsically intertwine; that is, we *write* memos in producing grounded theory *analysis,* and researchers accomplish much autoethnographic reflection (i.e., analysis) through construction of narratives or performances. Hence, in calling for multiple forms of analysis and genres, I realize I can invoke no clear standard for assessing researchers' adherence to this principle. The slipperiness of categories notwithstanding, making choices that maximize the variety of epistemologies represented in a qualitative text constitutes the goal that I urge authors to pursue, so that their readers can perceive (in some way) multiple ways of knowing.

A fourth principle is that crystallized texts feature a significant degree of reflexive consideration of the researcher's self in the process of research design, data collection, and representation. Reflexivity in research involves "thoughtful, conscious self-awareness" (Finlay, 2002, p. 532). Qualitative researchers traditionally conceive reflexivity as "a deconstructive exercise for locating the intersections of author, other, text, and world, and for penetrating the representational exercise itself" (Macbeth, 2001, p. 35). Macbeth (2001) divides reflexivity into two interdependent types: positional reflexivity, which attends to the author's identity, context of writing, discipline, and privilege, and textual, which focuses on the construction of representations that point to their own construction. He proposes that these cannot escape their Enlightenment roots in enhancing an account's validity through establishing credibility and certainty,[1] for "facts of every kind have their contingencies, including those recovered by critical self-reflection" (p. 55). Nonetheless, being open about research processes demonstrates researcher integrity and consciousness that "through the use of reflexivity, subjectivity in research can be transformed from a problem to an opportunity" for dialogue (Finlay, 2002, p. 531).

Many ways of representing reflexivity may be incorporated into crystallized texts, and depending upon the researcher's goals, explicit evidence of authorial reflexivity may be placed in an appendix, footnotes or endnotes, interludes, or even a separate, cross-referenced or linked text. Moreover, subtle cues enable authors to embed awareness of the author's role in some ways, regardless of the aesthetic demands of the text. For example, describing the researcher's interactions with participants can reveal aspects of their relationships through dialogue.

Fifth, crystallization eschews positivist claims to objectivity and a singular, discoverable truth and embraces, reveals, and even *celebrates* knowledge as inevitably situated, partial, constructed, multiple, and embodied. It brings together multiple methods *and* multiple genres simultaneously to enrich findings *and* to demonstrate the inherent limitations of all knowledge; each partial account complements the others, providing pieces of the meaning puzzle but never completing it, marking the absence of the completed image. Definitive claims of truth from "nowhere" (Haraway, 1988)—that is, from an objective, neutral, all-seeing stance—do not reflect the goals of crystallization. Surrendering an all-powerful stance may be difficult for researchers trained in positivist science, particularly those working within medical schools or other places where researchers hold objectivity and "hard" science as not only normative goals but also as the only valuable ones[2] (see Chapter 8 for a discussion on defending and promoting your work to colleagues at either end of the methodological continuum).

To surrender definitive truth claims involves acknowledging that knowledge is never neutral, unbiased, or complete. It may be easier to perceive how privileged researchers' perspectives shape (and limit) their understanding of participants' worlds than to acknowledge that participants also occupy specific standpoints that intersect with power and oppression; the subaltern (i.e., oppressed) is never an innocent position (Haraway, 1988). Thus, participants' voices should be respected and considered valid accounts of participants' experiences, and researchers should incorporate participants' perspectives into analysis, representing them in ways that honor their perspectives. At the same time, researchers should take great care not to romanticize participants' accounts as objective or somehow authentically true in their efforts to respect participants; all perspectives necessarily are partial, even severely marginalized ones. Releasing the burden of having to produce only Truth that, by definition, must compete with all other proposed truth claims may be quite liberating and affirming for researchers' schooled in positivism or immediate-postpositivism. Crystallization provides a framework in which to balance claims of truth with recognition of the intersubjective nature of all knowledge claims. At the same time, surrendering objectivity does not mean that we cannot make claims to know, recommendations for action, pragmatic suggestions for improving the world, and theoretical insights. All of these remain not only possible, but also more probable, because of the depth of consideration that went into the production of the crystallized text. While acknowledging that there is always more to know about our topics, we nonetheless produce extremely rich, evocative, useful accounts through crystallization.

Given its reliance on ideological critique of knowledge construction as situated, crystallization often explicitly incorporates critical stances such as feminist (e.g., Harding, 1991), critical race (Nakayama & Krizek, 1995), or queer (Sedgwick, 1990). Crystallization offers a way to circumvent, at least to some degree, the deconstructionist dilemma. That is, while critique sheds necessary light on the workings of power in society, it also often fails to offer any solutions or even positive insights—critique forms its own justification for being (Epstein, 1997). Critics often target feminists and postmodern scholars for always criticizing but not fixing anything. Crystallization enables sound critique to be coupled with other ways of knowing and of offering suggestions for theory, research, and practice. Such a pragmatic approach emphasizes that our findings are meaningful only insofar as they indicate "what conduct [they are] fitted to produce" (James, 1907, p. 45). Hence, the effectiveness of a critique not only does not weaken through crystallization, but may actually be strengthened when contextualized with evidence of a deep understanding of a group or place and of passionate dedication to positive action.

FACETS OF THE CRYSTAL:
TYPES OF CRYSTALLIZATION

I divided crystallization into two primary types: integrated and dendritic. *Integrated crystallization* refers to multigenre texts that reflect the above principles in a single, coherent representation (e.g., a book, a performance) and take one of two basic forms: woven, in which small pieces of two or more genres are layered together in a complex blend, or patched, in which larger pieces of two or more genres are juxtaposed to one another in a clearly demarcated series (see Chapter 5). *Dendritic crystallization* refers to the ongoing and dispersed process of making meaning through multiple forms of analysis and multiple genres of representation for those who cannot or do not wish to combine genres into a single text (see Chapter 6).

To further describe and distinguish crystallization from other qualitative approaches, I provide answers to frequently asked questions at the end of this chapter. I now turn to making a case for the specific advantages of crystallization and note some constraints as well.

STRENGTHS OF CRYSTALLIZATION

With crystallization, very deep, thick descriptions (Geertz, 1973) are possible. Multiple ways of understanding and representing participants' experiences not only provide more description, but more points of connection through their angles of vision on a given topic. Crystallization enables significant freedom to indulge in showing the "same" experience in the form of a poem, a live performance, an analytic commentary, and so on; covering the same ground from different angles illuminates a topic. As our goal in conducting qualitative research generally involves increasing understanding in order to improve dialogue among individuals and groups and to effect positive change in the world (e.g., Fine, 1994), enriching findings through crystallization may move us to fulfilling that goal.

Another benefit is that crystallization enables qualitative researchers to generate less naive representations. We can continue to engage in and learn from systematic knowledge production without simply perpetuating the remnants of positivism in our writing. Crystallization allows more freedom to portray accounts that reflect current sensibilities about the slippery nature of claiming knowledge without forcing us to give up systematic research methods. We read actively, as participants in the construction of meaning in the text, and we can read with and against expectations in the particular genres. Crystallization continually turns back upon itself, highlighting its own construction by showing that no one genre offers truth. By making and problematizing claims, crystallized texts gain a level of reflexive validity (see Lather, 1993).

Moreover, crystallization enables researchers to push the envelope of the possible, particularly as regards to linking or integrating narrative/poetic/ literary representations with grounded theory or other forms of systematic pattern finding. While disciplinary and professional conventions remain dominant forces, the success of some work that moves around, beyond, through, and alongside traditional work always benefits the field, because it reminds us of the constructed nature of all such norms and practices. Thus, disciplinary conventions such as APA style reflect not sacred commands but a fallible and limited set of regulations that serve important purposes best when they avoid stagnation or pointless rigidity. Like language, rules shift over time, and crystallization embodies one form of shift that may keep us thinking.

Finally, crystallization may gratify researchers personally as a mode of work that liberates, excites, and demands. Reinharz (1992) explains that feminist researchers (and others) engage in multimethod research in part because of their passion for their topics and their quest for fulfilling, engaging work that makes a difference in the world; crystallization can be one excellent path toward personal and professional fulfillment. No doubt many readers have been advised by mentors, textbooks, and colleagues that systematic qualitative analysis and creative analytic work essentially are incompatible and that researchers must (or at least really *should*) choose one. That (perceived) forced choice reflects a long history of honoring an art/science dichotomy in the academy, and my goal in this book is to explain how to circumvent that choice through carefully considered strategies—albeit not without costs.

LIMITATIONS OF CRYSTALLIZATION

Of course, like any methodology or genre, crystallization bears limitations. First, not everyone holds the capacity to be fluent in multiple genres and forms of analysis. Writing evocative and engaging narratives alongside insightful, well-organized analysis challenges even highly skilled researchers. When done poorly, autoethnography can degenerate into exhibitionism or pointless self-indulgence. Likewise, analysis can skim the surface, failing to detect subtle meanings or construct insightful interpretations. Crystallization requires a wide range of skills, and not many doctoral programs exist in any discipline that foster development of student expertise in narrative/creative writing, ideological/ philosophical criticism, and social scientific qualitative analysis. Authors can educate themselves on unfamiliar techniques through books, conferences, workshops, and mentoring, but acquiring needed skills is challenging, and researchers should not take lightly the need to respect the artistry and rigor of each genre, medium, or method on its own terms (see Chapter 3 for resources).

Second, crystallization involves a trade-off between breadth and depth. In a single article or book, using crystallization enables an in-depth experience, but breadth often suffers. Authors must make strategic choices about focus because of space limitations and demands for specificity of purpose. Embracing crystallization necessitates forgoing other representational opportunities. Crystallization takes a lot of space and time, and it comes with a cost. Even in a book-length manuscript, exploring the topic through crystallization without losing your ability to bring together a coherent text necessitates a high degree of specificity in the topic. Rather than be discouraged by this constraint, I urge researchers to embrace it as an inspiration to produce a variety of works that draw upon the same data (see Chapter 6).

A third limitation relates to the lack of recognition of crystallization as a viable methodological framework. Audiences often perceive multigenre projects, my own certainly included, as self-contradictory and inconsistent, leading to suspicious questions from reviewers about the legitimacy of research practices and the rigor of analyses. Many fields, such as medicine, offer limited acceptance of qualitative and interpretive methods anyway (for a notable exception, see Charon's [2006] work on narrative medicine), and are unlikely to soon embrace crystallization with enthusiasm either. Indeed, positivists may find crystallized texts even more threatening than inductive qualitative analyses, as they overtly deny the positivist paradigm while refusing to embrace a single alternative standard of truth either. I discuss ways to infiltrate mainstream venues with crystallized work (see Chapter 6), but I am realistic in acknowledging that many conventional journals will continue to resist broadening their scope. Nonetheless, critical and interpretive scholars have made tremendous strides in the last three decades, and the hegemony of positivism sports cracks and fissures that will continue to grow.

Finally, researchers have to be willing to set aside or change their beliefs about the rightness or correctness of any given method or genre. I consider this a limitation of crystallization because the willingness to truly appreciate a wide range of representations and methods of analysis on their own terms—beyond mere lip service to epistemological/representational equality—remains uncommon among practitioners at all points along the qualitative continuum. Researchers must remember what we typically forget and often even consciously purge from published accounts—that is, that scholarly communities *make up* generic and methodological standards, constraints, and practices. These norms constitute not sacred science, nor sacred art, but fallible human constructions. While I suspect most researchers know this on some level, many will find it quite a different matter to engage in serious genre and method play and have to overtly explore the degree to which all representations and practices (especially our own particular favorites) fail to transcend their partiality. This appreciative capacity differs from the analytic and creative skills to conduct good analyses and write in a given genre. Rather, practitioners of crystallization must have the cognitive and emotional capacity to both suspend belief in the rules of a given practice and implement a range of practices simultaneously. I find such an exercise mentally invigorating but also wearying and frustrating. At times, the perpetual "turning in on itself" of the project can feel like a descent into relativism—a sense that if no single standard for evaluating claims exists, then we must surrender and accept all perspectives as equally valid—a position I believe neither helpful nor inevitable. All researchers face challenges, and crystallization poses more than the typical number.

Obviously, this book attests to my relatively undaunted recognition of the above limitations of crystallization. All choices involve opportunity costs, and I prefer the costs of crystallization over those of other approaches. I turn now to a short introduction of two ethnographic studies that provide illustration for many of the ideas presented in the remainder of this book. An overview of Chapters 2 through 8 follows, along with an introduction to myself as author.

ETHNOGRAPHIC EXEMPLARS

Throughout this book, I refer repeatedly to two of my own ethnographic projects to illustrate various aspects of crystallization processes, products, and possibilities. Obviously I have the most in-depth knowledge of—and can speak with the most authority on—my own behind-the-scenes experiences in research that are integral to undertaking crystallization. I endeavored to include exemplars of others' work wherever possible, particularly in my explanations of the vast continuum of methods practiced and representations produced. However, a fairly limited number of scholars currently practice in ways that meet my emergent expectations for crystallization—that is, go beyond producing multiple forms of artistic representation (e.g., poetry and performance) or of social science (e.g., grounded theory and critical discourse analysis) to produce multi-genre work that cuts across the artistic/interpretive/social science epistemologies by including both a middle- or right-ground form of social scientific analysis of a data set *and* an artistic representation in the same project. Hence, some of the same exemplars reappear throughout the text. To reduce potential redundancy in presenting these exemplars in later chapters, I provide a brief overview of two ethnographic projects here.

The first research project described the daily world of the Interdisciplinary Oncology Program for Older Adults (IOPOA) at the Southeast Regional Cancer Center (SRCC; both pseudonyms). The IOPOA team consisted of two oncologists (one of whom also is program director), a nurse practitioner, two registered nurses, a registered dietitian, a licensed clinical social worker, a clinical pharmacist, and an administrative assistant. The team provided comprehensive geriatric assessment and treatment recommendations to each new patient over the age of 70 who came to SRCC for treatment or for a second opinion. Using more than 2 years of participant observation, formal and informal interviews, grounded theory analysis, ethnographic narrative, autoethnography, and feminist critique, I explored such issues as backstage communication among health care providers (Ellingson, 2003), communication issues and spirituality in the comprehensive geriatric assessment process (Ellingson, 2008b, 2008c), the roles of patients' companions in geriatric patient–health care provider communication (Ellingson, 2002), my cancer survivor positionality in the clinic (Ellingson, 1998), and embodiment issues in health care ethnography (Ellingson, 2006a). In addition, I published a multimethod, mixed-genre book, *Communicating in the Clinic: Negotiating Frontstage and Backstage Teamwork* (Ellingson, 2005a), that exemplifies the possibilities inherent in crystallization by exploring backstage communication among health care providers, its relationship to frontstage communication with patients, and intersections of power in health communication (and in feminist ethnography).

Another, ongoing ethnographic project involves studying communication within an outpatient dialysis unit that treats people with end stage renal disease (ESRD; i.e., kidney failure). Western Valley Dialysis (a pseudonym) owns and operates 14 units in the western United States. The unit employed about 25 people, including registered nurses, licensed vocational nurses, patient care technicians (PCTs), technical aides (TAs), clinical social worker, registered dietitian, head technician, unit secretary, and nurse manager, with per diem nurses and PCTs augmenting full-time staff. At the time of observation, the patient census fluctuated between 91 and 100 patients; patients endure the painful and fatiguing procedure to filter waste from their blood three times each week. The dialysis unit operated from 6:30 a.m. to roughly 6:30 p.m., with three staggered shifts of 3 hours each. The center had one isolation unit; the other 24 chairs were arranged around the perimeter of an open room, with a nurses' station in the middle. While I spent most of my time "on the floor" (i.e., in the treatment room) talking with patients and staff, I also observed in the patient reception area, staff break/conference room, staff offices, and water treatment facilities. After almost a year of participant observation, I conducted formal interviews of staff and patients and collected organizational documents. Using this data, I have produced a grounded theory analysis of routinization of communication (Ellingson, 2007), an interpretive analysis of hierarchy in dialysis communication (Ellingson, 2008a), a layered account (Ronai, 1995) of the experience of time in dialysis that alternates brief narratives of patients' embodied experience with theoretical analysis (Ellingson, 2005b), and a piece that integrates grounded theory and poetic transcription to explore paraprofessionalism among dialysis technicians (Ellingson, 2006b). I intend to develop at least three further manuscripts from this data. I produced no central, book-length manuscript; I explain in Chapter 6 the benefits of this multigenre, dispersed approach, which I term *dendritic crystallization.*

ORGANIZATION OF THIS BOOK

Chapter 2 explains the need to consider what claims we make as researchers and writers and our justifications for them, particularly insofar as crystallization often involves juxtaposing forms of representation that reflect differing, even conflicting, ways of knowing. Further, I connect epistemology to a consideration of the ethics of representation, including issues of power, embodiment, and speaking for others. In Chapter 3, I briefly explore many options for conducting and representing research across the continuum of nonexclusive possibilities in qualitative methods. I provide brief explanations of grounded theory analysis and a variety of creative analytic practices for readers who may be aware of but have limited familiarity with such forms, as well as citations of exemplars for readers desiring to learn more.

The next three chapters detail how to design and carry out a crystallized study. Chapter 4 explains how to go about selecting different forms of analysis and multiple forms of representation. I begin by providing suggestions on how to determine the best fit for your goals and audience(s). I then discuss the roles that theory may play in crystallization and outline a decision-making process. Chapter 5 presents specific strategies for using crystallization to combine multiple forms of representation into a single manuscript, media presentation, or other integrated text. Chapter 6 develops the process of dendritic crystallization. Here, I offer further strategies for envisioning crystallization as an ongoing and dispersed process for those who wish to embrace multiple outlets for fragments of their large project, a process that retains many of the benefits of multigenre texts and offers other advantages.

The final two chapters offer concluding advice and some lessons about crystallization. Chapter 7 discusses writing techniques, as well as structural, organizational, and creative ways to enrich the telling of qualitative research. I also encourage readers to enlarge the boundaries of acceptability in traditional publishing outlets. Chapter 8 explores several lessons of crystallization, and then takes a pragmatic approach to getting crystallized articles, pieces, monographs, live and/or filmed performances, art work, and books into publication or circulation. I also present suggested responses to likely criticisms of crystallized work from practitioners on both the artsy and the social science ends of the qualitative continuum.

Each of the chapters ends with an "interlude" that offers a narrative, pedagogical discussion, or reflection on some aspect of the crystallization process; I have purposefully avoided standardizing these sections in order to provide a greater range of representations. These interludes serve two functions. First, they enable me to explore some important issues that are somewhat tangential to the focus of the chapters but that benefit readers in understanding both my emergent approach and how crystallization relates to broader themes and issues in qualitative methodology. Second, the interludes provide me a space to crystallize this account of crystallization, interrupting the conceptual explication and methodical presentation of instructions and strategies with some more playful and personal segments as alternative ways of communicating ideas to readers.

CONCLUSION: FREQUENTLY ASKED QUESTIONS ABOUT CRYSTALLIZATION

I include a "frequently asked questions" (FAQs) section in this chapter as a way to differentiate my approach from that of others and to clarify my positioning of crystallization vis-à-vis other important concepts, methods, and trends in qualitative research. Following the FAQs, this chapter's interlude delves into my standpoint as author of this book.

Q: Is your articulation of crystallization the same as Richardson's?

No, this articulation of crystallization is my own. Although I gratefully draw on Richardson's (1994, 2000b) explanation of crystallization as a jumping-off point, I elaborated it to reflect my own goals and preferences, and she does not necessarily agree with every aspect of my further development of her initial concept into a framework for conducting multigenre qualitative research.

Q: Is crystallization the same as triangulation?

No, crystallization differs from triangulation and mixed-method design. In positivist and postpositivist research, triangulation involves an attempt to get closer to the truth by bringing together multiple forms of data and analysis to clarify and enrich a report on a phenomenon (e.g., Creswell & Clark, 2006). While such work often includes both qualitative and quantitative data or a range of different qualitative data or statistical measurements combined into a single report, the manuscript remains consistent with traditional writing conventions and does not include creative analytic genres. Crystallization in no way stands in opposition or mutual exclusivity to triangulation, but it does reflect significantly different goals. "Triangulation itself carries too positivist an implication, to wit, that there exist unchanging phenomena so that triangulation can logically be a check" (Guba & Lincoln, 1989, p. 240). Whereas triangulation seeks a more definitive truth, crystallization problematizes the multiple truths it presents. Unlike triangulation, crystallization is informed by postmodernism, meaning that it presupposes that no truth exists "out there" to discover or get close to, but only multiple and partial truths that researchers (and others) co-construct. Since researchers construct knowledge and representations (narratives, analysis, etc.), all accounts are inherently partial, situated, and contingent. Rather than apologizing for this partiality as a limitation, scholars using crystallization can celebrate multiple points of view of a phenomenon across the methodological continuum.

Q: Can I incorporate other forms of qualitative analysis or statistical data into crystallization?

Yes, crystallization could include other forms of analysis not discussed here. I practice and refer to grounded theory (e.g., Charmaz, 2000), but you may use other qualitative forms such as discourse analysis or rhetorical analysis, or even statistical analysis, provided that the researchers involved understand statistics as careful measurements that inevitably are expressed in language, grounded in culture, and represent (only) one form of knowledge construction. While I do not specifically address quantitative data in this book, it may be incorporated in mixed-genre texts in much the same way that grounded theory and other systematic, inductive qualitative analytic findings are included, that is, as one more perspective on a group or phenomenon.

Q: Is crystallization a type of autoethnography or performance ethnography?

No, crystallization is not synonymous with autoethnography or performance ethnography, although these may be parts of a crystallized project. Many researchers represent their findings in creative analytic genres such as autoethnography without combining more than one way of knowing or constructing data. Sometimes layered accounts or other hybrid genres (which are often autoethnographic and/or performative) involve strategies that could be considered crystallization. At the same time, crystallized work may not include explicit focus on the researcher(s) as autoethnography does, but instead may focus on analysis and creative representations of participants' experiences, with consideration of the researcher in a secondary role.

Q: Do I have to be a feminist or other critical scholar to use crystallization?

No, crystallization complements a range of ideological perspectives, but it does not require explicit invocation of one. Feminists and other critical theorists forged the way for much of the "crisis of representation" that has decentered positivism, and their work forms much of the justification/ foundation for crystallization (e.g., Hesse-Biber, 2007; Mies, 1983). However, researchers can conceptualize crystallization as an expansion of methodological triangulation into multigenre crystallizations within a social constructionist or postmodern framework that is not explicitly feminist, Marxist, queer, and so forth.

Q: Is crystallization the same as "immersion/crystallization"?

No, my development of crystallization is unrelated to the "immersion/ crystallization" approach described by W. L. Miller and Crabtree (1999) as one of four "analytic styles" in qualitative research and elaborated by Borkan (1999) as an "organizing style" that "consists of cycles whereby the analyst

immerses him- or herself into and experiences the text, emerging after concerned reflection with intuitive crystallizations until reportable interpretations
are reached" (pp. 180–181). When cited in method sections of qualitative
work, the process resembles inductive analyses such as thematic analysis or
a constructivist version of grounded theory (for exemplars, see Bertram,
Kurland, Lydick, Locke, & Yawn, 2001; C. H. Fox, Brooks, Zayas, McClellan,
& Murray, 2006). However, I do not practice this approach and cannot speak
about it with authority.

Q: Is crystallization specific to communication studies research?

No, crystallization is not limited to the field of communication studies, or
any other discipline, nor even the social sciences. Richardson (1994), a sociologist, introduced the idea. Scholars from education, nursing, social work/
human services, medicine, and the humanities may find it helpful, just as those
in anthropology, sociology, and psychology would. Throughout the book, I
draw on research from diverse fields within the social sciences, education,
health care, and human services.

Q: Is crystallization limited to written texts?

No, crystallization can be accomplished in virtually any medium—writing,
video, painting, performance art, computer generated images, and so on. Most
qualitative projects involve writing either as the end product (e.g., a book, a
journal article) or as a component of a mixed-media presentation (e.g., a performance script), but I offer no limits on what genres and media researchers may
include and do not specify that written text be one of them.

Q: Is crystallization an "all or nothing" proposition?

No, you do not need to chose between fully adopting crystallization as the
framework for your qualitative project or setting it aside completely. Rather,
reading and considering the ideas in this book can provide all researchers with
suggestions on thinking creatively and productively about their research processes
and representational choices.

INTERLUDE

Introducing the Author

Readers deserve to know a bit about who wrote this book, in order to understand the perspectives it reflects. With Dr. Laurel Richardson's blessing, I embarked on my own journey toward articulating a methodological approach that has become so much a part of who I am as a qualitative researcher. How did I get to this point? Here is a short version of the story.

As an academic-in-training, I was blessed with two primary mentors. The first was Dr. Patrice Buzzanell, a feminist organizational communication scholar who originally trained in quantitative methods and moved over to middle-ground qualitative research. As she guided me through my MA thesis on communication between women with breast cancer and their physicians, we focused on feminist theory and methods but also on qualitative rigor (Fitch, 1994; Tompkins, 1994) and producing clearly articulated and well-supported analysis with copious research citations, scrupulously written to adhere to APA style requirements. From Patrice, I learned to construct persuasive arguments, to interrogate my own standpoint, and to always pay attention to power in interaction. Dr. Carolyn Ellis became my second mentor, and she urged me to focus on my own stories and those of my participants, to make sense of data (and life) via narratives, and to focus on the evocative, unique, sensuous, and embodied details of lived experience. From her, I learned that stories are theories, autoethnography offers a path toward humanizing social science, and that art and science form not opposites but complementary and interdependent ends of a vast qualitative continuum. Unwilling to choose between my mentors' paths, I forged my own that brought together my favorite parts of both via crystallization. I consider Dr. Laurel Richardson a mentor-at-large; her ideas of writing as a method of inquiry, invocation of feminist poststructuralist theory in qualitative research, and crystallization profoundly influenced my work and my self. When I attended the Society for the Study of Symbolic Interaction (SSSI) Couch-Stone Symposium in Las Vegas as a blushing, nervous graduate student, she inscribed my copy of her book, *Fields of Play,* with a message so inspiring and optimistic that I have sought since then to live up to her expression of confidence in me. Like any account, my account of crystallization both results from and influences who I am. Here are some things readers might want to know about the author in understanding this book.

I am a feminist researcher. I ascribe to Marie Shear's notion that feminism is "the radical notion that women are people" (Shear, 1986, p. 6).[3] That means that I stand against oppression and violence toward anyone. I gratefully acknowledge that I came of age academically at a time when my foremothers and their allies had completed the foundational work of institutionalizing women's studies in academia. I earned a graduate certificate in women's studies while pursuing my PhD. Since 1996, I have been a member of the Organization for the Study of Communication, Language, and Gender, an interdisciplinary feminist group whose annual conference provides the highlight of my academic year (see www.osclg.org); and I served as president of OSCLG from October 2006 to October 2008. I tend to view the world in general and my research in particular through a lens of power—as it relates to gender hierarchies, of course, but also heteronormativity, ablebodiedism, White privilege, nationalism, and class oppression.

I have a liberal arts background. Before earning an MA in communication at Northern Illinois University and a PhD in communication at the University of South Florida, I did my undergraduate study in English literature and religious studies at the University of Vermont and earned an MA in writing with an emphasis in nonfiction at the University of New Hampshire. I came to the discipline of communication through debate; having been a debater in UVM's Lawrence Debate Union (and having married a former teammate), I was offered a chance to be an assistant coach for the NIU team. These two things—a background in writing and literature and a love of debate—profoundly influence how I understand research. I strive to construct clear and lucid arguments that are well reasoned with strong support from a variety of forms of evidence. At the same time, nothing pleases me more than engaging prose. I continue to privilege the written word, despite current attention to other formats and critiques by feminists (and others) of the patriarchal effects of elevating printed texts over oral and lived ones (e.g., Neufeld, 1999; Ong, 1982). I fully support less linear and fixed accounts presented as performance or as multimedia and video, audio shows, painting, and other forms, and I mention many of them here in this book. I have experimented myself with some performance and look forward to moving further in that direction (e.g., Ellingson, 1999). I encourage readers to explore any artistic genres that they want to work in. But I love words, specifically written ones, and I believe that the problem of suppression and marginalization of some voices lies less in written accounts themselves than in the mistaken, destructive authority granted to those accounts culturally (e.g., Roof, 2007). Of course, that acknowledgement does not let me off the hook of responsibility; when I choose to produce written texts, I uphold (willingly or not) the social and political power of the printed word and participate in the devaluing of orality. I address this issue further in Chapter 2 when I explore epistemology and ethics.

I trained in both middle-ground and artistic/interpretive approaches to qualitative methods and consider myself to be as much a qualitative methodologist as a health communication and gender communication scholar. I served as chair of the National Communication Association Ethnography Division and actively publish on issues in qualitative methods such as reflexivity (Ellingson, 1998), the continuum of qualitative methods (Ellis & Ellingson, 2000), embodiment in academic writing (Ellingson, 2006a; in press-a), applied communication ethnography (Ellingson, in press-b), and autoethnography (Ellingson & Ellis, 2008). Most of my research focuses on health communication, so most of my examples come from ethnographic studies of clinics that I described earlier in this chapter. I also conduct feminist research on extended family communication; currently, I am coauthoring a qualitative project with Dr. Patty Sotirin that explores communication between aunts and their nieces/nephews (Ellingson & Sotirin, 2006; Sotirin & Ellingson, 2006, 2007).

I came to both health communication and qualitative methods inspired by surviving bone cancer. I am an 19-year survivor of osteogenic sarcoma in my right leg. After 15 surgeries, 13 months of chemotherapy, and a zillion tests and procedures, I am well into remission and more or less mobile. The reconstructions to my leg necessary to remove the tumor and then to rebuild (and rebuild, and rebuild . . .) my knee have left my leg with an unusual appearance and quite a few limitations. A 22-inch-long scar flows down my leg, and skin and muscle grafts crown my knee. Assorted other smaller scars adorn my thigh. My knee bends slightly less than 90 degrees (i.e., just over half of what an average knee can do), and while I can walk, I cannot run or jump. My right leg is almost an inch shorter than the left one, requiring lifts in all my right shoes. I move through the world with a marked body that shapes my understanding of ethnography, contemporary health care practices, and all other aspects of my life.

Finally, I am White/European-American, come from a middle-class New England family, and maintain a committed heterosexual relationship with my partner Glenn with whom I share a house in the San Francisco Bay area. I am an ardent Red Sox fan, adore my cat Vladimir, take joy in being an aunt, enjoy cooking and scrapbooking, and believe that chocolate is a major food group.

NOTES

1. Macbeth (2001) suggests the ethnomethodological concept of "constitutive reflexivity" as an alternative productive focus:

> The essential reflexivity of accounts or how it is that our accounts of the world reflexively constitute the very affairs they speak of . . . points to the organization of ordinary sense and meaning—how order, fact, and meaning in everyday life are produced as practical objectivities, reflexively made of the social technologies for producing and detecting them. (p. 49)

2. Crystallization does not have to eschew quantitative data and claim making altogether, however. I acknowledge the potential for incorporating "hard" statistical analysis, particularly of social trends, to contextualize evocative portrayals. Stack's work

does this brilliantly, combining social and demographic research on education, poverty, immigration, and so on to contextualize the specificities of her in-depth ethnographic and interview data (Stack, 1974, 1997). I draw on quantitative research from health communication research and other fields to contextualize my claims. Such work improves when juxtaposed with other genres that clearly demonstrate that the disinterested tone of the research report is only one choice; it is not neutral, natural, or inevitable.

3. This quote is often mistakenly attributed to Kramarae and Treichler (1985), authors of *The Feminist Dictionary.* In fact, both Kramarae and Shear (personal communication, February 2, 2008) confirmed that Shear (1986) coined this definition of feminism in a book review of *The Feminist Dictionary,* which appeared in the *New Directions for Women* newsletter, in which Shear praised the book's efforts and offered several original definitions of her own.

TWO

ETHICS AND EPISTEMOLOGY

Assumptions Underlying Crystallization

———◄•◆•►———

Tell all the Truth but tell it slant—

Success in Circuit lies

Too bright for our infirm Delight

The Truth's superb surprise

As Lightning to the Children eased

With explanation kind

The Truth must dazzle gradually

Or every man be blind—

—Emily Dickinson

The question of what comprises "the truth" and how we go about discovering, constructing, or recognizing truth never poses an easy resolution. Most qualitative researchers are eager to share their truths, but are less certain over what would comprise "all the truth." I have always embraced Emily Dickinson's directive "tell it slant," as I have found straight-up versions of so many of my truths (e.g., as a cancer survivor, as a feminist) encounter less-than-warm receptions when shared outside select circles, an

alienating experience well documented among people of minority racial, ethnic, sexual, and ability groups (e.g., Hartsock, 1998). Crystallization provides
one mode for slanting our truths (I do wish Ms. Dickinson pluralized!). The
need to dazzle gradually—that is, to reveal knowledge as fragmentary, contingent, and irreducibly complex—manifests as a guideline for understanding
and practicing crystallization.

We need to consider the claims—about reality, our participants, and
ourselves—that we make as researchers and writers. Since crystallization's
raison d'etre involves bringing together multiple contrasting, even conflicting,
ways of knowing in order to make knowledge claims and problematize those
same claims, researchers must understand the ethical and epistemological
issues that arise in multigenre work. Of course, researchers also must act ethically in the field as they interact with participants; ethical concerns are not
limited to issues surrounding representation. However, as ethics in fieldwork
and data collection generally fall beyond the scope of this book, I recommend
readers read coverage on these important topics within qualitative methods
textbooks (e.g., Lindlof & Taylor, 2002) or in essays on research ethics (e.g.,
Preissle, 2007). Strategies for managing epistemological and representational
tensions in the crystallization process will be addressed in Chapter 4; this
chapter provides relevant background and further explains the perspective that
underlies this book. After defining epistemology and explaining epistemological
foundations for understanding crystallization as I conceptualize it, I explore
some of the ethical quandaries that arise in crystallized work and offer suggestions on how to construct ethical representations.

WHAT IS EPISTEMOLOGY AND
WHY DOES IT MATTER IN CRYSTALLIZATION?

Epistemology is "a theory of knowledge" that involves the examination of
"justifying beliefs" concerning what counts as knowledge or evidence (Harding,
1987), also referred to as "ways of knowing" (e.g., Belenky, Clinchy, Goldberger,
& Tarule, 1986; Potter, 1996). Qualitative researchers do not conduct research
based on a single set of principles about how we make sense of the world, that
is, a single epistemological foundation. Rather, understandings of what counts
as knowledge and how it can be produced exist along a continuum that ranges
widely from positivism to radical interpretivism (Ellis & Ellingson, 2000).

Building on my introduction of the qualitative continuum in the previous chapter, I briefly explore ways of knowing across the field of qualitative methodology.

At the far right of the qualitative continuum (see Figure 1.1, p. 8), emphasis on valid and reliable knowledge as generated by neutral researchers utilizing the scientific method to discover universal Truth reflects an epistemology commonly referred to as positivism (C. A. B. Warren & Karner, 2005). Historically, social scientists understood positivism as reflected in a "realist ontology, objective epistemology, and value-free axiology" (K. I. Miller, 2000, p. 57). Enlightenment views of science as discovery of objective truth form the basis for methodological triangulation; traditionally, researchers triangulate by combining multiple quantitative and/or qualitative measures to capture more effectively the truth of a social phenomenon (Lindlof & Taylor, 2002). Few, if any, qualitative researchers subscribe to an absolute faith in positivism, however. Many postpositivists, or researchers who believe that achievement of objectivity and value-free inquiry are not possible, nonetheless embrace the goal of production of generalizable knowledge through realist methods and minimization of researcher bias, with objectivity as a "regulatory ideal" rather than an attainable goal (K. I. Miller, 2000, p. 61). In short, postpositivism does not embrace naive belief in pure scientific truth; rather, qualitative research conducted in a strict postpositivist tradition utilizes precise, prescribed processes and produces social scientific reports that enable researchers to make valid, reliable, and generalizable claims about the social phenomenon under examination. Postpositivism forms something of a bridge between the right and middle ground in qualitative work, as others whose methods characterized as middle ground (and reflecting social constructionism) also invoke the term postpositivist.

In the middle ground, qualitative researchers move another step past (post) positivism and adopt a social constructionist or postmodernist-influenced perspective of meaning as intersubjective and co-created (Ellis & Ellingson, 2000). From this perspective, objectivity reflects a damaging myth, an unwarranted claim made by those who have enough power to reinforce their perspective as the correct/normative one (Gergen, 1999). Claims of truth always remain mired in (among other things) the politics of research funding, the indeterminacy of language in which authors express claims, and the fallibility of human sense making. Rather than apologizing for being subjective or pretending that researchers do not influence findings, middle-ground qualitative researchers interrogate their subjectivity to shed light on how their race, class, gender, sexuality, and other identities and experiences shape our research processes and results. Moreover, such researchers largely refuse a relativistic position in which "anything goes" and all interpretations gain equal validity simply because neutrality and complete truth prove unattainable (see Epstein, 1997). Instead, rigor, depth of analysis, and reflexivity constitute important criteria for evaluating middle-ground qualitative research quality (Fitch, 1994).

Still others believe in the value of humanistic, openly subjective knowledge, such as that embodied in stories and poetry (Ellis & Ellingson, 2000). At the artistic end of the qualitative continuum, truths are multiple, fluctuating, and ambiguous. Autoethnographers, performance studies scholars, and others engaged in creative analytic practices embrace aesthetics and evocation of emotion and identification as equally or even more important than illumination of a particular topic (Richardson, 2000b). Literary standards of truthfulness in storytelling, that is, verisimilitude, replace those of social scientific truth at the left/artistic end of the continuum (Ellis, 2004).

MAKING KNOWLEDGE: AN
EPISTEMOLOGICAL BASIS FOR CRYSTALLIZATION

Richardson (2000b) grounds the theoretical basis for doing crystallization in postmodernism and in poststructuralist theory. I understand it largely in terms of social constructionism (P. Berger & Luckmann, 1966; Gergen, 1994, 1999). These theoretical positions overlap; indeed, most social constructionists draw heavily on principles from postmodern, poststructuralist, feminist, and other critical theorists (see Holstein & Gubrium, 2008). Readers need not be familiar with the subtleties of critical theory; however, several basic axioms concerning knowledge production underlie crystallization and warrant brief discussion.

First, meaning is constructed in communication, through language and nonverbal cues (Gergen, 1999). Meaning thus resides not *in* any one person, but *between* people who continually (re)negotiate it. Hence, meanings of words are not fixed or predetermined, nor can they be assumed to be equivalent among people. Culture reflects ongoing meaning making that both forms the context for interpretation and in turn is shaped by those interpretations (Hacking, 1999).

Second, we constitute our sense of ourselves as comprising various identities (e.g., woman, father, Latino, bisexual) through repeated performances, rather than simply perceiving essential aspects of a unitary, fixed self (Butler, 1997; Goffman, 1959). We know our identities through comparison and interaction with others (P. Berger & Luckmann, 1966). Those performative selves-in-flux are not false or artificial but rather constructed, maintained, and transformed through communication. Personal experience thus provides a good form of evidence, but we should be careful not to romanticize it. As Scott (1991) argues, no unmediated experience exists; we socially construct our perceptions, and we learn to see and be in the world in particular ways. Thus, our identities and experiences as qualitative researchers and the identities and experiences of our participants mutually inform each other and the intersubjective truths we generate.

Third, qualitative methods and approaches (including crystallization) exist both as constructions themselves and as means of understanding cultural constructions of meaning. That is, qualitative methods both enable us to learn something about a group or a setting *and* tell us about the researcher and the process of studying that group or setting (C. A. B. Warren & Karner, 2005). Each methodology constructs meaning somewhat differently and comes with its own constraints, opportunities, epistemologies, and aesthetics; indeed, in qualitative analysis and writing, "each practice makes the world visible in a different way" (Denzin & Lincoln, 2000, p. 4). Each genre privileges one or more epistemologies (e.g., Denzin, 1997; Richardson, 2000b); in the same way, each knowledge claim reflects specific "situated knowledges," that is, perceptions of the world from an individual's particular standpoint (Haraway, 1988).

Fourth, when we produce an account of research, we indulge in temporarily "forgetting" the socially constructed nature of the conventions of establishing truth in each genre (Ferguson, 1993). That is, we write evocative and coherent stories, edit an emotionally wrenching documentary film, or clearly articulate and support analysis according to the conventions that make them recognizable as a particular genre, ignoring or setting aside our awareness of the artificiality of those rules while we produce them (e.g., that stories should have a beginning, middle, and end). But Ferguson cautions us *not to forget that we forgot,* meaning that we must not become so enchanted with our evocative story or eloquent analysis that we romanticize an account as embodying Truth, instead of recognizing its inherent partiality. Crystallization provides one critical way of *not* forgetting. The existence of contrasting genres implicates the other forms as not objective, as not the only way to represent findings. Themes or processes (grounded theory) reflect the presence of specific incidents in the data upon which researchers form generalizations; incidents selected for telling as stories imply larger social issues and systems of sense making in the details of the story. The contrasts among genres make evident their mutual dependence for definition; put simply, we cannot have good without evil or narrative without analysis—the absence of one renders the other incomprehensible. Likewise, we recognize personal, openly subjective accounts as subjective *because* more detached accounts exist. Bodies typically remain absent in grounded theory analysis *because* they feature prominently in narrative ethnography, *because* autoethnography highlights them as intricately involved in the production of knowledge, and so on. Describing multiple genres of a text as mutually productive, mutually dependent constructions that provide equal utility and yet remain equally partial troubles the rigid methodological hierarchy of "hard" research over "soft," and "scientific" over "interpretive." In doing so, we resist dichotomous views of research methods.

A fifth underlying principle of crystallization is that researchers cannot escape systems of power; my position as author cannot be innocent or disconnected from the politics of academic publishing, for example (Haraway, 1988). *All* research and writing reflects a will to power over truth (Foucault, 1977), or the power to present a particular version of reality as an (or the) authoritative one. In circumventing traditional divisions of art and science, I engage in resistance to disciplinary power. At the same time, I invoke authorial power in order to claim the legitimacy of an alternative approach—a truth of juxtaposing and deconstructing generic boundaries to simultaneously problematize and celebrate them as thoroughly partial through crystallization. Hence, crystallization does not escape its authorship any more than any other framework or account does. It functions as one good way to present complex qualitative findings while actively reflecting on the constructed nature not only of the findings but of the entire research enterprise.

Finally, crystallization reflects a grounding of knowledge production in the body, not as in reflecting Cartesian dualism, or the mind/body split. Crystallization troubles many distinctions, among them those between mind, body, and spirit. I encourage readers to think of crystallization as always already embodied, resisting the disembodied voice that characterizes traditional academic prose. The performance of "disembodied researcher" has been repeated for so long that it functions as a set of naturalized norms that privilege a masculine mode of being (Ellingson, 2006a). Western culture has continually reaffirmed the mind/body split and the association of male or masculine with mind and female or feminine with body: "Embodiment is relegated to the female, freeing the phallocentric Idea to transcend the material, creating the deadly split between epistemology and ethics" (Lather, 1993, p. 682).[1] Since science traditionally defined the production of knowledge as the province of men, bodily knowledge has been systemically denied as oxymoronic; indeed, "it is as if 'facts' come out of our heads, and 'fictions' out of our bodies" (Simmonds, 1999, p. 52). However, disembodied prose comes from nowhere, implying a disembodied author (Haraway, 1988). The powerful enjoy the privilege of leaving their bodies unmarked; mainstream journal articles tend to reflect social science norms that frame the researcher's body and other sources of subjectivity as irrelevant. Unlike earlier historical periods during which visible signifiers conferred prestige, today the privilege of being unmarked, of having your own positionality obscured as normative, signifies power (Thomson, 1997). Members of marginalized groups (e.g., people of color, LGBTQ community members) tend to recognize that bodies are always political and cannot be separated from the selves that produce knowledge (e.g., Davis, 1990). That is, bodies cannot reflect neutrality but rather form "maps of the relation between power and identity" (Rose, 1999, p. 361). When researchers' bodies remain unmarked—and hence naturalized as normative—they reinscribe the power of scholars to speak *without* reflexive consideration of their positionality, while others' voices remain silent or marginalized by their marked status (Ellingson, 2006a).

Coffey (1999) argues that fieldwork constitutes an embodied practice (as do all methods) and that the researcher's body—its position, appearance, what social groups or classifications others perceive it as belonging to—matters in the production of qualitative accounts. Even with the embracing of qualitative methods and the broadening of academic writing conventions (e.g., permitting or requiring use of first person rather than passive voice) by many contemporary qualitative researchers and journals, consideration of the researchers' and participants' bodies remains largely absent from accounts of such research. Embodied autoethnography, narrative inquiry, and other creative analytic writing (Richardson, 2000b) in this vein largely appears in journals that focus on interpretive methodology rather than a specific topic area or discipline (e.g., *Qualitative Inquiry, Journal of Contemporary Ethnography*) or are segregated into edited collections of interpretive work (e.g., Harter et al., 2005).

Researchers have used the power of academic discourse to define their own bodies as essentially irrelevant to the production of knowledge (Denzin, 1997). The erasure of researchers' bodies from conventional accounts of research obscures the complexities of knowledge production and yields deceptively tidy accounts of research (Ellingson, 2006a). With crystallization, we embrace a holistic view of knowledge production as always a mind/body/spirit enter-prise. The field of qualitative research benefits significantly from embodied writing by reflexive researchers who implicate their bodies as essential com-ponents of research design, data collection and analysis, and the creation of representations. In my own ethnographic work, I strive to bring my body into my research as a site of knowledge production as a means of highlighting the slipperiness of distinctions between patients (who are experts on their bodies and experiences) and health care providers (who also suffer illness in their lives), as well as between ethnographers (who participate/interact in their research sites) and participants (who engage in sense making about their lives and about the researcher). My own sense of embodiment keeps me deeply rooted in the awareness that knowledge is not produced by the disembodied voices that speak in official accounts of research in professional journals and books, but by researchers whose bodies unavoidably influence all aspects of the research process and of knowledge production (Ellingson, 1998). As a patient/scholar/ethnographer, my body provides many subtle pieces of data (e.g., standing up all day in a clinic is physically exhausting) as well as many insights into that data (e.g., I physically shudder when I witness patients in pain, experiencing an embodied reaction to their suffering). Crystallization can (and should) reveal, illuminate, and problematize research findings as fully embodied phenomena.

In sum, what we claim to know about a given person, group, culture, or phenomenon cannot be separated from our beliefs about what constitutes knowledge, nor from the processes through which we produce knowledge. Moreover, how we define knowing also reflects our beliefs about ourselves-in-relation (Gergen, 1994), our ethical responsibilities toward others involved in and/or impacted by our research, including our research participants, the schol-arly communities we work in, local and national policy makers, and other audiences and stakeholders.

VOICING OTHER AND SELF: ETHICS OF REPRESENTATION

What do we do when we choose to speak for others? Is that possible? Desirable? "The questioning is important, the answers less so" (M. Wolf, 1992, p. 5). Feminists and other critical theorists have warned against the dangers of speaking for others, that is, of appropriating the voices of marginalized others for our own academic ends (e.g., Fine, Weis, Weseen, & Wong, 2000). Reframing our participants' words within our theoretical frames benefits us far more than them, and may even serve to harm participants. Certainly, no matter how well intentioned, the process of representing others' experience remains fraught with significant challenges. A profoundly ethical debate endures as scholars wrestle with ethical tensions surrounding researcher and participant intentions, political and ideological implications, and social justice imperatives of representing the Other (see Denzin & Giardina, 2007). The issue concerns not merely an academic dilemma of how to enrich or complexify our accounts. Rather, material and relational consequences of our representations affect our participants and ourselves as researchers. "The ethics of representation is the good or ill that results from how participants are represented in publications, presentations, and other reports of research" (Preissle, 2007, pp. 525–526). Of course, we should first do no harm and obtain informed consent of participants (not a simple matter[2]); while necessary, these prove insufficient to ensuring an ethical account.

Crystallization offers some advantages over single-genre accounts as a way of addressing ethical concerns in representation. I will discuss several ethical strengths of crystallization.

First, when we disrupt the taken-for-granted norms of research writing, we avoid simply reifying existing power relations and instead complexify issues of authorship and representation, enticing readers to stop and reflect on the constraints of each genre and making them difficult to ignore. Pointing to an example of a crystallized account, Preissle (2007) suggests that authors can illuminate many of the complications of representation through juxtaposing "multiple and competing" accounts (p. 526). In this way, "rather than try to 'reflect truth' in a traditional fashion, research itself becomes an instrument for emancipation or intervention. It generates a critical posture toward the taken-for-granted" (Gergen, 1994, pp. 136–137). For example, M. Z. Miller, Geist-Martin, and Beatty (2005) intertwine academic essay and the first author's narratives and reflections with poems and letters written by young participants in a program that promotes peace and seeks to end violence among children. The beauty, tragedy, and vulnerability embodied in the children's words is breathtaking, and the tremendous impact of the program on the authors truly inspires. This piece embodies the possibilities of dialogue as a way to build community and promote peace, showing how much children have to say about their worlds and demonstrating that peace is a dream that can be made real.

Second, crystallization constitutes one means to provide a forum for voices that dominant discourses often silence. Although not exclusive to crystallization, a benefit of this approach is that it enables authors to combine poetry, conversation, photographs, stories, and other genres that detail the experiences of marginalized voices obscured by powerful others. For example, multigenre texts take readers to unseen or ignored spaces such as the sidewalks of Greenwich Village in New York City where primarily men without homes survive in the economic margins of society by selling used books and other scavenged materials (Duneier, 1999).

Third, writing in multiple genres can be one path to promoting social justice and serving communities outside of academia; we can effect change in the material world, and many qualitative scholars argue that we hold a responsibility to do so. Fine, Weis, Weseen, and Wong (2000) describe writing in multiple genres as an ethical imperative, urging scholars to heed

> our fiercest injunction: that we have an ethical responsibility to retreat from the stance of dispassion all too prevalent in the academy and to educate our students toward analyzing, writing, and publishing in multiple genres at one and the same time—in policy talk, in the voices of empiricism, through the murky swamps of self-reflective "writing-stories," and in the more accessible language of pamphlets, fliers, and community booklets. That is, if we are serious about enabling our students to be fluent across methods, to be engaged with community struggles, and to theorize conditions of social (in)justice, we must recognize that flickers and movements for social change happen in varied sites . . . and therefore through varied texts. (p. 128)

Crystallization provides a path toward bolstering efforts for social justice by reaching out to a variety of constituencies to explore options, invite dialogue, and spark creative interchanges and collaborations. An excellent example of this includes work done by Dr. Lynn Harter and her colleagues with Passion Works, a nonprofit agency that fosters collaborative artwork by people with and without disabilities. Harter's team wrote journal articles (e.g., Harter, Scott, Novak, Leeman, & Morris, 2006), a lengthy report for the agency's needs, and narratives for the Web site to reach out to the public (Harter, Norander, & Young, 2005).

FIRST, DO NO HARM: SOME ETHICAL CAUTIONS

Qualitative researchers must remain cognizant that crystallization cannot wholly circumvent the ethical challenges of representation, despite its strengths. Creative analytic, multigenre "reports" of research findings involve just as much sense making as writing conventional analytic accounts (M. Wolf, 1992). Literary narratives reflect just as much construction by the researcher as academic narratives; experimental texts do not escape their authorship (Haraway, 1988). Stories create and inscribe meaning through the imposition of order on unordered events (Bochner, 1997). While stories invite readers to more directly fashion personal, multiple meanings, the author's positionality still underlies decisions on what to include and exclude. We still accomplish representation of others via the author's power, even if that power alters and/or diminishes somewhat through inclusion of large portions of participants' transcribed words, or as stories fashioned out of dialogue with participants (e.g., K. V. Fox, 1996). No matter how well crystallized a text, it inescapably remains an invocation of authorial power and control.

> Whereas experimenting with strategies of representation has produced some alternatives, it is doubtful that these forms of representation are distinctly different from others, since the end product does not necessarily appropriate less and does not shift the balance of power or the benefits. Despite important efforts to experiment with strategies of representation and authorship, the basic power differences and distribution of benefits remain the same. (D. L. Wolf, 1996, p. 34).

I am keenly aware when I write narratives of the details I include, those I leave out, and the consequences of those decisions for how I construct others and myself. Lather and Smithies (1997) brilliantly articulate their approach to negotiating their authorial power in their book about women living with HIV/AIDS:

> To look with restraint as we bear responsibility to the women who have told us their stories: this is our task as we accept the gift of witness proffered to us by this study. As such, this work has made a claim on us to not drown the poem of the other with the sound of our own voices, as the ones who know, the "experts" about how people make sense of their lives and what searching for meaning means. Hence the book is organized as layers of various kinds of information, shifts of register, turns of different faces toward the reader, in order to provide a glimpse of the vast and intricate network of the complexities of cultural information about AIDS in which we are all caught. (p. xvi)

The rich and complex "glimpses" of the women's worlds, voices, and meanings provided in the multigenre text reflect the researchers' recognition and even celebration of the women's expertise. Not merely a rhetorical strategy for enriching the account, the authors constructed their book as a feminist collaboration with "ones who know" about living with HIV/AIDS. Never decoupling their own responsibility, the authors nonetheless privilege their participants' voices, literally placing the women's words above their own on the page in an effort to be ethical in their treatment of the women who have entrusted their stories and experiences to them.

STRATEGIES FOR ETHICAL
DECISION MAKING IN CRYSTALLIZATION

Although I have no single answer to the question of how to be ethical in your representation of others, I do suggest a profound awareness: It helps to keep in the forefront of your mind that every time you make a claim as you crystallize, you do just that—you *make a claim* on the trust of your participants, on the reader's time and attention, and on the collective body of knowledge in your own and related disciplines. As you make claims about how the world is, was, or could be imagined through multigenre representations, resist the urge to "forget you forgot" (Ferguson, 1993)—continually remind yourself of the constructed nature of all accounts and the ethical responsibility to do no harm and to write in ways that promote social justice. I offer strategies for ethical representation, independent of your choice of genres.[3] You will find each of these more or less pertinent depending upon the types of work you produce.

Reflect, reflect, reflect. I introduced reflexivity in Chapter 1 as a central principle of crystallization. I return to the topic here specifically in the context of ethics to make the point that reflecting upon yourself, your practices, and your representations relates not only to production of useful and illuminating work, but also to attending to the ethical implications of these processes and products. Fine et al. (2000) offer a series of insightful questions to ask ourselves as we work with our data collection, analysis, and writing. Of course, these do not occur in an linear fashion but as iterative practices throughout the research process. Fine et al. described these questions as intended to foster reflexive consideration of any qualitative project, and I gratefully acknowledge their applicability to crystallization as framework for constructing a multigenre text. Ask yourself:

1. Have I connected the "voices" and "stories" of individuals back to the set of historic, structural, and economic relations in which they are situated?

2. Have I deployed multiple methods so that very different kinds of analyses can be constructed?

3. Have I described the mundane?

4. Have some informants/constituencies/participants reviewed the material with me and interpreted, dissented, challenged my interpretations?

5. How far do I want to go with respect to theorizing the words of informants?

6. Have I considered how these data could be used for progressive, conservative, repressive social policies?

7. Where have I backed into the passive voice and decoupled my responsibility for my interpretations?

8. Who am I afraid will see these analyses? Who is rendered vulnerable/ responsible or exposed by these analyses? Am I willing to show him/her/them the text before publication? If not, why not?

9. What dreams am I having about the material presented?

10. To what extent has my analysis offered an alternative to the "commonsense" or dominant discourse? What challenges might very different audiences pose to the analysis presented? (pp. 126–127)

Using this guide in combination with your own intuitions, fears, joys, and thoughts, reflect on how you have chosen to construct your practices and representations as you engage in crystallization. Your goal in these exercises is not to somehow circumvent all potential risk that harm to anyone will ever result from your work (sadly, an impossibility) but to fulfill a moral obligation to take as much care as possible to treat others with dignity and care.

Resist easy categories. Avoid simple appropriation of the experience and voices of others, reinforcing damaging myths through oversimplification, or ignoring manifestations of power and resistance (Zimmerman & Geist-Martin, 2006). Fine (1994) advocates that we "work the hyphens" when we write, dispelling stereotypes, providing space for marginalized voices to be heard (not merely broken into small bits), highlighting intersections of identities over essentialist categories, and contextualizing claims to illustrate the complex intertwining of individual experience and larger social realities. This move becomes especially critical when your representations describe incidents or quote words from participants that present participants in an unflattering manner.

> In instances where your advocacy position or the position of your consultants places them or Others in a questionable or negative light, you must consider the context of their lives in relation to the structures of power that constitute their actions, culture, and history. (Madison, 2005, p. 137)

Such consideration spurs the production of nuanced accounts that promote compassion, dignity, and (ideally) motivation to effect positive change, rather than easy ammunition for those defending the status quo to appropriate for their own uses.

Conduct member checks. I highly recommend that you invite some or all of your participants to respond to your findings, a process also referred to as meeting the standard of *recalcitrance* (Tompkins, 1994). Invite them to comment, edit, and otherwise provide feedback, in order to enhance (albeit not equalize) their voices in the research process. Since participants frequently contribute valuable insights, member checking enhances the credibility of your claims, particularly of patterns or themes in the data (C. A. B. Warren & Karner, 2005). Member checking also somewhat demystifies the process of meaning making, demonstrating to them (and reminding you) that research constitutes a messy, imperfect, and exciting process of constructing, reconstructing, and co-constructing meaning. This process can be engaged in any number of ways: for example, through a focus group discussion, by distributing copies of the draft manuscript to individuals for their written comments, in (formal or informal) one-on-one interviews, via e-mail discussions, or by presenting findings in a public forum with participants present and then recording or taking notes on the conversations that ensue. Further, you can incorporate participants' ideas into your representations in a variety of ways. Ellis (2004) suggests that researchers can place divergent voices in a footnote or appendix, incorporate them into a dialogue, or present parallel narratives that illustrate differing perspectives (see also Fine et al., 2000). Video and multimedia representations offer further alternatives for enabling participants to "speak back" to researchers' analysis and representations. The flexibility of crystallization enables a wide range of practices that make room for representing contradictions, dialectical tensions, and multiple points of view.

Share your process. Consider including a section in your work for owning the complexities of producing and sharing ethical representations. That is, rather than asserting the conclusions you reached on how to represent your work ethically, invite your audience to witness (some of) your journey toward those conclusions through an autoethnographic account or writing story (Richardson, 2000b). Alternatively (or additionally) you might write a separate reflection on the topic for a methodological journal or the commentary section of a research journal (e.g., Adelman & Frey, 2001). Demystifying our messy research processes functions as a way of highlighting and further exploring the ambiguities inherent in all qualitative research. Moreover, such accounts constitute a crucial service to new researchers (and to those wondering why their research never seems to go as smoothly as it appears in others' published accounts) who benefit from their fore-researchers' experiences as maps of the territory. I find tracing our paths particularly crucial with crystallized projects because of the huge number of ethical and representational choices involved. You need not limit exploration of process to written texts. Wheeler's (2006) "The Making of Sandrah's Thesis," a playful yet sharp "mockumentary" riffs on "indie" film conventions to explore the tensions of producing feminist, deconstructive work. Wheeler hopes to extend the work of feminist and postmodern theorists

> by raising critical questions about style-guide-ruled academic writing at the pre-published level. In this way, a fictional performance of some purposeful misunderstandings concerning the form of thesis writing allows me to highlight form and style guidelines for the student writer that seem to be at odds with the feminist spirit of communication. This open spirit of communication insists on a forum that responds to questions such as: Who gets left out when form becomes too regulated? Who is invited to speak and identify through stylistic convention? Who do we risk marginalizing by (mis)representing univocality? (Wheeler, personal communication, September 13, 2007)

Using hilarious puppets, nature footage, and dramatic "reenacted" scenes from her thesis process, Wheeler problematizes both her own involvement in knowledge production and the limits of the forms we use to contain knowledge.

Remember that no innocent position exists (Haraway, 1988). That is, resist the urge to romanticize your participants' voices as though they reflect one-dimensional heroes or victims. Continually work the hyphens, not relying on stereotypes and stock tales of oppression; instead, strive to present people in all their complexity (Fine, 1994). I have struggled with this one myself, since I instinctually spring to patients' defense whenever I witness ineffective patient–health care provider communication. Given the oppressive hierarchy of the U.S. health care system, the top-down power distribution places patients firmly at the bottom of the pecking order. But patients are not powerless; where power manifests, so does resistance (Foucault, 1977). And quite frankly, a few of the patients I met at the dialysis unit engaged in quite active, hostile, even violent resistance. I worked to present their unpleasant behavior in the context of the oppressive Medicare system, limited choices, poor quality of life, poverty, and other barriers, but I also refused to render them simple victims in my narratives (Ellingson, 2005b). In both the geriatric oncology clinic and the dialysis unit, I learned that health care providers are human, with all the complexities of patients, neither good nor bad but imperfect. This in turn has transformed some of my personal stories of illness, as I have humanized health care providers I had hitherto presented as one-dimensional monsters (Ellingson, 1998). The same remains true of any participants; we all inhabit complex intersections of privilege and oppression, of power and resistance (McIntosh, 1988), and no one can claim the right to speak or to represent others' speech from a position of omniscient validity, truth, or neutrality. Crystallized accounts should always implicitly—and generally explicitly—reflect the complexity of all people's standpoints as manifesting intersections of power and privilege.

Consider collaborative forms of research. Collaborative strategies, such as partic¬ipatory action research, involve projects in which more than the usual amount of power sharing occurs to mediate researchers' privileged perspective by situating participants as co-researchers in designing and carrying out a research project, including making decisions about representation(s) (for a helpful overview of par¬ticipatory approaches, see Kemmis & McTaggart, 2005; for exemplars, see Frey & Carragee, 2007a, 2007b). Participants potentially can be involved in or even pro¬duce one or more of the genres in a crystallized project. Feminist researchers developed and continue to utilize many participatory approaches to research (Lykes & Coquillon, 2007). For example, the photovoice technique, in which par¬ticipants photograph aspects of their lives and engage in sense making about and display of the images, reflects a participatory ethic (López, Eng, Randall-David, & Robinson, 2005). Walker and Curry (2007) co-developed a booklet of narratives of survival with the clients and staff of a domestic abuse shelter, complexifying the relationship between researchers and participants in social justice projects.

Continue to work with and to represent others. My final caution reflects my most ardent concern: Please do not give up on the project of researching the experiences of less powerful others because of fear of exploitation, appropriation, or otherwise unethical representation. Some researchers have responded to the crisis of representation (Denzin & Lincoln, 2000) by retreating (to varying degrees) from the practice of researching marginalized others by focusing primarily on their own lives rather than on illuminating the experiences and meanings within a group of research participants (e.g., Richardson, 2007; Richardson & Lockridge, 2004). Of course, writing about yourself inevitably involves revealing the lives of intimate others—friends, family, colleagues—but not of formally designated research participants. I am fully aware of and in agreement with critiques by feminists and others of the dangers of speaking for others, of co-opting their voices, taking their stories out of context, and exercising our power as researchers in ways that benefit us but benefit our participants little or not at all (e.g., Fine et al., 2000; Hesse-Biber & Brooks, 2007; Reinharz, 1992; Roof, 2007). However, we cannot get off the hook of duty and passion by surrendering the practice of writing about others. Our surrender leaves the study of suffering and striving—and of survival and triumph—among marginalized people to those most vested in the status quo and least interested in transformation. "Your *angst* and *guilt* about your benefits [from representing Others in your work] cannot eclipse or cloud your *responsibility* to do meaningful work" (Madison, 2005, p. 135, original emphasis). Rather, with great care, humility, and good will, we must continue to work with the Other in order to build understanding (see exemplars in Perry & Geist, 1997).

CONCLUSION

Crystallization represents one powerful way to speak with, about, and on behalf of others and to connect those voices with those of more powerful others, challenging dominant discourses in vital ways through multiple forms of analysis and multigenre representations. Ethical representations are not limited to particular methodological strategies; all methods and genres raise ethical and epistemological questions about representing others. In the next chapter, I survey options for analysis and representation across the continuum of qualitative methods.

INTERLUDE

**The Limits of Genre—An Exercise
About Ethics and the Construction of Claims**

Imagine, if you will, sitting in a hard, not very comfortable chair with attached desk in my bland, beige classroom in the Arts & Sciences Building at Santa Clara University. We sit in a wide circle, and I, your professor, cheerfully expound on the inherent ethical and epistemological quandaries of qualitative methods, including crystallization. You and several of your classmates have begun to shift restlessly, remaining nonresponsive to my invitation to ask questions. The time has come to shift gears a bit, to show after so much telling.

In this section, I adapt an exercise I use regularly in my qualitative methods course to illustrate the ethics of representing a brief interaction through multiple genres. Three lenses provide contrasting images of "what happened"—a transcript of an interaction I recorded during fieldwork, a formal analytic description of the corresponding category of communication, and a portion of a narrative that depicts the interaction, each of which I drew from my *Communicating in the Clinic* ethnography of an interdisciplinary geriatric oncology team (Ellingson, 2005a). I explore this case study as a way to illustrate for readers the dramatic influence of genre on researchers' ethical representation of others (see also M. Wolf, 1992). Following each account, I offer some insights about its partiality; I then conclude with some final thoughts.

Representation #1: Audio-Recording Transcript [Excerpt of an interaction between the author (LE), a registered nurse (RN1), and a geriatric oncology patient (Ms N.) and her adult son (Son)]

LE: Hi, This is —. Dr. A's nurse.

Ms. N.:   Oh.

RN1:   Nice to meet you.

Ms. N.:   Nice to meet you.

Son: I'm——, how are you?

RN1:   Fine how are you? Um, today you're going to seen by Dr. A.

Ms. N.:   Um um.

RN1:   On our first visit with our patients we do the red carpet treatment. We have a whole team of people to see you. You may not think so, when we start taking all day

Ms. N.:   [chuckle]

RN1:   but you'll be here a while but we actually evaluate you in and out so we can get the best possible treatment plan for you. And we use a team of Diet um dietitians, a nurse practitioner, pharmacist, social worker. We now have Laura. [chuckle] So they evaluate you, give all their information to Dr. A and then he'll come in and see you near the end. Um, that way you know we can give you something that isn't generic, we need to look at your whole history

Ms. N.:   Um um

RN1:   history and everything and make sure everything is fine.

Ms. N.:   These are the pills that I take.

RN1:   OK.

Ms. N.:   Um there are some that I only take when absolutely necessary.

RN1:   OK. The pharmacist will go through all of those with you and ah [unintelligible 1 second] You can have any questions, um take that up with her, talk to her

Ms. N.:   OK.

RN1:   about different things; because the dietitian is very important you know. Depending upon whatever is going on with you right now, pharmacist will review everything. Um let's see, your social worker will evaluate and make sure then that everything is good for you at home, financially, emotionally, everything. And then [pause 5 seconds] probably Dr. A. I'm your case manager. I will come back in again.

Ms. N.:   OK.

RN1:   I will evaluate and make sure that you don't have any other questions um if you do then if I can answer them for you otherwise I'll get the other team members, or Dr. A back in. And I'll give you my card cause I'm the one you will contact if you have any questions in the future.

Ms. N.:   Oh OK.

RN1:   OK I'll see you then.

Ms. N.:   OK, what's next?

RN1:   bye-bye

Son: OK.

Transcripts have an aura of credibility; their format lends them face validity as scientific data (Mishler, 1991). Stripped of most nonverbal interaction cues and with no descriptions of the participants or setting, standard transcriptions of naturalistic encounters such as this one (or of research interviews) focus on accurately representing spoken language, placing rhetorical emphasis on the verbal content while ignoring the differences between oral and written speech. The excerpt begs an infinite number of questions about, among other things, the setting in which the interaction took place, the appearance of the people and their positions vis-à-vis one another in the room, and the tone of the discussion. Since people communicate over 90% of meaning nonverbally through cues such as facial expressions, tone of voice, and gestures (e.g., Adler & Towne, 2005), this account obviously presents only a very partial representation of "what happened," and of course it does not favor all participants equally.

This version of the story privileges the perspectives of the health care providers over those of patients in a number of ways. For example, it documents that the nurse provided information about the process of assessment to the patient in a reasonably intelligible manner. Lacking any indications of nonverbal kindness or a friendly manner—or lack thereof—it reinforces the primacy of the biomedical imperative of curing (transmission of information from patient to provider and back again) and deemphasizes caring and compassion, which people primarily express through facial expressions, touch, and tone of voice. The primary benefit or strength of this account is its rendering of conversational turn taking via notation of words exchanged by the provider, patient, patient's son, and me.

Representation #2: Analytic Account

The following excerpt provides an analytic summary of the process of orienting patients to the assessment process.

> Patients underwent a thorough medical history, a physical exam, and a psychosocial evaluation. Additionally, each new patient was screened for depression, cognitive processing deficits, risk of polypharmacy (over-medication or drug interactions), physical impairment or disability, and malnutrition. All of these assessments affected the treatment plans that the oncologists developed. As team members

cycled through each of the patients' rooms (typically three patients were scheduled simultaneously), they communicated with each other (and other cancer center personnel) in the halls and desk area. (Ellingson, 2005a, p. 5)

Again, the partial nature of the account should be apparent; so much remains absent from this summary. In this version, readers encounter no individuals, only description of general routines. I—the researcher—am arguably the one who most benefits from this account; its partisanship veers toward promoting a social scientific agenda of establishing the authority of my analysis by providing sufficient explanatory details to set the stage for my analysis. I demonstrate how carefully I have observed and how capable I am of summarizing key points. This account is not incompatible with providing helpful recommendations for theory and practice—I could even argue that such analysis functions as a necessary intermediary step to generating implications—but in itself, this analytic summary provides no benefit to the health care providers and little potential benefit to patients since I did not frame it as an introduction to the assessment process from a patient's perspective. This version of the story begs questions of how patients and health care providers experienced the process described; it also implies questions about how patients were scheduled in this manner and for whose convenience. The main benefit the account offers consists of concise summary of information.

Representation #3: Ethnographic Narrative

"Hi! I'm Beth, Dr. Armani's nurse," she says to Mrs. Davenport and the younger man sitting next to her. "It's nice to meet you."

Mrs. Davenport smiles. Her grayish-white skin and wig indicate that she has been having chemotherapy, but her rosy lipstick and the equally bright swaths of blusher on her cheeks give her a festive appearance. "Nice to meet you too," she says. She turns and looks deliberately at her son, who puts down the stack of papers he is reading.

"I'm Rick," he says politely. "How are you?"

Beth shakes his hand. "Fine, how are you? You've met Laura?" At their nod, she continues. "Um, today you're going to be seen by Dr. Armani. On our first visit with our patients, we do the red carpet treatment. We have a whole team of people who see you. You'll be here awhile, but we evaluate you in and out so we can get the best possible treatment plan for you. And we use a team of a dietitian, a nurse practitioner, pharmacist, social worker, and now we have Laura too."

Mrs. Davenport chuckles agreeably, her dark eyes sparkling behind her oversized brown glasses. "All right," she says. Rick has returned to reading what looks like a stack of reports. He gives the appearance of a busy executive who doesn't like to waste time.

"So they evaluate you, give all their information to Dr. Armani, and then he'll come in and see you near the end. That way we give you something that isn't generic; we look at your whole history and make sure everything is taken care of." Beth pauses and studies Mrs. Davenport's face to see if she looks confused or concerned. She appears quite pleased, however.

Nodding, Mrs. Davenport reaches into her colorful tapestry purse and pulls out a zipper-top plastic bag containing several bottles of pills. "These are the pills I take," she says, holding the bag out to Beth. Thinking to myself that Mrs. Davenport must want to be perceived as cooperative, I smile reassuringly at her.

Beth nods. "OK. You can—"

"There are some that I only take when *absolutely* necessary," continues Mrs. Davenport.

Again, Beth nods. "Yes, you can hold on to those. The pharmacist will go through all of those with you and answer any questions you have."

"OK," says Mrs. Davenport cheerfully, placing the plastic bag on the floor by her seat.

"After everyone sees you," continues Beth, "I will come back in and make sure you don't have any other questions, and take care of anything at that time. And I'll give you my card, 'cause I'm the one you will contact if you have any questions in the future." The primary nurses are the de facto case managers, spending extensive time trouble-shooting and coordinating treatment, tests, and information flow once patients leave the new patient clinic.

Beth looks questioningly at Mrs. Davenport who nods cheerfully again. "OK, that's fine, I'll see you then," she says.

"See you then," repeats Beth, opening the door to exit.

"OK," says Rick, looking up briefly. (Ellingson, 2005a, pp. 22–23)

Naturally, the narrative representation feels no less partial than the others and is perhaps the genre most obviously constructed by me. Its partiality lies in the obviously interpretive descriptive statements that I provide. I have left an infinite number of details out (e.g., the colors of the examination room), but nonetheless, I have provided more of a picture. The issue of course centers on whether the reader trusts that those details I have included, especially those more dependent on my impressions, memory, and notes of those impressions, and subsequent interpretation of their meaning. This account favors the patient and her reality more than the other two; I include a lot more description of her and her eagerness to please, presenting her in a positive light as a likable and cooperative patient. At the same time, this account reinforces the current medical establishment expectations of patient compliance to health care provider directives (e.g., Polaschek, 2003); my account normalizes those expectations by portraying an obedient patient as a good one. We could problematize this account by asking: How authentic is the patient's happy demeanor? Is it possible she acted this way out of fear, socialization, respect for medical authority? What key nonverbal signals have I left out: How close did people stand or sit to each other, for example? On the other hand, this account boasts some strengths in its more holistic and humane presentation of the actors and richer descriptions of their interaction.

Overall, this brief analysis and comparison demonstrates that no genre can claim objective representation. Crystallization does not offer an easy way out of ethical responsibility; every genre features strengths and limitations, and when we combine them, we only multiply the representational quandaries. On the other hand, the juxtaposition of multiple genres makes it difficult for readers to take for granted the premises of truth reflected in any one genre. Rather than finding frustration in an endless descent into relativism—that is, just give up since we can never really tell a completely comprehensive, balanced account—I urge researchers instead to take seriously the need to ponder ethical questions and to do the very best they can do to promote justice and minimize potential for direct and indirect harm.

NOTES

1. Lather draws here on the work of Irigaray (1985) to support her argument about the possibilities of a "voluptuous" or "maternal/feminine" validity as an alternative to traditional foundationalist (masculine) conceptualization of methodological validity.

2. Ascertaining the degree to which participants have the capacity to give truly informed consent and judging whether or not the consent actually has been given forms a persistent and deeply troubling problem with no clear resolution (e.g., J. A. Fisher, 2007; Veatch, 1995).

3. For guidelines on the equally important issue of ethical behavior in the field, see Berg (2007), Ellis (2004), and Lindlof and Taylor (2002).

⊰ THREE ⊱

ILLUMINATING OPTIONS FOR ANALYSIS AND REPRESENTATION ACROSS THE CONTINUUM

———•◆•———

In the beginner's mind there are many possibilities, in the expert's mind there are few.

—Shunryu Suzuki (1973, p. 21)

According to Zen teachings, the beginner's mind is childlike—open, curious, capable of wonder, and compassionate. We narrow our ability to understand when we get caught up in being the knowledgeable expert, an authority passing judgment. Conceptualizing qualitative methods as encompassing a continuum—and as forming part of a larger continuum of methods that includes quantitative methods—frees us from the unproductive strictures of a fixed and definitive set of practices in favor of a continually changing map of the territory.

No sufficient excuse exists any longer for qualitative researchers to deny the range of their options in designing, collecting, analyzing, and representing qualitative data. The crisis of representation persists as less a crisis than an ongoing patrol of borders, and we have made the narrative turn from which no practical hope of fully turning back remains. Ideological critiques of method, theory, and truth are widely expected, even if not welcomed by all, and a plethora of textbooks document the incredible diversity of practices that fall under the rubric of qualitative methods (e.g., Berg, 2007; Lindlof & Taylor, 2002; C. A. B. Warren & Karner, 2005). In this chapter, I briefly explore many options for analysis and representation across the continuum of qualitative methods, from conventional social science reports through artistic representations and much in between. I intend this overview for readers who are aware of but have limited familiarity with the variety of forms; extensive bibliographic citations provide readers with resources to locate further information and exemplars. I advocate that readers embrace the possibilities of moving fluidly along a continuum of nonexclusive possibilities.

TRADITIONAL FORMS OF ANALYSIS

Forms of analysis cannot be completely separated from decisions about representation. At any point on the qualitative continuum, a set of assumptions about epistemology (i.e., about what knowledge is and what it means to create it) influence choice of data collection and analysis method, which in turn foster particular forms of representation. While a thorough overview of qualitative data collection and analysis methods is beyond the scope of this project, I will touch on two conventional forms of inductive, qualitative analysis: ethnography and grounded theory.

Ethnography

Ethnography is a broad methodology that encompasses many practices and philosophies. The methodology is difficult to define, and no consensus exists within communities of ethnographers on its ideal definition or description (see Atkinson et al., 2001; Potter, 1996). Ethnography is generally thought of as "primarily a process that attempts to describe and interpret social expressions between people and groups" (Berg, 2007, p. 134). Classically, ethnographers conceptualized the collection, analysis, and representation of data as all being ethnography; one conducted ethnography, analyzed the data ethnographically, and produced an ethnography. Ethnography requires immersion into a culture and generally relies on inductive analysis of detailed fieldnotes and often informal and/or formal interviews of participants. Ethnographers achieve "intimate familiarity" with their data by rereading it many times, making notes on emergent trends, and then constructing themes or patterns concerning aspects of the culture (C. A. B. Warren & Karner, 2005). This is not to say that careful consideration of the ethnographic production of knowledge claims did not happen, only that research reports highlighted issues of data collection and did not typically include detailed descriptions of systematic analytic procedures labeled as techniques other than ethnographic analysis. Such an approach assumed a relatively straightforward (i.e., postpositivist) conceptualization of analysis that acknowledged the role of the researcher in sense making but largely took for granted a shared understanding of data analysis procedures. Contemporary realist (reflecting middle-to-right areas of the continuum) ethnographers sometimes follow this model of understanding and reporting their analytic processes, giving few if any details of how data lead to findings (e.g., Barker, Melville, & Pacanowsky, 1993; Brooks & Bowker, 2002; Meyer, 2004; Novek, 1995). However, with the burgeoning of alternative approaches to analyzing and representing data (and the blurring of lines among those processes), many ethnographers now describe their works in terms of more formally defined inductive procedures, of which they provide significantly more procedural details (e.g., M. Miller, 1995; Wright, 1997; Zoller, 2003).

Grounded Theory

Qualitative researchers commonly analyze qualitative data inductively to derive a typology of themes, patterns, or categories, a process often referred to as *grounded theory* or *constant comparison.* That is, rather than beginning with a theory and examining the ways in which data support and/or refute the tenets of a given theory (i.e., deduction), the researcher grounds findings in the data itself (i.e., the participants' words and experiences) by reasoning inductively, thus using theory to explain and contextualize findings rather than using findings to test the theory. Researchers use many other forms of inductive analysis that differ in significant ways from grounded theory (e.g., discourse analysis).[1] However, I concentrate here on grounded theory because the method is widely used across the social sciences, allied health and human services fields, and education and because its premises allow for examination of the same broad epistemological goals reflected in all forms of inductive qualitative analysis.

Glaser and Strauss (1967) steeped their original formulation of grounded theory methods in positivist notions of "discovering" themes that "emerge" from the data in "valid" ways, so long as researchers properly employed the method. Later, grounded theory was recast in a postpositivist vein that acknowledged the role of the researcher but still emphasized validity and conventional research writing (Strauss & Corbin, 1990). More recently, Charmaz (2000, 2005) situates grounded theory methods within social constructionist theory, developing the constructed nature of all knowledge claims as arising out of relationships; meaning resides not in people or in data, but *between* them. Researchers can "form a revised, more open-ended practice of grounded theory that stresses its emergent, constructivist elements. We can use grounded theory methods as flexible, heuristic strategies rather than as formulaic procedures" (Charmaz, 2000, p. 510). Charmaz's formulation is particularly amendable to feminist commitments and to scrutinizing our own positionalities in relation to the themes we generate in ethnographic data. Even further down the qualitative continuum past postpositivism, *situational analysis* points out the potential within grounded theory methods to reflect postmodern sensibilities and goes further to develop those connections drawing upon Foucault and other theorists (Clarke, 2005). Although none of these methodologists combines creative analytic representation with traditional writing forms, social constructionist and postmodern frameworks go a long way toward opening up grounded theory to be combined with other forms of analysis and representation, because they highlight the partiality and culturally specific nature of all knowledge.

Regardless of which paradigm you situate inductive or grounded theory analysis within, the basic processes of data analysis remain similar. The steps of grounded theory research outlined by Strauss and Corbin (1990) and Charmaz (2000) include coding data, developing inductive categories, revising the categories, writing memos to explore preliminary ideas, continually comparing parts of the data to other parts and to literature, collecting more data, fitting it into categories, noting where new data does not fit and revising the categories (theoretical sampling), and continually refining the typology using constant comparative analysis. To learn more about the practice of grounded theory, see Charmaz (2000, 2005, 2006); for exemplars of grounded theory, see Farrell and Geist-Martin (2005); Kwok and Sullivan (2007); Larsen (2006); M. Miller (1995); Miller-Day and Dodd (2004); Montemurro (2005); Sacks and Nelson (2007); Sandgren, Thulesius, Fridlund, and Petersson (2006); Townsley and Geist (2000); Wilson, Hutchinson, and Holzemer (2002); Wright (1997); and Zoller (2003).

Systematic inductive analysis through ethnographic and grounded theory analysis lends itself to traditional research report forms that facilitate documentation of patterns through literature reviews, explanation of method, careful explication of themes or categories buttressed with data examples, and a discussion of theoretical and practical implications of analyses. This style of writing continues to proliferate in academic journals, and I practice it commonly myself.

SAME OLD, SAME OLD: THE VALUE
OF TRADITIONAL QUALITATIVE WRITING

Critics take to task many aspects of the conventional forms of writing that traditionally report grounded theory analysis findings. Richardson (2000b) pointed out how boring so much otherwise "good" qualitative research can be to read. And certainly the number of researchers who are not willing or able to write engaging prose remains unfortunately large. Denzin (1997) sums up these critiques of analytical methods (such as grounded theory and narrative analysis):

> These methods of analysis risk reproducing the fallacy of objective reading. . . . This framework presumes a fixed text with fixed meanings. . . . These methods fail to address language's radical indeterminacy, the slipperiness of signs and signifiers . . . and the fact that language creates rather than mirrors reality. . . . These methods fail to examine the text as a meaningful whole. (p. 244)

To be fair, such critiques of mainstream academic writing generally are on target; we can get too enamored of our constructions and forget how partial, situated, and messy they really are (Ellingson, 2005a). I acknowledge the strength of Denzin's and others' position on the limitations of analytical qualitative methods; if left unexamined, unproblematized, and not complemented by other genres, detached and analytical writing offers only limited (and potentially harmful) entry into understanding researchers' and participants' worlds and sense-making processes.

However, as apparent in my choice to include grounded theory analysis in this text, I disagree that such genres *necessarily* are unacceptable from an interpretive perspective. I hear in this statement echoes of critics of narrative research who assert that unscientific, personal, messy writing "must be avoided." No genre should be declared off-limits; a plurality of genres—and the many ways in which they can be read—can only strengthen the social sciences. Authors do not solely construct their texts; readers and writers co-construct the meanings of texts: "We should remember that readers are always active participants in the construction and application of the conditional knowledge we share" with them in our research (Rawlins, 2007, p. 62). Our goal should be to encourage a multitude of points of entry:

> Authorship is about increasing the opportunities for different readings. The reader becomes significant, not as a consumer of correct results—the right intended meaning from the text and its author(ity)—but in a more active and less predictable positioning, in which interesting readings may be divorced from the possible intentions of the author. (Alvesson & Sköldberg, 2000, p. 171)

Therein lies the possibility for learning from an analytical report while simultaneously engaging in a subversive reading of the text. Hence, readers of realist analytical texts can (and I do) read findings as partial, situated, and reflecting the positionality of the writer, of the reader (myself), and of the particular time and context in which the text was written and in which I read it. I do this even if (especially if) the author does not acknowledge her or his positionality or influence on the findings. Some strategies for reading subversively include

• Noting the authors' institution and discipline; as you read, reflect on how disciplinary socialization likely shapes topic focus, methods, and writing practices.

• Reflecting on your own disciplinary, methodological, and ideological leanings and try to be conscious of how they direct your attention, enable you to take statements for granted, or conversely lead you to question a statement.

• Carefully reading (or note the lack of) descriptive details of research participants; be conscious of whose truths are (claimed to be) reflected in the aggregated data and conclusions.

• Questioning findings, not in order to disprove them in an aggressive/attacking stance but to ask: What else? What's left out? How does the form reflect the specific sociopolitical moment of the text's creation? What does this text say about its authors?

- Reading against the genre to reveal the text's construction. If the findings are more implied in an artistic representation, try to form a one-sentence explanation of the text's message; if the message is explicit in a research report, imagine how those findings could be re-presented poetically.

I thus problematize the claim that traditional texts reproduce an image of the positivist reader. The text can not reproduce an image on its own; it requires the reader's involvement. I agree that a text may offer more or fewer cues as to the type of reader it projects (certainly medical journals offer more suggestions of a positivist reader than do medical humanities journals, for example), but all texts still remain open to different reading positions. Analytic knowing must *not* be the only form of approved knowing in the social sciences, and neither should narrative knowing, or any other single approach.

Writing academic research reports (preferably reflecting a social constructionist or postmodern perspective, written in first-person voice) remains valuable after the interpretive turn for many reasons. First, patterns and themes represent a rich way of arranging collective stories. While not exhaustive or perfect, themes help us to understand what happens in a context or within a group. Inductive analysis constitutes a far more efficient way to share findings than attempting to present all aspects of your data, an impossible goal. Patterns help us to digest information, and as long as we do not labor under the illusion that a set of patterns constitutes a singular, valid reality, we benefit from systematic overview of phenomena.

Second, inductive analysis provides useful insights to a discipline's knowledge base. Being able to explain patterns and illustrate them with rich exemplars provides important descriptive and analytical knowledge on topics of interest. In my case, information about communication processes contributes to our interdisciplinary research on team communication that may prove helpful for other health care teams as they seek to revise and improve their modes of practice (Ellingson, 2003).

Next, although seemingly conventional among qualitative researchers, the language and style of grounded theory provides a way to introduce qualitative research in disciplines characterized by statistical research. For example, qualitative research pushes the boundaries of the positivist biomedical orientation that dominates medicine and medical research to incorporate more interpretive findings. At the same time, this genre uses language that fits fairly well within the norms of medicine, helping to make the findings intelligible and more

palatable, and easing scientific readers into consideration of qualitative perspectives rather than plunging them into a radically different mode of data representation (e.g., poems or narratives) that they likely will reject out of hand.[2]
Rawlins (2007) calls such passing in mainstream journals "guerilla scholarship"
(p. 59; see Chapter 6 for more on guerilla scholarship).

Finally, the grounded theory genre enables researchers to articulate concrete
arguments, to make claims and support them with data and with connections to
relevant research literature. As M. Wolf (1992) argues, "I still see my ethnographic responsibility as including an effort to make sense out of what I saw, was
told, or read—first for myself and then for my readers" (p. 5). Grounded theory
offers one useful form of making sense that appeals to the desire for analysis and
less ambiguous claims than those possible in artistic writing.

AESTHETICS AND ANALYSIS:
HYBRIDS OF ART AND SCIENCE

Taking a step to the left of constructivist grounded theory and traditionally
structured academic prose lands us in the realm of art/science hybrid representations. At no one point do we abruptly cross over from constructivist social
science to art; endless numbers of ways to blend art and science exist, with
more being developed all the time. Moreover, systematic inductive analysis
simply does not radically depart from creative analytic work as some maintain.
Rather, forms of sense making share many commonalties: "There is magic
within the method of qualitative data analysis" (Hunter, Lusardi, Zicker, Jacelon,
& Chandler, 2002, p. 388), and "there is artistry in identifying and interpret-
ing meaningful actions in the ongoing activities of others" (Harter, Norander,
& Quinlan, 2007, p. 110). At the same time, producing artistic representations
requires analytical thinking, conscious reflection, and strategic choices concerning which details to include, what the artistic account's purpose and audience are, and what moral or lesson it portrays.

One way to achieve art/science hybrid accounts is to re-present conventionally derived findings. Inductive qualitative analysis can be showcased in
other ways besides traditional research reports: Carr (2003) used poetry to further explore her grounded theory analysis of data on vigilance of patients'
loved ones. Gray and Sinding (2002) wrote and produced a performative piece
based upon focus groups and interviews with women living with metastatic
breast cancer and with oncologists. Hybrids also integrate inductive/grounded

theory analysis with other methods of data collection, such as photography (López et al., 2005) and participatory action research (Teram, Schachter, & Stalker, 2005).

Another way to overtly blend the voices of art and science is to weave them into a single representation. *Layered accounts* move back and forth between academic prose and narrative, poetry, or other art, revealing their constructed nature through the juxtaposition of social science and artistic ways of knowing (Ronai, 1995). Layered accounts often connect personal experiences to theory, research, and cultural critique and/or to discussions of methodological matters (e.g., Ellingson, 1998; Jago, 2006; Magnet, 2006; Markham, 2005; Ronai, 1999, Saarnivaara, 2003). For example, Jago (2006) explores both her own experiences of father-absence and the process of doing research with and representing women raised without fathers, who must construct and inhabit "a livable personal narrative through 'a primary act of imagination'" (p. 398), weaving together narratives, theory, and related research findings. Alternatively, hybrid accounts can feature a single narrative followed by a section containing analysis and/or a review of relevant literature (or vice versa), presenting two ways of knowing sequentially rather then repeatedly moving between them (e.g., Ellis, 1993).

As with more conventional modes of writing, hybrid accounts that weave together academic voices with those of art embody representational advantages and disadvantages. On the plus side, these forms provide the best of both words: analysis and story, entry into a richly evoked world, and a critical view of it, show and tell. Ronai (1995) articulates the possibilities of such blended formats for addressing particularly painful and complex topics, such as child sex abuse. The primary drawback of such boundary-spanning accounts is their relatively limited publication outlets. Also, although interweaving voices works well in some cases, it potentially can become tiresome and distracting for readers. Authors face a significant challenge when they seek to construct a coherent account that maintains focus and clarity while abruptly shifting between ways of knowing and representing.

AESTHETIC POSSIBILITIES: CREATIVE ANALYTIC PRACTICES

At the left end of the qualitative continuum, creative analytic representations of social science work take the form of stories, painting, sculpture, poetry, and performance (Richardson 1994, 2000b). A. W. Frank (1995) urges us to think *with* stories, not simply *about* them as we subject them to analysis. The advantage of artistic representations lies in their capacity for readers to empathize with writers' experiences. Like all art, creative social science representations enable us to learn about ourselves, each other, and the world through encountering the unique lens of one person's (or a group's) passionate rendering of reality into a moving, artistic expression of meaning. At its best, art engages our hearts and minds, sparking compassion and inspiring people to change themselves, their communities, and the world (Ellis, 2004). The limitation that art cannot (and should not) escape is the glorious indeterminacy of meaning that forms its very strength. Art shows, and showing is not always best; sometimes, an occasion calls for telling. You do not have to reject an art form to acknowledge that it cannot serve the need for a technical manual, for example. Some have critiqued artistic representation as self-absorbed and of limited utility to the knowledge building enterprise (e.g., Atkinson, 1997). Others clearly find fault with creative analytic accounts on an individual basis as reviewers and editors of the many mainstream journals across the social sciences, education, and health and human services that police their boundaries to exclude any work that violates conventional research report standards. Doubtless still others simply ignore artistic work, dismissing it in favor of reading and citing more conventional social scientific accounts. I embrace artistic accounts as useful in their own right, but primarily utilize them myself in multigenre work.

At the artistic end of the qualitative continuum, I sketch out a variety of popular approaches to integrating art into social science. These categories are loose and overlapping, not discrete, with tremendous variation within each category. Moreover, my list represents only some of the possibilities out there. I hope readers will use this as a jumping-off point for their explorations in creative analytic practices, not as a destination.

Autoethnography

Autoethnography is research, writing, story, and method that connect the autobiographical and personal to the cultural, social, and political—it is both a process and a product (Ellis, 2004, p. xix). It involves the study of a culture of which you are a part, integrated with your relational and inward experiences. The author incorporates the "I" into research and writing, yet analyzes self as if studying an "other" (Ellis, 2004; Goodall, 2000). Autoethnography displays multiple layers of consciousness, connecting the personal to the cultural, often utilizing a layered format of representation. Autoethnographic texts appear in a variety of forms, although the predominant form consists of stories written by researchers who systematically introspect and record their experience with the intent of evoking emotional response from readers (L. Berger & Ellis, 2002). In these texts, authors express the workings of the self emotionally, physically, and cognitively. These texts feature concrete action, emotion, embodiment, spirituality, and introspection, which appear as relational and institutional stories impacted by history, social structure, and culture, which themselves are revealed dialectically through action, feeling, thought, and language. Autoethnography portrays meaning through dialogue, scenes, characterization, and plot, claiming the conventions of literary writing (Ellis & Bochner, 2000). For example, Lee's (2006) autoethnographic article details her emotional struggle when informed of a loved one's suicide and her grief in the context of her ongoing life. See Ellis (2004) for detailed lessons on conducting autoethnography; for other exemplars, see Kiesinger (2002), Rambo (2005, 2007), Secklin (2001), and Spry (1997).

Poetry and Poetic Transcription

The creative analytic practice of poetic representation of findings provides rich modes for artistic expression of research (Faulkner, 2007; Richardson, 1992a, 1992b, 1993, 2000b). Variations include research poetry wherein authors present poems but do not contextualize them with analysis or methodological details (e.g., Chawla, 2006; Richardson, 1994) and a "hybrid poem" that is a "grafting together of narrative research, qualitative methods, and poetic representation" (Prendergast, 2007, p. 743; see also González, 1998). Austin (1996) represents her relationship as an African American doctoral student with an African woman anthropology doctoral student as a "narrative poem" that "celebrate[s] [her participant] and the unique relationship we developed through dialogue and conversation in the context of interactive research interviews" (p. 207). Hartnett (2003) offers "investigative poetry" that explores the horrors and hope within the U.S. prison-industrial complex.

Other researchers engage in poetic transcription of interview data. Although an artistic, interpretive sensibility informs poetic transcriptions of data, this process produces texts that "move in the direction of poetry but [are] not necessarily poetry" (Glesne, 1997, p. 213). Willis (2002) echoed this distinction, stating that the poems he developed from data, which he called "reflections in verse," "tended to be more elaborated and lacked the implicit and oblique character of more developed poems" (p. 4). Of course, poetic representations reflect no less researcher construction than do snippets of data interwoven into analytic explanations; interpretations shape the poetic representation of the participants' words. "Poetic transcription disintegrates any notion of separation of observer and observed. These categories are conflated in an interpretive space" (Glesne, 1997, p. 215). Researchers follow a variety of rules when engaging in "poetic transcription." While Richardson stated only that she retained her participant's words, syntax, and grammar while editing the transcript (Richardson, 1992a), Glesne (1997) elaborated on her process, explaining that she began with a traditional qualitative analysis to identify recurrent themes, and coded and sorted her data accordingly. Like Richardson, Glesne used only her participant's words. She further chose to select phrases from anywhere in her transcript and juxtapose them, but sought to retain her participant's speaking rhythm.

I differed slightly from Glesne's approach in my poetic transcriptions of dialysis technicians' understandings of professionalism (Ellingson, 2006b). I selected chronologically ordered excerpts from my interview transcripts which I then condensed and physically arranged (e.g., line breaks, spacing) on the page; also, I poetically transcribed transcripts of several different participants, rather than focusing on a single participant as others have chosen (e.g., Carr, 2003; Furman, 2006). For example, I transformed this bit of interview transcript,

> everybody he would treat wrong. It took me a week or so until I figured him out. Give him a bad time. Argue with him and it makes him happy. That's him. You've got to be—I hate to say it. To him its not disrespectful, but you got to be kind of like disrespectful towards him and speak to him basically in his own language in order for him to be happy. And he has to complain to be happy . . . ha ha . . .

into a portion of a poem:

> It took me a week or so until I figured
> him out.
> Give him a bad time, argue with him
> and it makes him happy. That's him.

I hate to say it.

You got to be kind of like

disrespectful towards him

and speak to him in his own language

in order for him to be happy.

And he has to complain

to be happy

Poetry and poetic forms offer rich opportunities for highlighting larger segments of participants' words than usually occurs in conventional reports that rely on very brief snippets of participants' words. Although different in form, poetry reflects much of the same artistic sensibility as narratives.

Narratives

The lines between ethnographic narratives and autoethnographic narratives continually slip and blur. We can most productively think of them as existing along a continuum from being primarily about the author at the autoethnographic end, to being primarily about participants/others at the ethnographic end, with a lot of fertile ground in between (see Van Maanen, 1988). Narratives constructed from fieldnotes, interview transcripts, or other data enable readers to think with and feel with a story, rather than only analyzing its meaning (A. W. Frank, 1995). Narratives enable qualitative researchers to show rather than tell, and such narratives enhance a number of different formats. Some authors weave brief narratives into the aforementioned layered accounts, while other ethnographic narratives stand as self-contained accounts. For example, the narrative chapter of *Communicating in the Clinic* portrays a "day in the life" of the oncology program staff and patients in which I am a character, and the focus is on the rhythms of the clinic. Given their length and difficulty in condensing evocative representation, ethnographic narratives often require or at least lend themselves readily to book-length publication. Drew's (2001) ethnography of the world of Karaoke combines vivid narratives of performance with critical commentary on the popular music industry, celebrity culture, and social norms surrounding public performance. Other exemplars of ethnographic narratives include Tilmann-Healy's (2001) book on friendship between gay and straight people, Abu-Lughod's (1993) study of the lives and stories of Bedouin women, Trujillo's (2004) ethnographic portrait of family relationships that centers on his grandmother, and Diamond's (1995) intimate ethnography of a nursing home.

Article-length ethnographic narratives appear in journals less frequently, presumably due to space constraints. Parry's (2006) short stories based upon her interviews with women negotiating pregnancy, birth, and midwifery within the highly medicalized, "fetocentric" culture of North America and Parry's (2004) short stories of women negotiating infertility provide two excellent exemplars. Other examples of this genre include narratives of aging Muslim women immigrants in Canada (Dossa, 1999), tales of a soup kitchen for homeless and near-homeless people (D. L. Miller, Creswell, & Olander, 1998), short stories about street kids in Brazil (Diversi, 1998), and an impressionist tale of "peer de-briefing" during a program evaluation (Cooper, Brandon, & Lindberg, 1998).

Fiction

Like the line between narrative and autobiography/autoethnography, the line between "factual" narratives and fiction similarly proves elusive. The truth/fiction dichotomy pervades Western cultures but ultimately breaks down as scholars inevitably fail to make any definitive distinction between the categories. Fiction often feels profoundly true in its representation of some aspect of life, while established facts often fail to communicate anything close to the complex realities of a situation: "Facts don't always tell the truth, or a truth worth worrying about, and the truth in a good story—its resonance with our felt experience, as Walter Fisher says—sometimes must use imaginary facts" (A. Banks & Banks, 1998, p. 11, see also Rinehart, 1998). Some scholars, nurtured in graduate school with notions of research as a search for definitive truth involving careful avoidance of error, may feel threatened by the use of openly fictional accounts in the name of social science. Such work may seem a hopelessly relativistic surrender to the impossibility of making any authoritative claims. However, "the imposition of fiction into the divide between fact and error doesn't negate the possibility of a real world; all it does is recognize the impossibility for authors to be objective" in their descriptions of that world (Stephen P. Banks, quoted in A. Banks & Banks, 1998, p. 13). That is, we can represent the world in truthful ways, regardless of whether the narrative reflects facts that bear less than direct correlation to others' perceptions of an event.

One strong example of the use of fiction to tell truthful fiction is *Opportunity House: Ethnographic Stories of Mental Retardation,* a collection of fictionalized stories about adults who are developmentally disabled and live in a residential community (Angrosino, 1998). Through fiction, Angrosino both protects the anonymity of his cognitively disabled participants (whose capacity to give informed consent is questionable) and uses the freedom of the genre to communicate truths of the varieties of experience of his participants, demonstrating the differences among the participants, rather than simply lumping them all into a single, pitiful category. Quite to the contrary, the stories portray his characters as articulate, wily, perceptive, and wonderfully human. For other, article-length exemplars see the groundbreaking collection *Fiction and Social Research: By Ice or Fire,* which includes fictional stories and essays about fiction in ethnographic work (A. Banks & Banks, 1998), as well as Athens's (2006) two tales from a novel about ethnic conflict, Gerla's (1995) ethnographic fiction that compares the experiences of students at wealthy and poor schools in Texas, K. Frank's (2000) short fiction based on fieldwork in strip clubs, S. P. Banks's (2000) five fictional holiday letters, and Ross and Geist's (1997) truthful fictions of women's experiences of pregnancy and miscarriage.

Video Representations

Visual social scientists use three different types of sources of images in their work: images created by participants, those created by researchers, and preexisting images that are part of the group or culture with whom researchers are engaged (C. A. B. Warren & Karner, 2005).

Many of these visual forms of representation involve participatory methods. For example, photovoice, based on the work of Freire (1970/2000, 1973/2002), is designed to empower by having participants take photographs of their lives, providing space for reflection and discussion of the images, and ideally empowering participants to act on their own behalf (Carlson, Engebretson, & Chamberlain, 2006; see also McAllister, Wilson, Green, & Baldwin, 2005; Nowell, Berkowitz, Deacon, & Foster-Fishman, 2006; Singhal, Harter, Chitnis, & Sharma, 2007; Singhal & Rattine-Flaherty, 2006; Wang & Burris, 1994). White (2003) provides an exemplary overview of a variety of approaches to participatory video making in which participants create or co-create films as critical and potentially liberatory projects that reflect and spark grassroots organizing. Projects described in White's volume focus on such diverse groups as

Arab women (Underwood & Jabre, 2003), Guatemalan Mayan women (Guidi, 2003), and Columbian domestic workers (Dudley, 2003).

Other video representations of ethnographic data can resemble documentary filmmaking. Such accounts provide rich views into worlds often marginalized in mainstream discourse. Examples include *Heart Broken in Half: Chicago's Street Gangs* (Siegel & Conquergood, 1990), a gripping portrayal of the hopes and realities of gang members; *Beyond Consumption: Retail at the Edge* (Shaw & Adelman, 2001), an ethnographic video that blends marketing, consumption, and social support and highlights major themes revolving around well-being and consumerism by focusing on "Venus," a consignment shop for large women, and "Toys in Babeland," a sex toy-shop that caters primarily to women; *The Pilgrim Must Embark: Living in Community* (Adelman & Shultz, 1991), an ethnographic video documenting life in a residential facility for people living with AIDS (Bonaventure House, Chicago, IL) that focuses on the inherent tensions of community living that permeate the practical, personal, and communal lives of residents; and *Between Two Worlds: The Hmong Shaman in America* (Siegel & Conquergood, 1985), which captures rare and dramatic footage of a Hmong shaman in the United States from Conquergood's ethnographic fieldwork, explains the traditions of this displaced people, and portrays a people caught between two worlds.

Scholars also write and perform visual work in video and photography that features primarily their own lives and experiences. For example, one performance studies scholar created a video he described this way:

> Inspired by the music of Laurie Anderson, "lenses" explores the filmmaker's own personal history: a child creating a place for himself; a teenager coming to terms with his homosexuality; and an adult finding love and grieving its subsequent loss. Four women—each representing different facets of his personality—take the viewer on a surreal odyssey of expressionistic, iconic imagery painting an emotional landscape of psyche and gender identity. Ultimately, the filmmaker uses an experimental narrative structure to better understand his past and as a means for personal catharsis. With an approximate running time of 45 minutes, "lenses" is told solely through images accompanied by a score of Anderson's music and stories. (Santoro, 2004)

Videos also are increasingly available via Web sites. One outstanding source is the online, peer-reviewed journal *Liminalities: A Journal of Performance*

Studies, a wonderful source of archived video and audio performances. For example, Issue 2.3 contains gems such as: "Just the Funny Bits" (Galloway, 2006), a video of hilarious and poignant performance selections about her life as a deaf woman; visit the journal at http://liminalities.net/archives.htm.

Live Performance

Many researchers create live performances (which may be taped and screened again) based on autoethnography, ethnographic fieldnotes, and/ or interview data (Spry, 2001). Such performances function as fictional theatre does by engaging audiences and inviting them into the experience of the stage. Gray and Sinding (2002) detail the development of two live performances based on studies of women living with metastatic breast cancer and men living with prostate cancer. They developed the performances to educate and inspire dialogue among health care providers, patients' groups, and larger community; the book comes with a videotape of the live performances.[3] Another research team developed a "dramatic production" entitled *Expressions of Personhood in Alzheimer's* (Kontos & Naglie, 2007). The performance serves as a teaching tool for medical practitioners to humanize the experience of Alzheimer's patients from a person-centered perspective with attention to aesthetics, thus producing an engaging experience to foster learning and dissemination of qualitative research findings (for more on ethnodrama, see Mienczakowski, 1996, 2001).

CONCLUSION

In sum, many opportunities exist along the qualitative continuum that provide representational diversity for producing crystallized accounts. I have scratched only the surface here. I hope readers embrace the joy and the challenge of working in genres reflecting contrasting epistemologies across the qualitative continuum. This chapter's Interlude illuminates the limitations of dichotomous thinking as a way to further demonstrate the relationships among the many forms of representation discussed in this chapter. Chapter 4 outlines strategies for making choices about selecting and combining genres as you design and develop your crystallized project.

INTERLUDE

Resisting Dichotomy, Embracing Continuum

I address the limits of dichotomous thinking early in the qualitative methods course I teach, right after introducing social constructionism as the epistemology that underlies the methodological continuum. "The central premise of social constructionism," I tell my students, "is that meaning is not inherent. The central concerns of constructionist inquiry are to study what people 'know' and how they create, apply, contest, and act upon these ideas" (Harris, 2006, p. 225).

My undergraduate students sit with their desks arranged in a circle, faces not yet drooping with late-term fatigue, but more than a few evidencing the mild resentment born of taking required courses. I discuss the politics of the field of qualitative research, and how hotly contested many issues are within the field, referencing their reading by Potter (1996). My students look at me with naked disbelief when I add with a smile, "And some of us actually care so deeply and passionately about this stuff that we have ongoing debates and dialogues and even get *mad* at each other sometimes!" The students shake their heads, mystified as to how anyone could care so much about such a topic.

I share an exercise that I use each quarter with methods students. I give them a list down one side of a sheet of paper with the following words: Hard, Man, True, Rational, Objective, White, Right, Good, Mind, Strong, Father, Science, Quantitative. I ask them to quickly and without thinking too hard to just list the opposite of each of these terms on the other side of the paper. And every quarter, with the rarest of exceptions, every single student replies with the same list in less than a minute: soft, woman, false, irrational (or emotional), subjective, black, wrong, bad (or evil), body, weak, mother, art, and qualitative. So ingrained in our minds is the ideal of thinking in terms of dichotomies—that is, paired opposites—that students do so easily and without questioning my seemingly odd request.

I ask them why they think women are the opposite of men and to explain all the ways in which we are opposite. "What of the ways we are similar? How are they reflected?" I ask. We discuss the limits of dualistic thinking. Likewise, the art/science and quantitative/qualitative dichotomies limit our ability to think through the "way it is" or, at least, the way it could be. "Becoming qualitative researchers is in large part about rejecting dichotomies," I tell them.

The idea of rethinking the world in terms of continua takes the vast majority of my students by surprise. "You have to learn how to see what is in between the extremes," I tell them, "since that is where we live most of the time. Most people are neither wrenchingly poor nor lavishly wealthy, but somewhere in between. Most people aren't all masculine or all feminine in their characteristics, but an intriguing, androgynous blend of the two. Many problems facing our society today cannot be reduced to right/wrong, good/bad; they are too complex. It is in the complexities that the richness of experience is experienced and hence can be explored."

Then I tell them that making sense of the world through dichotomous thinking is unproductive. "Dichotomies are pervasive in Western thinking," I add, warming to my topic, my excitement growing. The circle of students remains quite unexcited, but I continue undaunted. "Knowledge is not 'out there' waiting to be found. Instead, we socially construct knowledge in relationships, through formal channels (such as academic journals) and through informal, interpersonal interaction with others (Gergen, 1994). Unfortunately, we are so schooled in some ways of thinking that we no longer notice how limiting those mental patterns can be. There are three ways in which dichotomies limit our thinking. You'll want to take notes on this and ask me questions if you don't understand, since this isn't in the reading, and it will be on the exam."

This last comment brings them to rapt attention, and they poise their pens above their notebooks as I explain, "First, dichotomies present as opposites what are actually interdependent. Socially constructed opposites actually *depend* upon each other for existence; without women, there would be no men, only people; without hard, there would be no soft, only a single texture.

"Second, dichotomies limit the possibilities to two and only two, negating the near-infinite possibilities present between any two poles. Thus, we can resist the limitations of femininity and masculinity as mutually exclusive opposites and imagine them instead as poles between which there are many degrees of androgyny, blended identities, and possible performances of sex, gender, and sexuality.

"Finally, when we limit possibilities to only two, one will inevitably be valued over the other. It is not possible to view the world in terms of equal opposites; one side is *always already* privileged." As I finish the statement, I notice I am leaning forward, gesturing enthusiastically, my voice effortlessly projecting throughout the room. One of my students, a lovely young woman who works in my department office, looks up at my impassioned soliloquy and gives me an amused smile.

As my students dutifully scribble away, I think about how Ellis (2004) charts qualitative research with the squiggly, broken line down the middle between the art and science sides. "Qualitative as art and qualitative as science," she writes, "are endpoints of a continuum. You have to decide where you want to locate yourselves in terms of your identity and in every research project you do. That location will determine your goals, the procedures you use, and the claims you make" (Ellis, 2004, pp. 25–31). Inspired by her approach (see chart in appendix II in Ellis, 2004, pp. 359–363) and our essay that mapped the qualitative continuum that my students also read (Ellis & Ellingson, 2000), I developed my own figure that I pass out to my students, illustrating not only the ends of the qualitative continuum but also articulating much of the rich middle ground (see Figure 1.1, pp. 8–9). After discussing the breadth of options across the continuum, I organize the students into groups and pass out a set of research article abstracts and a sheet with several small, blank continua on them. I ask them to examine the language, practices, and claims made in the abstracts and then, based on their impressions, to mark where on the qualitative continuum they would place each study and to justify their choices. This exercise engages students in critical thinking and facilitates them becoming more familiar with the central premises of the three main designations (right, middle, left) of the continuum.

NOTES

1. Other researchers conduct qualitative analyses that resemble grounded theory in the sense of being inductive and discerning patterns, but do not follow precisely the guidelines. Deriving themes was one way of describing inductive analysis; for instance, Apker (2001, p. 121) "reviewed [data] for emergent themes," and Gillespie (2001) employed Owen's (1984) criteria for themes (repetition, recurrence, and forcefulness) to determine which ideas were representative in the data (see also Meyer & O'Hara, 2004). "Patterns" is another term invoked to describe inductive analyses (e.g., Braithewaite, 1997; Morgan & Krone, 2001). While significant differences do exist among these forms of inductive analysis, I do not explain them here since they are not germane to my purpose of constructing a broad map of the qualitative continuum. Any systematic qualitative analysis procedure potentially can be combined with artistic accounts through crystallization.

2. Acceptance of narrative perspectives is on the rise in medical communities, and medical humanities programs enrich medical education to encourage holistic learning with art and literature (see, e.g., *Journal of Medical Humanities*). However, practitioners and scholars in medicine still largely consider the production of narrative and artistic work to be pedagogical or stress-management techniques; medicine largely frames art as a complement to research, but not as constituting research itself. While clearly having made a step in the interpretive direction, biomedical views of science continue to pervade medical research and medical culture (e.g., du Pre, 2005).

3. I witnessed *Handle With Care?* (the performance focusing on breast cancer) at the 2000 SSSI Couch-Stone Symposium, in St. Petersburg, Florida. It was a moving and inspiring performance; although painful, it also was a blessing to encounter such empathetic renderings of cancer experiences. As A. W. Frank (2002)—also a cancer survivor—says of the performance in the foreword to the volume,

> this research does what so many social scientists talk about in principle but few are able to effect in practice: it listens. . . . When I saw this play, I knew this was the research report I wanted those who might someday care for me to have seen, so that they would *care* for me, not just treat me. (p. viii)

FOUR

STRATEGIES FOR DESIGN

Putting Crystallization Into Practice

———•◆•———

*More important than attempting to include everything—or as much
as possible—is to have a well-thought-out pluralism and a balanced
multiplicity in the perspectives that the empirical landings offer.*

—Alvesson and Sköldberg
(2000, p. 188)

C rystallization does provide a tempting openness to casting a wide net
when composing a text, but that does not mean that more is necessarily
better. As in the quote above, authors should aim for pluralism and balance,
not simply for a laundry list of different representational forms. The trick, of
course, remains finding and maintaining that balance between richness and
diversity of perspective on one hand, and coherence, aesthetic appeal, and clarity
on the other. At the same time, all authors confront limitations on their skills
in any given genre.

No formula for crystallized design exists. Instead, opportunities and constraints abound, and researchers should expect, even embrace, an organic evolution of their projects. Janesick (2000) encourages us to think of qualitative
research as being both like a precise, orderly, scripted minuet *and* like a free-
flowing, responsive, creative improvisational dance. Training and careful planning prepare you to enter the field, but equally vital is embracing opportunities

73

as they arise and adapting to the needs of the people and context in which you work (see Janesick, 2003). You have no need at any given point in your project to decide "once and for all" what methods of collection, analysis, and representation you will use; plans should remains always open to revision and amendment. Nonetheless, you may find it helpful to map out preliminary goals and ideas about analyses and genres to provide a working vision of a project.

This chapter leads readers through the initial design processes of a project utilizing crystallization. I begin by outlining a reflection process, suggesting questions to guide you in exploring a myriad of considerations about the best fit among your goals and audience(s), as well as your personal strengths and weaknesses. I then offer several guidelines for weighing your options for analysis and representations. I discuss the role of theory in different types of qualitative research and suggest ways of managing its inclusion in various forms of representation. Finally, I advise determining a thesis statement or statement of purpose for your crystallized project, mapping the project, and then looking to the future. Of course, none of the steps outlined here are fixed in a linear progression; I invite you to think of crystallization as an iterative process and to forge your own creative paths.

WONDERING

Regardless of how improvisational a research project turns out to be in data collection and analysis, all good research begins with preparation (Janesick, 2000). We must have training and planning, even if we then set aside the plan once in the field.

> The aha, the path to illumination, does not just happen. The creative leap is
> at best a wish, more likely an illusion. The creative person does not leap to
> illumination. Extensive preparation is required to lay the groundwork for one
> to be creative. (Hunter et al., 2002, p. 396)

Crystallization likewise requires preparation in order to set the stage for whatever opportunities may arise. In addition to reading relevant methodological, theoretical, and topic-specific materials, I also suggest that researchers explore their goals in a process I call *wondering*.

To prepare, explore the answers you generate to the following questions in deciding how to engage in crystallization for your project. I heartily encourage journaling or free writing on these topics, using writing as a method of inquiry (Richardson, 2000b). Questions to ask yourself about your project goals, intended audiences, own abilities and interests, and data should address your data collection and ongoing analysis, topics of investigation, preferred audiences, your own preferences and desires, and the genres through which you could express your ideas.

Data/Analysis

- What cases, events, stories, or details come to mind immediately when I think about my data?

- What have I learned about my data by immersing myself in it?

- What contradictions, inconsistencies, or exceptions to the rules do I notice in my data?

- How does my identity relate to my work? How do my age, gender, race/ethnicity, nationality, abilities and disabilities, special talents, formative experiences, and so on shape how I understand my data?

- How do I think my participants perceive me?

- What have my participants taught me about their worlds? About mine?

- How is power revealed and concealed in my data?

- How am I complicit with systems of power in my data and analyses?

- What truths seem to be missing from the preliminary analyses and accounts I have worked on?

Topics

- What are the key content claims I want to make about my topic?

- What patterns do I wish to explore?

- What is/are my thesis statement(s) for this project?

- What political implications of my project do I want to explore?

- What pragmatic suggestions for improving the world have I developed? Or in what areas do I detect a need for improvement that I might be able to shed light on with my study?

- What questions do I still have about my setting, participants, and processes?

Audiences

- What academic audiences do I want to reach with my work?
- What community, lay, or popular audiences could benefit from my findings?
- What would my favorite auntie [insert friend/relative of your choice] want to know about this topic?
- What nonprofit or government agencies could benefit from my project?
- What policies could be improved using ideas from my project?
- Sharing with which audiences would bring me the most satisfaction? Why?

Researcher Desire

- What is my favorite thing about my data? What makes me smile when I think of it? What makes me cry? What makes me angry?
- What would be fun to write?
- What process issues or ideas come up in my journaling that intrigue me?
- What strong emotions do I have about my participants, their stories, and our relationships?
- Whose research do I admire? Why?
- What about my study embarrasses me or makes me feel self-conscious? Why?
- What am I most proud of in my data?
- If one of my mentors asked me about my project, what would I want to tell her/him?

Genres

- What new forms would I like to experiment with?
- What types of writing am I good at?
- What nonwritten forms could I collect or represent my data in?

- What genres do I enjoy reading? Why?

- With what genres are my participants most familiar and comfortable?

- What texts could I produce that would benefit my participants?

- How do accounts I have written or produced (e.g., fieldnotes, transcripts, photographs, e-mails, memos) shape each other?

Using these questions, explore the project you see (or hope to see) taking shape. Stream-of-consciousness writing about an issue may help to get your mind rolling. You can also talk these issues out with a supportive friend or colleague; for example, my friend and colleague Leigh Berger Serrie and I had weekly "chai chats" at a café where we took turns processing out loud with each other issues that we were facing in the development of our book manuscripts. Any manuscript requires innumerable decisions about content, language, and style. The freedom of moving beyond generic constraints through crystallization makes this process exponentially more complex, but also invigorating. Wondering enables you to explore options throughout the duration of qualitative projects as new opportunities, insights, and relationships develop. I urge you to set aside time for wondering and (re)answer these questions throughout data collection, analysis, and writing and/or producing art in other media.

WEIGHING YOUR OPTIONS

You can choose from among an infinite number of formats for crystallization, which can both excite and overwhelm researchers, even experienced ones (certainly myself among them). I recommend several strategies to help you along as you consider how to analyze, represent, and format your text(s).

First, intentionally move beyond your comfort zone in at least one area. Embrace crystallization as an opportunity to expand your repertoire of tools and techniques: Try a different genre or medium, engage in a new form of analysis, consider incorporating critical theory, experiment with ways of juxtaposing genres, play with the physical layout of words and voices on the page. Remember that you do not have to choose among your loyalties; you can have your analysis and your narrative too. Ideally, you will produce good work in a variety of genres, but even if you do not produce publishable material in a new genre you experiment with, you still benefit: The exercise will undoubtedly enrich your understanding of some aspects of your self, participants, data, and/or research processes.

Or consider studying a topic area far removed from your current perspective/ daily world. Much good research comes from being able to offer a fresh perspective based upon an outsider's view, often referred to in ethnography as the "etic" point of view, in contrast to the "emic," or insider, perspective (C. A. B. Warren & Karner, 2005). While few endorse old models of the privileged, colonialist scholar going to a community to judge the "natives" according to the (unstated) norms and values of the scholar's (imperialist) culture, that does not mean that ethnographers cannot do excellent work in areas completely new to them. Often an outsider can detect the taken-for-grantedness of daily practices within a setting. Here are a few ideas to get you started in a new area:

- Focus on burning political, moral, or religious questions that intrigue you and for which you long to find (or build) an answer; see where those questions lead you.

- Take a good long look at your everyday life and the thousands of taken-for-granted elements of communication that you unthinkingly use every day; explore one of them.

- Talk to someone you admire about their passions and interests; join in one of their activities and see if it engages you.

- Volunteer in your community. Not only will doing so likely lead you to opportunities to study the experiences and needs of a group of (under-served) people, it will also make you realize how blessed you are.

- Take someone over the age of 70 out for coffee and really listen to them—what they care about, questions they have, places they went, decisions they regret, choices they relish, chances they took. If you don't have older relatives, borrow a friend's, or visit a senior center to invite conversation.

If you decide to go and then to write about (or otherwise represent) where you have never gone before, I suggest you do so in a spirit of humility, posi-tioning yourself as a respectful, grateful student of those whose cultural exper-tise you would like to learn about. Do not patronize participants by trying to minimize (or conversely to prove) your intelligence or accomplishments; instead, emphasize how much you value the opportunity to learn about the par-ticipants' world. In a new setting, you are likely to find both shared ground and moments of disconnect with participants. That push-pull of identification and difference may lend itself to multigenre expression in which your multiple (perhaps conflicting) perspectives on a setting are each captured via a different genre (Ellingson, 1998).

Second, listen to your data. In each study I have conducted, certain elements, moments, stories, and questions have tugged at my heart and/or my mind, and on more than one occasion, my spirit. Consider what tugs at you in terms of both form and content, and what pops into your mind when you are grocery shopping or driving. Pay attention to those flashes of insight, and they will lead you to the heart of what you need to address. For example, one of the challenges of my ongoing dialysis project that continually tugs at me involves the endless repetition of behaviors in the unit—the same patients come for the same procedure at the same time, with the same group of staff members, three times a week for months or even years (Ellingson, 2007). I find it challenging to form coherent and engaging accounts when, frankly, not much happens most of the time. At the same time, I learned that the unit always buzzes with thousands of tiny signals sent and received among the staff and between patients and staff in such a routinized manner as to give the *illusion* that nothing happens. This endless (re)enactment of routine intrigues me on an intellectual level, but pushes the limits of my writing skills. Engaging representation of the culture of the dialysis unit hinges on the ability to evoke the beauty and pain of the most excruciatingly mundane of actions, such as the rapid stripping of the clear plastic tubing from the dialysis machines following each patient's treatment, or the way the patients weigh themselves at the beginning and end of each treatment. A lengthy narrative (e.g., well-developed short story) of this unit eludes me; I bore myself. So far, I have had the most success with brief anecdote-length narratives that portray moments of interaction between staff and patients, poetic transcription (each constituting a series of fragments), a layered account, and one systematic analysis of routinized communication (Ellingson, 2007).

In contrast, the rhythms of daily life in the geriatric oncology clinic I studied were much more varied and dramatic in nature. Description of the interdisciplinary team felt more compelling when structured to tell a lengthy story of a day in the unit, showing the staff and patients interacting in a myriad of incidents that actually occurred on different days but which I recontextualized into a seamless narrative (see Chapter 2 in Ellingson, 2005a). So many different types of interaction and of consequences of patient diagnosis/prognosis facilitated character development and plot. The contrast of these two health care ethnographies demonstrates the complexities of the links between form and content of representation. While I can offer researchers no formula for crystallization, I am confident that each project contains the potential for multiple genres of representation, and that clues to those possibilities can be found through careful study of and listening to the data.

Next, try to bracket the voices in your head that tell you that your work blasphemes whichever methodological guru/mentor/program trained you. Such negativity can drown out the voices within your data and your own gut instincts. I do not mean to suggest that you ignore or reject your training or mentors, only that you learn how to set that training and socialization aside temporarily in order to contemplate and experiment with possibilities from a different angle. Writer Anne Lamott (1995) offers a wonderful exercise she recommends for handling critical voices that also lends itself to the type of bracketing I describe here: Close your eyes and picture your advisor, colleagues, journal editor, or whomever as a mouse. Pick this mouse up by the tail and drop it into a large, clear glass jar; repeat for all the disparaging or limiting voices you hear, and then slap a lid on it. Imagine turning the volume up all the way so you can hear a cacophony of voices criticizing you, guilt-tripping you, confusing you. Then turn the volume all the way down and go back to writing. Remember that the "if you're not for us, you're against us," "us/them" mentality reflects a false dichotomy. We can be for more than one methodological approach. Once you have wondered about your project, carefully considering your goals, audiences, and options for your work, commit to producing whatever genre draws you. Set aside your critics and worry about your work's reception later, *not* during the creative process. When you finish, if people tell you that they find your work inconsistent, contradictory, or hypocritical, you can explain yourself using one or more of the specific strategies for promoting and defending crystallization provided in Chapter 8. Of course, they may also simply find your experimental work lousy, a risk we take when we try new genres and media. For now, however, consciously set these outside voices aside.

Additionally, consider balance: Ask yourself how can you show *and* tell, talk *and* listen, move forward *and* step back, portray the personal *and* the political. Try to formulate a text or series of texts that provides not just multiple perspectives but a range of perspectives—group, societal, individual, dyadic, critical, appreciative, and so on. Resist limited notions of abstract or universal "fairness" or "equity" and instead think about what balance best serves your goals for this particular study. For example, I represent the voices of staff members more than those of patients in *Communicating in the Clinic*. That choice surprised and bothered me for a long time, especially since I empathized so deeply with patients. Further, Dr. Armani and I had (and continue to have via e-mail) rousing debates about my choices to invoke feminist theory in my accounts of him and the rest of the geriatric oncology team. Ultimately, I determined that those representational choices embodied my vision for the book as one that both applauds the work of the team and highlights the limitations of the hierarchical culture of medicine—providing a balance between appreciation and critique.

Moreover, I urge researchers to embrace your own personal satisfaction as an important factor in making choices: Formulate a text or series of texts that reflect and feed your quest for constructing knowledge, helping others, taking political stands, self-exploration, and artistic expression. A text can be about you without having to be *all* about you. Of all the myriad of topics available to me in the geriatric oncology clinic, I chose backstage communication in large part because of its forbidden fruit quality. Having spent years as a patient myself, the behind-the-scenes interactions among health care providers fascinated me. I felt delicious guilty pleasure at witnessing a culture that patients almost never encounter. All researchers have personal reasons for choosing the topics they pursue (Bochner, 1997); I recommend consciously making those reasons part of your decision-making process rather than pretending they do not exist so that no one will accuse you of being biased.

Next, engage in serious play. Stepping outside of the box scares most people. That box can be positivism/validity, the methods and approaches you feel most comfortable with, patriarchal institutional norms, or other familiar routines. Even "experimental" work can function as a limiting box, if that constitutes your usual mode of scholarship. Experimenting with different forms of representation in service of diffuse goals such as enriching our understanding of the world and of our modes of knowledge production seems risky at best, even foolish. You may quite reasonably reason that if your methods are not broken, you need not fix them. But since crystallization provides no one way to proceed, some trial and error always proves necessary. I prefer to think of this process in terms of serious play, rather than in terms of making errors. Play is *fun,* first of all, a concept that often gets lost as we work in academia. A sense of playfulness can help us to enjoy the process of considering our options (Sandelowski, 1994) and potentially assist in avoiding "analytic interruptus," or stopping before we have achieved deep, complex analyses of data (Lofland, 1970, p. 35). Set guilt and loyalties aside and concentrate on what seems like it would be invigorating to do; drudgery does not yield morally, aesthetically, or intellectually superior work, counter to the impression fostered by some number of academics.

Furthermore, consider other aspects of your life—hobbies, previous careers, family traditions, rituals or routines, friends, community organizations you support, spiritual or religious practices—that might provide insights into the possibilities, both literally and figuratively. Bochner (1997) and others have warned that keeping our personal and professionals lives artificially separate forms a fruitless and painful pursuit, and undoubtedly work has crept into our private time on numerous occasions. So reverse the trend; let your "other" interests influence your ideas about representation.

> I have used plays, poetry, pastiche, quilting, and mobiles to help me construct the magic in the phenomenon. . . . Making meaning of data is very much like making magic. . . . To capture the meaning, the gestalt, of the data, one must tap into the creative, magical self. (Hunter et al., 2002, p. 395)

I love scrapbooking, for example, at Friday night gatherings of women who come together to share their week's experiences while sorting and decorating photos. Pasting together disparate pieces of data with decorative and explanatory "embellishments" into a scholarly "scrapbook" forms an apt metaphor for crystallization. Following the rules of a sport while improvising with your own moves also works. Cooking a variety of dishes that together compose a delicious meal hints at yet another way of envisioning crystallization. Invite those metaphors in to your mind to shape your practices. Direct connections may also be possible; video or multimedia photo exhibits could be a great form for an arts-and-crafts devotee or family photographer to explore.

Each of the above suggestions provides a starting point for considering your options for analysis and multigenre representation. Consider several possibilities initially and then narrow, widen, and/or shift your focus as you proceed with your project and encounter new opportunities.

RE/CONSIDERING THE ROLE OF THEORY

In crystallization, "method and theory are reciprocally linked yet necessarily distinguishable" (Madison, 2005, p. 18). The role of theory in qualitative research varies widely, but most qualitative reports draw upon at least some theoretical insights or refer to a specific paradigm in order to contextualize their findings within ongoing scholarly conversations and situate their findings among those of published research. Moreover, researchers cannot approach analysis or compose narratives (or other artistic representations) completely apart from our store of theory and concepts from our disciplinary training and socialization: "'Reality' is *always already* interpreted. Thus, data never come in the shape of pure drops from an original virgin source; they are always merged with theory at the very moment of their genesis" (Alvesson & Sköldberg, 2000, p. 17, original emphasis).

Of course, myriad ways of defining theory exist. Simply put, a "theory is a consciously elaborated, justified, and uncertain understanding" of phenomena (Babrow & Mattson, 2003, p. 36). Professional standards make it pretty much impossible to publish qualitative analyses in many (even most) scholarly venues without an explicit theoretical framework; this remains especially true in medicine and related health fields, although exceptions exist. On the other hand, if you wrote stories for an organizational Web site, you would probably not include overt references to formal theory, since academic jargon presumably would not engage the public (your intended audience) as well as more accessible prose.

Many qualitative researchers use theory as a guiding framework. Such frameworks serve a number of functions, including "to (1) focus a study, (2) reveal and conceal meaning and understanding, (3) situate research in a scholarly conversation and provide a vernacular, and (4) reveal [the theory's] strengths and weaknesses" (Anfara & Mertz, 2006, p. 192). Theory performs similar functions within projects that involve crystallization, often explicitly in more conventional research reports and implicitly in artistic representations, where theory forms part of the context in which the researcher generated the artwork. I illustrate the functions of theory in Anfara and Mertz's typology as they relate to crystallization using Tracy's (2004a) layered account of emotional labor among correctional officers as an exemplar.

To begin, theories provide focus. Projects seeking to crystallize findings often necessitate even more tightly focused purposes than other qualitative projects because of the complexity of tying together disparate, and often fragmented, representations. Multiple angles illuminate, but they can also obscure and confuse if researchers do not provide sufficient tools for connecting them. A discussion of theory—whether in essay form, a series of quotes, an anecdote that exemplifies theoretical axioms, or what have you—can serve the vital function of making clear the focus of the inquiry. Tracy (2004a) invoked Hochschild's (1983) emotion labor theory, signifying that the scope of her ethnographic inquiry focused on the ways in which correctional officers experienced, controlled, and expressed emotions in what society considers to be stigmatized "dirty work" (see Drew, Mills, & Gassaway, 2007). Moreover, Tracy seeks to complexify this theory, which "has largely relied on a dichotomous portrayal of real and false self (Tracy & Trethewey, 2003)," by problematizing the real/false duality with postmodern theorizing about discourse and the self; "philosophies from Foucault can assist in explicating the role of discourse in constructing and harnessing emotional identity" (Tracy, 2004a, p. 525). Intersections of emotion labor theory with Foucault's (1977) work on the creation and disciplining of identities map out a territory for Tracy's inquiry into the socially constructed world of correctional officers. Both the narratives and the academic prose highlight a wide range of emotions, including anger, disgust, fear, excitement, pride, confusion, pity, amusement, and embarrassment.

Second, theories reveal and conceal meaning, a function particularly suited to complex crystallized representations that play with conventions of revealing and concealing through choices of genre. In the same way that narratives foreground particularities of individual experience while backgrounding larger patterns of meaning, theoretical frameworks draw readers' attention to certain aspects of meaning and in so doing necessarily deemphasize others. Concealing is not a weakness; indeed, it constitutes an inevitable cost of sense making, since you can never equally foreground all aspects of a story, academic or otherwise. Emotion labor theory and Foucault's (1977) theorizing on discipline and identity foreground the role of institutions such as prisons on the identities of those within the institutions and how emotional expression both reflects and creates identities. Tracy acknowledges the partiality of her account and the impossibility of fully representing all perspectives, such as that of the inmates and of the general public, in her study of correctional officers. Her choice of theoretical framing offers an intelligible means for highlighting the types of performances that interest her:

> In devising performances that attempt to achieve [organizational] expectations, officers not only engage in their own brand of stoic emotion labor but also play a part in constructing organizationally harnessed emotional identities—identities that are marked by paranoia, withdrawal, detachment, and an "us-them" approach toward inmates. (Tracy, 2004a, p. 529)

Tracy does not merely describe these performed identities analytically, she invites readers to experience them by offering narratives of her ethnographic experiences. Her description of an incident in which officers found a prisoner in possession of drugs provides an illustration:

> Officers Brankett and Jones are writing up reports on the strip searches, urinalyses, and cell shakedowns. . . . The officers, who are usually so no nonsense and tough with the inmates, are excited, almost girlish. Jones looks in my direction and squeals, "This was a *really* good bust!" . . . Brankett explains to me, "We search them and search them and usually find nothing. This one, finally, was a good bang for the buck!" I note Jones's use of the sexual metaphor as well as the duo's goofy, giggly, flirty demeanors as they reconstruct the events of the evening. (p. 527)

At the same time, Tracy deemphasizes important issues outside the purview of her inquiry, for example, the role of public perception of crime and punishment on the regulation of the prison-industrial complex by state and federal government and the impact of prison reform activists on correctional officers' training.

Theory's third function involves providing scholarly contextualization and a vernacular—in other words, a set of common tools particular to a defined scholarly speech community. In crystallized texts, vernacular or jargon provides a means for shorthand communication, provided that readers know the speech codes of the community. Researchers should take great care in defining or at least citing references for all terms that may exclude members of the audience they want to reach. Achieving clarity without bogging down in excessive definitions constitutes a major challenge in crystallization, because different genres require varying vocabularies. For instance, the term "embodied ethnography" immediately conjures for trained ethnographers images of a participant observer in the field carefully noting smells, tastes, textures, temperature, and other sensuous details within fieldnotes. For others—including intelligent, learned, creative others—this term holds no clear meaning, and its use may function at best as a sign of disinterest toward the audience's needs or at worst one of intentional exclusion of nonexperts. Reading unfamiliar jargon may also simply bore readers. For example, I have struggled to reach medical and allied health audiences who cannot be assumed to understand standpoint theory (Harding, 1991), Foucault's (1977) analysis of the relationship between power and knowledge, or feminist critiques of bureaucracy (Ferguson, 1984). Nonetheless, I value the vocabularies provided by communication theory and research, as well as those from medical sociology, anthropology, women's studies/feminist inquiry, nursing, social work, education, medical humanities, and medicine. Like any tool, theory proves useful for some tasks and not others; terms enable us to label, explicate, compare, and differentiate among ideas, making it possible to highlight subtle shades of meaning. Tracy's (2004a) examination of correctional officers utilized the terms emotion work, voyeurism, and differentiation, drawn from emotion labor theory, as well as Goffman's concept of "total institutions" to explain her findings. Tracy also utilizes scholarly concepts to explain aspects of her methodology, such as when she states, "I interrogated and problematized my own role in the story I presumed to collect—a process that Fine et al. (2000) call, 'coming clean at the hyphen' (p. 123)" (p. 521).

Moreover, jargon can also serve a function even when its meaning remains less than fully clear (or completely opaque) to readers by problematizing the authority of the author. While this technique potentially alienates readers, elitist, power-laden discourse nonetheless provides a sharp contrast with narratives and other more accessible genres, serving a deconstructive purpose by reinforcing the partiality of the theoretical account. Crystallization reveals the wholly constructed, nonnatural status of scholarly jargon as an academic game. While not a game without value, theoretical analysis and argumentation also cannot claim a naturalized status as objectively real. In other words, asserting jargon that your audience may not understand helps to resist the dominating effects of science if the audience sees through the attempt.

Let me offer a funny story that illustrates the potential for jargon to backfire, rendering itself ridiculous, or at least suspect, rather than authoritative. I participated in a strategic planning meeting with a group of people who did not know each other very well. The facilitator invited us to engage in an "icebreaker" activity called "two truths and a lie." The idea was for group members to get to know each other by having each member share with the others two truths and a lie about themselves. The group members then tried to guess which one of the person's three statements was the lie. During my turn, I said: "I have had fifteen surgeries, my husband Glenn and I spent our honeymoon in France, and I am writing a book on a form of postmodern methodological triangulation called qualitative crystallization." Every person in the room guessed that I lied about my book project, when actually I had lied about the location of our honeymoon. When I laughed and asked why, they said that such a jargon-laden sentence could not possibly be *real;* it sounded too "made up." I share this story not to encourage researchers to risk alienating their readers by drowning them in abstract theoretical ruminations but to assure them that some obscuring effects of social science prose (when used strategically) can potentially reinforce the crystallized validity of multigenre texts by emphasizing the contrasting epistemologies underlying the contrasting representations. All representational conventions are "made up"—none exists in an independent reality.

Finally, theories reveal their own strengths and weaknesses when used as frameworks, and this too may be evident in and benefit crystallization. Juxtaposition of poetic and artistic accounts with social science prose points to strengths and weaknesses. We need not dismiss the weaknesses of a given theory in crystallized accounts as mere "limitations" of the inquiry that must be begrudgingly acknowledged at the end of the standard research report. Instead, such weaknesses become more data for analysis, another part of the picture, another node in the network of meaning. Rather than apologizing for inevitably partial accounts (including theories), we can celebrate them as additional points of view or facets of the crystal. Tracy's (2004a) account of the complexities of correctional officers' identities and emotional performances reveals the strength of emotion labor theory in accounting for the intense work involved in producing appropriate displays of emotion in a difficult environment. At the same time, readers perceive the weaknesses of the theory in narratives that illustrate how much else goes on in correctional settings.

I do not advise slapping a theoretical frame onto a multigenre text if it does not fit and enhance the project's goals. On the other hand, if a specific theory or perspective guided your project, by all means include it in some way in your crystallized text. Ideally, the theory will help you to make a persuasive account of your ideas: "A useful theory is one that tells an enlightening story about some phenomenon. It is a story that gives you new insights and broadens your understanding of the phenomenon" (Anfara & Mertz, 2006, p. xvii). Many possibilities exist for useful theories in qualitative research, any of which can then potentially be used in a crystallized account. Social constructionism (e.g., Gergen, 1994, 1999; Hacking, 1999; Holstein & Gubrium, 2008) provides a broad basis for qualitative inquiry, while many other theories may illuminate certain aspects of a given project. I provide a brief overview of theoretical perspectives, cautioning readers that these are intended merely as jumping-off points, not as circumscription of possibilities.

Theoretical perspectives on power and knowledge are common in qualitative research; for instance, Foucault's (1977, 1979, 1980) work on disciplinary power and resistance (e.g., Edley, 2000; Gillespie, 2001; Zoller, 2003) and Croft's use of Fiske's (1993) theory of imperializing and localizing power. Researchers also widely employ feminist theories of the gendered nature of power and resistance, including the feminist case against bureaucracy (Ferguson, 1984), feminist standpoint theory (Harding, 1991), subaltern counterpublics (Fraser 1990–1991), and strategic essentializing (Spivak, 1988). Performance theory, drawing on such theorists as Butler (1990; e.g., Lindemann, 2007, 2008; Morgan & Krone, 2001; Murphy, 2001; Tracy, 2002; J. T. Warren, 2001), and dialectical theory (Adelman & Frey, 1997; Alemán, 2001; Geist-Martin, Carnett, & Slauta, 2008) provide other common perspectives. Other examples of theories used to guide qualitative research include symbolic convergence theory (Lesch, 1994), play theory (Brooks & Bowker, 2002), structuration theory (Howard & Geist, 1995), and peer cluster theory (DeSantis, 2002).

Some qualitative studies seek to extend existing theory or models. M. Miller (1995), in her study of a family of four generations of women who had attempted suicide, extended the "basic suicidal syndrome outlined by Breed (1972)" (p. 264) with a model of communication that described the "intersubjective experience of the mother–daughter relationship and the perpetuation of the suicidal tradition" (p. 268). Similarly, in my research on a health care team (Ellingson, 2003), I extended the bona fide group perspective (Putnam & Stohl, 1990) with the concept of "embedded teamwork," that is, work done in dyads and triads of team members outside of formal meetings (see also Lammers & Krikorian, 1997). Finally, Tracy (2004b) extended theoretical perspectives on framing by developing a model of framing techniques for organizational tensions that suggests that employees commonly frame tensions as simple contradictions, complementary dialectics, or pragmatic paradoxes.

Theory also can lurk in the background in crystallized accounts, informing without taking center stage. Lather and Smithies' (1997) work with women living with HIV/AIDS used no overarching theory, although it wove references to published research and some brief mentions of concepts from theorists such as Foucault (1979) and Benjamin (1968). I found that Goffman's (1959) framework could also offer useful concepts without unduly restricting my ability to accomplish several descriptive, critical, and analytical goals at once. In fact, Goffman and other social constructionist or symbolic interactionist frames tend to work quite well with crystallization projects that combine creative and analytic representations, since such frameworks highlight the performance of self in interaction, mirroring the goal of showing and telling through contrasting epistemological claims embedded in multiple genres.

Finally, theory can be a form of personal and social intervention. Feminist theorist bell hooks explains that she

> came to theory because I was hurting—the pain within me was so intense that I could not go on living. I came to theory desperate, wanting to comprehend— to grasp what was happening around and within me. Most important, I wanted to make the hurt go away. I saw in theory then a location for healing. (hooks, 1994, p. 59)

Like hooks, we need to make sense of our everyday experiences in our embodied, situated lives, and theory can help us to do that. Theory can be accessible, helpful, and potentially empowering, not just intellectual, and it can play a vital role in the process of crystallization. Theory may provide concepts and angles of vision that serve as useful tools to the practitioners, public, or other stakeholders to whom we bring our crystallized research in a variety of genres. Theoretical sensibilities also can be a vital tool offered by academics in dialogue with research participants (A. W. Frank, 2005).

Some issues to reflect on as you decide on what role theory will play in your crystallized project:

- *Audience:* Who are my intended audiences, and what are their expectations for theory? How does setting up a theoretical framework provide a useful foundation for my account? How can I explain key terminology to those unfamiliar with it?

- *Your theory toolbox:* What theories am I familiar with that might help me to frame my analyses? What theories seem to emerge as relevant as I immerse myself in my data?

- *Connections/situating your work:* What disciplinary, professional, and critical discourses do I invoke with my use of a particular theory? Am I comfortable with those alliances? Why and/or why not?

- *Representation:* How would theory get in the way of my ability to make claims, tell tales, or otherwise creatively and evocatively represent my ideas? How would theory facilitate or enhance these same processes? Where else could I put theory, in addition to within the main narrative— endnotes, appendices, parallel voices on the page?

Again, I suggest journaling to play with these questions and urge researchers to think outside the box for creative ways to include theory in crystallized texts.

DECIDE ON A DESIGN

At some point, you must come to a preliminary decision on the scope and form of your project. I advise that you write it down and that your decision have three parts: thesis statement(s), genre selections, and a plan.

Thesis Statement(s)

As a holdover from my training as a college policy debater and my years of teaching public speaking, I favor clear, concise thesis statements. You need a well-articulated thesis statement, or perhaps a few of them if you pursue a book-length manuscript. While you need not include this statement in your work per se (depending upon your choices of format, genre, etc.), your ability to write it down for yourself as a guide for your project is paramount; if you cannot do this, you have insufficient focus and direction for your project and need to do more reflection. The statement can be adapted at any time, but it must exist as a focal point for your project. As an illustration, consider the role clearly articulated thesis statements played in the production of a book-length ethnography. In the process of writing *Communicating in the Clinic,* my examination of team communication evolved slowly into an exploration of backstage clinical communication. Once I devised a set of three definitive claims that formed the foundation for my book, I had a much easier time making other analytic and representational decisions. I went back and refined the statements as I worked through the project until I completed the final version of the manuscript. I elected to include my thesis statements in the introductory chapter to my book in order to set the stage for the remainder of my crystallized account. I considered this particularly important because the next chapter took the form of an extended narrative, and I wanted readers to encounter that story with my conclusions in mind.[1] My thesis statements for the project included

- Teamwork must be recognized as taking place outside of designated team meetings, through informal communication channels, and in dyads and triads of team members, rather than as primarily occurring within full team meetings.

- Backstage team communication (communication among team members without patients present) is interwoven intricately with frontstage (health care provider–patient communication); the boundaries between these are fluid and permeable, not sharply delineated as they are currently theorized.

- Team communication is heavily constrained and shaped by persistent gender, racial, class, and disciplinary hierarchies in the medical establishment; structural and individual inequalities are not natural, neutral, or inevitable, and they are integral to the daily enactment of teamwork through communication. (Ellingson, 2005a, p. 8)

The narratives, analysis, and critiques I wrote all centered on these statements and the intersections thereof. I opted to include them in just this form to enhance the clarity of my book. You must decide for yourself whether such an explicit statement increases the clarity of your work, needlessly or even harmfully bashes readers over the head with a definitive interpretation, or perhaps could be integrated into the account in a more implicit manner. Regardless of how you use it, however, I strongly advise articulating your thesis statement before you go too far along, and periodically revisit it as you progress.

Genres

Based upon your consideration of the questions and issues raised in your design process in the previous chapter, make a decision about the approximate length, genres, and types of outlets (journal, book, literary magazine, etc.) you will target. As with your thesis statement, you can (and should) remain open to change down the road as ideas emerge, but you need at least a starting point. I know many writers would not agree with me, preferring to allow "writing as a method of inquiry" to be quite a literal process of simply applying pen to paper, fingers to keyboard, or brush to paint and see what comes up. Extreme openness can be overwhelming and immobilizing, however, and I recommend using journal writing as the space in which to write as inquiry and to come up with ideas for structure and genres, at least in the beginning. I recommend that you consider genres as you collect and analyze data, make an initial selection, start writing, and then make changes to generic choices if needed.

For example, in my study of the interdisciplinary geriatric oncology clinic, I considered writing the manuscript in the form of an extended layered account or having one or two lengthy narratives in each chapter that exemplified the analytical concepts in the chapter. I finally decided that moving back and forth so frequently among genres and forms of evidence would be too distracting and make too many demands on my readers over the course of a book. I selected four genres, each of which would characterize one chapter: ethnographic narrative, grounded theory analysis, autoethnography, and feminist critique. I chose them because they spoke to my disparate scholarly and ideological commitments, fit with my data, and supported the thesis statements about which I felt most strongly. Moreover, I reasoned that if I could not find a publisher open to publishing my crystallized account as a multigenre text, I could separate each of the chapters into articles (albeit with some loss of meaning) and publish them in qualitative methods, applied communication, and feminist journals, respectively. Keep in mind the audiences and types of publication venues you wish to reach as you chose your genres.

Plan

Create an informal outline, or what Madison (2005) calls a "muse map" (p. 183), a list of what you are going to do and the approximate order in which you plan to do it. I recommend mapping whether you plan to pursue an integrated multigenre text (see Chapter 5) or a series of related but separate texts (dendritic crystallization; see Chapter 6), or both. This can be informal; feel free to shed complex alphanumeric structures and create your own flexible, heuristic format that helps you get your ideas organized. Visual representations may also prove helpful, not just listing but mapping and modeling ideas in order to understand their relationships to each other (Hunter et al., 2002, p. 392). Visualizing relationships among your thesis statement(s), genres, data, theory, and research literature may help you not only get organized but deepen your understanding of your project (see Clarke, 2005).

The map becomes an important resource for you as you write any project, but especially in crystallization because the complexity of your representation necessitates careful coordination. The map is not the territory, but in this case, it can be at least partially constitutive of the territory. We do not map external realities, but create them. As you build a map, you provide yourself with a representation. No fixed reality exists for you to capture through your research; instead, endless opportunities abound. You build a world as you represent your choices on a map, and you can always change those choices. But to try to go without a map is to go not just into uncharted territory, but often into a void. Instead of freeing you, it can bind you, leaving you lost among your data and ideas. As you co-create your world, map its contours. At the same time, do not be afraid that a map will overly constrict you; no matter how carefully you follow a map, you will always notice unexpected side roads, landmarks will appear suddenly, or the view around the corner will prove stunning and you will pause to explore it in much greater detail than you planned. The informal outline or map remains flexible throughout your project; you can and will deviate from it.

You should feel free to make your map in any analog or digital format in which you enjoy working. I prefer to use the hyperlinked capabilities of an inexpensive software program for Macintosh computers called "Voodoo Pad"[2] that enables hyperlinked cross-referencing between ideas, outlines, project status notes, "to do" lists, and any other textual or visual data you want to add. Other people prefer colored pens and notebooks, spreadsheet software, drawing paper, or copious use of sticky notes. Wander through a stationery, office supply, or arts supply store to see what is available, and then experiment to find what works best for you.

As part of the mapping process, I also recommend that you have a place to store ideas for the future, both related to your current project and to potential new ones. As I plan, reflect, write, and map, I often receive new insights. Through the construction of multigenre texts, I encounter a range of social scientific/empirical, theoretical, critical, narrative, poetic, and performance texts and experiment in a hands-on manner with the constraints and possibilities of genres and truth claims and positioning of myself as an author. This in turn opens up new vistas of reading and writing. Ideas pop into my head unbidden as I read and write. I recommend keeping a journal or file where you note these ideas down for later consideration. Productivity guru David Allen (2002) calls this a "someday/maybe" file and advises people to check through it on a regular basis to discard, add to, and act on ideas stored within it.

CONCLUSION

The design processes sketched here do not constitute discrete steps that begin when collecting data ends, but ongoing processes that precede, overlap with, and follow data collection. The looseness of the processes should not cloud their importance to producing a high-quality qualitative research project. The following two chapters provide further detail on engaging in crystallization to produce coherent multigenre texts/representations (Chapter 5), a series of dispersed texts/representations illuminating a qualitative data set (Chapter 6), or both.

INTERLUDE

Beware the Law of the Hammer

The law of the hammer states that if you have a hammer as your only tool, you tend to search for opportunities in which to hammer things, rather than looking for interesting opportunities and then choosing an appropriate tool. Many of you may be familiar with Lee Hay and Pete Seeger's (1958) famous folk song, "If I Had a Hammer," which joyfully suggests hammering morning, noon, and night. Hammering can be useful, but only in some circumstances. The hammer swinger sees many nails, but few screws, threads, plants, foodstuffs, or other items that cannot best be addressed through repeated bonking with a blunt object.

I invoke "the law of the hammer" as a playful—and hopefully memorable—metaphor to encourage methodological pluralism. Nonetheless, this lighthearted label refers to the serious issue of limiting the types of questions we can answer about the world to only those that fit a single methodological tool. For many scholars, a method such as statistics, grounded theory, narratives, or performance became their methodological or representational hammer, and they now hit every question they propose with that tool, even if another tool may prove vastly more suitable to illuminating the nuances of a particular topic, problem, or setting. This tendency fails to surprise me; no one receives training in all methods, and of those we are taught or teach ourselves, we inevitably prefer some over others. Moreover, we are attracted not only to certain types of methods, but to specific types of questions that tend to fit with our preferred methods. In other words, these preferences develop iteratively, and often our preferred method also fits our posed questions. Furthermore, reliance on a single hammer is not limited to those working within positivist or postpositivist paradigms; researchers across the expanse of the qualitative continuum uphold the law of the hammer.

However, when we employ a variety of tools, we can address a broader range of questions; you could hammer a nail/question, but if you had a set of pliers, you also could bend the nail and use it to fashion a hook, for instance. Thus, if you work primarily in grounded theory, I urge you to reflect about what else could be done to interpret and represent your data more evocatively. For example, in the same way that many of us excerpt part of our data set as case studies (e.g., Buzzanell & Ellingson, 2005), you could also excerpt an individual participant's story as a narrative (e.g., Ellingson, 2008c), write some poetry or poetic transcript of interviews, or produce a performance piece for your participants and/or other audiences. If you generally produce artistic work, I encourage you to reflect on what patterns in your data could be highlighted, what systematic questions you could ask and answer in order to add to the body of knowledge in your discipline, persuade policy makers, provide informational resources to your participants, generate practical advice for practitioners serving those participants or others like them, and/or gain a new perspective on the larger sociopolitical context of your evocative accounts, connecting the local to national or global trends.

Keep in mind that disciplinary and methodological loyalties are not moral in nature; dallying in other representational arenas constitutes ethically sound practice. Indeed, such intellectual and creative variety may improve your understanding of the workings of habitually favored methods (Fine et al., 2000; Richardson, 2000b). I have often felt self-conscious about my divided loyalties, which I tend to think of as between the health communication community and the ethnographers. But some ethnographers conduct grounded theory (e.g., Tracy, 2002, 2004a), and some health communication scholars engage in narrative work (e.g., Harter et al., 2005). Put down the hammer and pick up a tool box, and you can do a lot of good. Of course, you can also make mistakes; learning a new tool often proves difficult, and all research methods should be approached with respect and after securing guidance from a more experienced tool wielder. Early efforts may not net work of publishable quality for some time. Do not let that trouble you; no education or experiment is ever wasted. However, you must also balance such experimentation with good judgment. Students, junior and contingent faculty, and others particularly vulnerable to negative consequences of devaluation of their work should be sure to complete some work with representational comfort zones that meet institutional scholarly standards while exploring other tools in the methodological box.

NOTES

1. Of course, I could also argue for the benefit of readers delving into the narrative without the preparation of my agenda for the account. Certainly their experience of its meanings varies according to whether they have in mind how I want them, in part, to interpret the interactions I portray. And readers' interpretations are further reshaped upon reading the next three chapters, which offer more analysis and more narrative, further complexifying the reading of the narrative—this is a strength of crystallization.

2. Voodoo Pad resembles an Internet "wiki" but remains contained on your personal computer rather than online. It is available for trial downloads and for purchase at www.flyingmeat.com. I receive no financial consideration from the producers of this product, and share it only with the hope of others finding it useful.

FIVE

BRINGING IT ALL TOGETHER

Integrated Crystallization

———◆◆◆———

[Researchers] do jump across traditions, we do straddle metatheoretical camps, and (unfortunately) we do let paradigmatic "definitions" constrain our work. . . . [I want to] allow for comfortable jumps and straddles and to loosen some of these constraints.

—K. I. Miller (2000, p. 48)

I too wish to facilitate more jumping, straddling, and loosening among qualitative methodologists. Thinking of straddling genres as a process of crystallization provides a means of directing our efforts to enlarge the possibilities of qualitative research. I divide approaches to crystallization broadly into two main types: *integrated* and *dendritic*. *Integrated crystallization* involves producing a written and/or visual text consisting of multiple genres that reflect (and straddle) multiple points on the qualitative continuum (for guidelines on composing a series of separate pieces within a *dendritic* crystallization framework, see Chapter 6). I develop the metaphor of quilting as a heuristic for imagining the process of bringing genres together. Extending the process begun in Chapter 4, I provide specific strategies for combining multiple forms of representation. I then take readers through a number of multigenre texts to explore two types of integrated crystallization, which I term *woven* and *patched,* including both article- and book-length representations.

CREATING A COHERENT MULTIGENRE TEXT

Thinking about your goals, audience(s), epistemology, and the role of theory sets up the context for creating the crystallized text. Quilting constitutes an apt metaphor for thinking through the construction of a multigenre text. Traditional masculine metaphors characterize scientific research, framing inquiry as voyage, exploration, conquering, and wresting truth from nature or subjects (Flannery, 2001). While these metaphors serve useful functions, they nonetheless reflect a limited conceptualization of the formation of knowledge. Knowledge cannot be separated from the means through which we construct and represent it (Haraway, 1988). Hence, feminists (and others) consciously invoke complementary metaphors through which to produce knowledge, framing alternative research processes and suggesting other types of knowledge (Harding, 1993). Feminists have invoked quilting as a metaphor for women's and other social movements, for life (as an alternative to journey metaphors), and as a way of

> conceiving of feminist theory and feminist theory-building on the metaphor of quilting: individual persons located in different historical and socioeconomic circumstances who quilt quilts (or patches for quilts). The quilts (or patches) tell unique, individualized stories about the quilters and the circumstances of their lives; they are candidate patches for a larger, global mosaic . . . [that] collectively represents and records the stories of people of different ages, ethnicities, affectional orientations, race and gender identities, and class backgrounds committed to [feminist principles].
> (K. Warren, 1994, p. 186)

Given these characteristics of quilts, Flannery (2001) suggests quilting as a feminist metaphor for science, drawing a number of intriguing parallels between the processes, products, and communities of the two enterprises (pp. 633–637). Both research and quilting involve drawing on the work of a larger community that passes down styles, norms, terminology, and traditions; learning the craft through apprenticeship with an emphasis on tacit, "hands on" knowledge; endless numbers of decisions in design and procedure; a tension between conformity (to a pattern or paradigm) and creativity; improvising out of necessity and out of a desire for innovation; and products that conceal as much as they reveal—"Just as the backing hides a great deal about the construction of a quilt, such as the rough edges where pieces were sewn together, a research article hides as much as it reveals about the process of science" (Flannery, 2001, p. 636).

Likening the processes and products of crystallization to quilting embraces many positive associations: The making of a quilt involves creating art and producing a functional object by piecing together bits of fabric into a holistic pattern that beautifies, warms those who use it, reflects the artistic voice of its creator, and often provides a social outlet during its creation, via quilting bees and sewing circles.[1] Likewise, crystallized qualitative projects produce both aesthetic and functional products that benefit a range of stakeholders and reflect the voices of both researchers and participants. Crystallization uses "scraps" of data, often reflects collaborative processes, and embraces improvisation with form and content that depend upon what comes available. The construction of a quilt also brings personal satisfaction, pays homage to cultural and familial traditions, evokes an appreciation of domestic or local materials, and can embody important social and political statements (Williams, 1994; see also this chapter's interlude on quilting as social activism). Keeping an image of a quilt in your head while creating a crystallized, multigenre text may aid in simultaneously envisioning the big picture of your social, political, and scholarly goals for your project, while also enabling you to focus on one particular patch of work at a time. Because quilts are often passed down through generations in families or made as gifts to celebrate occasions such as birth and marriage, quilts also may carry legacies of love and passion in their creation and in the giving; similarly, qualitative work conducted with love and passion also may reflect "threads in a quilt stitched from the heart" (Chapman Sanger, 2003, p. 29).

One of the most exciting aspects of crystallization involves the infinite possibilities for how to practice it, just as with quilting. Freedom also forms a constraint, however, and it can be intimidating to make the long series of creative decisions. While I encourage readers to think of this process as nonlinear, iterative, and improvisational (which is how I experience it), I nonetheless provide some steps as a jumping-off point for understanding how you might incorporate crystallization into your own ongoing or future projects. These steps are not necessarily linear, exhaustive, exclusive, or sequential.

Selecting and Organizing Material

How much material you need (or more likely, how much you can bear to leave out) depends upon many of the questions addressed in Chapter 4. For now, let us assume that you have chosen an approximate length for your manuscript (e.g., a chapter in an edited collection) and thus have some idea of an appropriate amount of material needed for your manuscript. If you plan a book, you are fine taking up lots of space. If you anticipate an article or monograph, scale down accordingly; I generally plan about 30 manuscript (double-spaced) pages for journal articles and chapters. As with any qualitative researcher blessed with a rich data set, I find it challenging to select incidents about which to write narratives, to chose examples with which to illustrate analytic themes, and to decide which theories and research to cite. During my study of the interdisciplinary geriatric oncology team, I had collected hundreds of pages of fieldnotes and transcripts of interactions between patients and health care providers, in addition to staff interviews. My dialysis project likewise generated a sizable pile of data. After numerous experiences selecting from these large data sets (and several smaller ones), I developed some general guidelines for selecting illustrative material.

First, consider the research question or issues to be addressed and the genres you have chosen for the particular multigenre text (see Chapter 4). Reflect and do some journal writing on what you most want your audiences to get out of the text—what the "take away messages" of the text will be—and then make sure that every example or incident chosen clearly embodies one or more of these messages. Save interesting but peripheral instances for later use.

Second, indulge by selecting at least some of your favorite moments, quotes, or examples for lengthier representation. Tell your favorite fieldwork stories in narrative and poetic writing and keep the exemplars and instances that are representative but more easily broken into snippets to illustrate themes for analytic accounts. With a crystallization project, planning ahead about which stories or incidents you want to develop narratively avoids boring and unhelpful repetition of the same incidents in both your creative analytic representations and your more social scientific pieces. Obviously, this proves especially important when producing a single multigenre text because you want to highlight the range of experiences rather than reusing a few incidents.[2]

Next, think in terms of which stories (and/or poems, photos, etc.) can be shared and commented upon with a manageable amount of background information. Oftentimes qualitative researchers find themselves in the position of not being able to include a narrative or telling detail in an article because it would not make sense to readers unfamiliar with other aspects of their data, and insufficient space exists to fully contextualize the interaction. For example, I had some revealing interactions with the first nurse practitioner of the geriatric oncology team I studied (Ellingson, 2005a) surrounding her qualitative doctoral research. However, her research was unrelated to her job as a nurse practitioner and team member, and as I tried to construct a narrative of one of our fascinating conversations about data collection, sense making, and power, I got bogged down in providing sufficient background details on the research we were discussing. This made the anecdote about our conversation less of a helpful illustration of backstage communication in a clinic and more of a distracting tangent. Similarly, some examples, taken out of context and serving as one of only a few representations of your participants in a particular manuscript, may characterize your participants in ways that you do not intend or support. Thus, you want to chose examples in part based on their comprehensiveness and their transportability.

Finally, when writing grounded theory or other systematic analyses, consciously endeavor to illustrate themes with examples from different forms of data (e.g., transcripts, fieldnotes, organizational documents) and from a range of participants. Incorporating variety in this way when possible adds richness and interest to your findings.

Mutual Influence

During and after your material selection process, continually reflect on how writing or creating in one genre impacts your representation in other genres: "For research descriptions to be thick and rich, researchers must be able to view their data from several perspectives. The more experience they have in multidimensional thinking, the more ways of making meaning they have at their disposal" (Hunter et al., 2002, p. 394). Multidimensional thinking may spring from multigenre representation, as each genre offers a different way of knowing about your topic. As we move back and forth among constructing narratives, writing personal reflections, and inductively deriving analytical categories and processes, we play with the constraints of various genres and epistemologies by allowing each to inspire and shape the others. That is, we place the modes of thinking and writing into conversation with one another. In the process of constructing *Communicating in the Clinic,* I realized that the narrative and autoethnographic accounts were informed by my inductive analysis of the data, which in turn shaped the sense making of narrative construction. The narrative and autoethnographic accounts had as their goal to show the worlds of the clinic, which differed from my goal in the grounded theory analysis of "telling," that is, of declaring my analytical thoughts on how the team functioned in the clinic. Thus, the storied accounts do not rest on claims of systematic analysis, but rather on claims of narrative truth and ethical responsibility to both portray what I believe went on there and to do no harm to the people who shared their lives with me. At the same time, the narrative and autoethnographic accounts also affected the construction and representation of my grounded theory analysis. As I constructed stories, ideas and images came to me that resulted in further revision of my analytical schema, particularly in the noting of exceptions to a norm or less common events that I nonetheless considered vital to understanding the clinic.

The narrative at the beginning of *Communicating in the Clinic,* for example, shows the team acting together to deal with an emergency situation. A patient with severe cardiac distress was not a "typical event," but emergencies did arise periodically, and the ways in which the team members worked together to address them revealed critical aspects of their individual personalities and ethics of care (Ellingson, 2005a). After composing this narrative, I went back to my schema and rethought how emergency situations function as part of the backstage communication I had described. Narratives also focused my attention on some events and diverted attention from others. Ordering events constructs meaning(s) for them, and these subsequent meanings affected my analytical process as well. The reflexive relationship among different forms of analysis and narrative representation constitutes an analytic strength of crystallization, and I encourage others to explore how their writing and analysis processes mutually influence one another.

Considering Options for Formatting

For those opting to compose an integrated crystallized text (see Chapter 6 for dendritic forms of crystallization), formatting options abound. Moreover, many readers will invent their own. By this, I do not refer to selection of genre, as discussed in Chapters 3 and 4, but to choices about physically formatting words on a page, images on a screen or canvas, and so on. I urge researchers to innovate, but offer the following three considerations to guide those innovations.

Perhaps the primary formatting concern is to ensure that your format embodies your work's purpose. That is, the form should reinforce the content, providing another form of evidence or support for your main argument or another answer to your central question. For example, in my layered account of the experience of time in the dialysis clinic (Ellingson, 2005b), the alternating social science prose and narratives embody the multiple expectations concerning the experience of time that co-exist in that space. Confronting differing experiences of time in a tightly scheduled and controlled environment disconcerted me, particularly at first, when I lacked familiarity with the dialysis unit's norms. The form of this account reflects the complexity of overlapping and not always congruent experiences of time among staff, patients, patients' family, the organization's administration, and regulatory agencies (e.g., state of California). The abrupt shifts between perspectives captures (some of) the sense of disconnection experienced by participants when they encountered someone else's understanding of, or experience of, time.

A second formatting concern centers on choosing a structure that enables you to show *and* tell about a phenomenon under investigation in an effective manner. These goals are not mutually exclusive, of course; stories can also tell and analysis can show in the midst of explication. However, multigenre accounts should embody balanced portrayals. Balance cannot be reduced to a mathematical equation of 50% poetry and 50% literature review or analysis; instead, think of showing and telling as existing in productive tension; each one picks up where the other leaves off. Many authors now rely on some variant of the layered account that alternates narrative and academic prose (Ronai, 1995) or the "open-faced sandwich" structure (Ellis, 2004) in which a review of theory and research follows a narrative or poetic account (e.g., Ellis, 1993). Examples of layered accounts that show a world through particularly evocative accounts while also telling solid analytic arguments include Magnet (2006), Markham (2005), Ronai (1999), and Saarnivaara (2003). In each of these, the author presents a balance of showing and telling that does not necessarily accord equal length to each style but instead ensures a symbiotic relationship between the styles that serves to illuminate the central point of the article.

One final formatting caution: Researchers should keep in mind the risks of reader fatigue; some very fragmented and/or complexly formatted texts, while effective for highly motivated readers, can lose their luster over the course of a lengthy text. Parallel narratives reinforce the duality of perspective, for example, but they also require the reader to either move back and forth between the two narratives or go through each section twice (e.g., Lather & Smithies, 1997). Fragments jar the reader intentionally, but too much jarring may be pointlessly unpleasant. Avoid making mere novelty of format its own goal and instead make choices that enable your readers to comprehend and engage your material as fully as possible.

I will now explore the two types of integrated crystallization—woven and patched—in turn, and then discuss exemplars of each.

BLENDING GENRES AND BLURRING
BOUNDARIES: WOVEN CRYSTALLIZATION

Crystallization involves blending, juxtaposing, and weaving genres, and over time, I developed some strategies for ways to enhance the analytic portions of manuscripts that were intended to be read in combination with narrative or other literary genres. Practitioners of crystallization must make judgment calls about how best to accomplish the integration of artistic and social scientific work. In *woven crystallization,* we deliberately weave different genres into a single text in which the contrasting genres mix, frequently moving readers back and forth between several genres in small excerpts and pieces as a larger picture is constructed, much like the small pieces of a quilt or scraps in a collage together form a coherent work. Although assembling woven texts primarily necessitates having a clear central point for the work, researcher's intuition, and a good deal of trial and error, I nonetheless provide some general guidelines to assist in constructing woven texts.

Manageable Chunks

When weaving or blending, think in terms of small- or medium-size bites rather than huge mouthfuls of analysis or theory to mix with poetry, story, film, and so on. Of course, the actual length of an excerpt varies according to the overall structure and length of the manuscript in which you include it. But it bears remembering that as you ask readers to actively navigate a crystallized manuscript in a more conscious way than a single-genre work requires, you should aid them by breaking the paper into coherent, relatively self-contained, intelligible pieces. Of course, you could artfully incorporate some mystery and consciously withhold some information or offer ambiguous statements, but this should be deliberate and not the result of authorial sloppiness, arrogance, or apathy. The reader and author jointly construct meaning, and authors should meet readers (at least) halfway by presenting their analytic work in digestible pieces.

(Dis)connections

When you combine narratives, poems, and so on with analytic prose, think carefully about breaking points and transitions. Like a sitcom that leaves viewers hanging before the commercial break, you should give readers an expectation of the story continuing to unfold or another piece of the literary puzzle to be put in place following each shift in genre. If you provide pieces of one continuous narrative, leave each section with a provocative statement or a pause in the middle of action, or a hint as to where the story goes next. If using a series of related incidents as anecdotal-length narratives, poems, field-note excerpts, or other forms of data/representation, it may not be possible to leave a "cliff-hanger," so you may want to emphasize a more abrupt "jump" to the next bit of analytic prose to emphasize the deliberate disconnect between and juxtaposition of the contrasting forms of representation. After switching back and forth a couple times, your readers should be able to catch the rhythm and follow you expectantly.

Contextualizing

Although it may seem dramatic to plunge readers into an evocative scene of a narrative, the same seldom proves true of analysis and theory. Notwith-standing artful arrangements of intriguing quotes or other thought-provoking tidbits, authors should provide sufficient explanation of any theory, research, or other expository information we choose to include in multigenre texts. Crystallized texts run the risk of disorienting readers, and while some degree of that risk reflects a deliberate attempt to reveal the constructed nature of all knowledge and representation, too much may serve to frustrate and alienate readers. As you compose the analytic portions of your texts, stop and consider what you leave out, what leaps of logic you make or aspects of theory and research context you omit that your readers may need in order to make sense of your argument. I find that after I am immersed in a project for a long time, it becomes difficult to step back and bracket my own familiarity with my data and related theory and research. I often exclude vital pieces of information, taking for granted my readers' familiarity with the topic and expecting them to fill in the enthymemes of my argument for me. Be on guard not to fall into this trap; have someone else read your work and/or read it yourself carefully with this question specifically in mind.

Inform on a Need-to-Know Basis

One impulse when writing narrative work designed to be combined with more conventional analysis is to treat the story like the introduction and literature review of a report and cover all your bases up front to set the stage for the "results" to come. Resist the temptation to introduce all your characters or all the details of the setting in the first creative analytic moment of your piece. Let your work unfold as a story. Moving back and forth between genres sparks wonderful ideas, but it can also make it difficult to remain true to the goals of any one genre. Stories unfold and analysis speaks directly; very rarely should stories be overly direct. Woven crystallization requires authors to manage the unfolding and the explicit in one text, and this presents an ongoing challenge.

On a related note, as you pull together and revise your multigenre work, continually review the sequence of information and ideas you reveal to discern whether you have arranged them in the most helpful order. Again, try to step back and consider the readers' path through your work, ask yourself what your audience needs to know in order for your exploration of a given issue or event to make sense in the overall context of your argument.

Signposts

Letting your readers know your current location in the overall structure of your argument helps them to follow your line of reasoning. I learned this guideline during my years of teaching public speaking to scores of undergraduates, many of whom had great difficulty organizing an introduction, a few main points, and a conclusion in a 4-minute speech. You should never underestimate the value of a "heads up" signal that reminds your audience what you have discussed and what remains to be explored; this gives a helping hand to all of us multitasking readers, and we may be grateful enough to keep reading. You can accomplish this goal in any number of ways, from simple numbering of your points (e.g., first, second, next), to more complex internal previews (e.g., "I will discuss the following six categories . . .") and summaries (e.g., "Having explained the eight forms of backstage communication, I now turn to . . ."). For those who want more subtle and graceful connections, transitional or orienting sentences at the beginning of analytic paragraphs serve a similar purpose without being quite as explicit in labeling.

I now explore several exemplars of *integrated crystallization* to highlight some of the many possibilities. Of course, none of the books and articles I examine invoke the concept of crystallization to explain their approach, although their work reflects its principles as I outline them, and the authors may well

refuse the label as I propose it. My goal centers not on retroactively categorizing these works but on pointing to the possibilities for the conscious use of
crystallization in future projects.

WOVEN CRYSTALLIZATION EXEMPLARS

In this section, I discuss a range of exemplars. I begin with projects published as books, then explore those published as journal articles or chapters
in edited collections.

Book-Length Exemplars

One way to form a coherent integrated text involves layering participants'
voices into the text in as "raw" a state as possible. Lather and Smithies (1997),
in their book about women living with HIV/AIDS, used an ingeniously nonlinear format for their book. The authors placed edited transcripts of interviews
with participants at the top of the page with an ongoing dialogue between the
researchers below that, visually reinforcing the focus on the participants' sense
making and privileging the voices of the women. Lather and Smithies wanted
to empower women with HIV/AIDS by making their voices more visible, and
they did this by placing their words higher on the page than the researchers'.

> While this book is not so much planned confusion as it might at first appear,
> it is, at some level, about what we see as a breakdown of clear interpretation
> and confidence of the ability/warrant to tell such stories in uncomplicated,
> non messy ways. . . . By moving from inside to outside, across different lev-
> els and a multiplicity and complexity of layers that unfold an event which
> exceeds our frames of reference, we hope to create a book that does justice
> to these women's lives, a book that exceeds our own understandings, some
> widened space to speak beyond our means. Via a format that folds backward
> and forward, the book moves toward a weaving of method, the politics of
> interpretation, data, analysis—all are embedded in the tale. Challenging any
> easy reading via shifting styles, the book positions the reader as thinker, will-
> ing to trouble the easily understood and the taken-for-granted. (p. xvi)

Moreover, the authors "interrupted" the parallel texts with boxes containing demographic, medical, and other information about the impact of HIV/
AIDS on society and photos of AIDS-inspired artwork. This powerful refusal

of linear narrative order institutes an alternative, more egalitarian, productive order. The text never becomes chaotic, however; a meaningful order exists and challenges readers without abandoning them. The authors never surrender (nor claim to surrender) their control over the material, but rather seek to put forth claims while problematizing those same claims through an artfully disruptive, but still coherent, text.

Another outstanding exemplar of woven crystallization is Thorp's (2006) book about a participatory action project involving creating and caring for a garden at a diverse, underresourced, primary school that serves urban children, the majority of whom live in or skirt the edges of poverty. Thorpe used what she calls "a methodology of letting go, getting lost, and finding my way" in which she let the kids and teachers "have their way with" her (p. 117). Refusing a linear, tidy account of her experience with the kids and teachers that would be a comfort for readers, Thorp explains:

> I wish I could write a happily-ever-after story—a "comfort text"—for these are children with basic needs going unmet. These are children with little or no access to fresh, nutritious food. Not to mention love and attention, literacy and health care, clean water, security and safety. It is a profusion of needs. Overwhelming, ever present. There is little comfort to be found. . . . And so I deal with this excessive otherness that defies all analysis and representations with messy texts, polyvocality, poetry, and performance ethnography. (p. 125)

The book combines photographs, fieldnotes, poems, and analytic prose generated by the researcher with digital images of children's journals, drawings, and diagrams. All of these are jumbled artfully together, interrupting, layered one over the other, yet cohering in a story that moves deeply and offers profound truths about how we fail our children, our teachers, and our planet. Perhaps the most fragmented and visually disruptive exemplar of work reflecting what I conceive of as woven crystallization, Thorp's (2006) work interrupts a single narrative thread with visual images in a variety of fonts, many of them handwritten. The black-and-white photos offer a window into the world she describes and invites us to witness suffering and joy.

A final example of a book-length woven crystallization, Bach's (2007) multigenre exploration of the "evaded curriculum" of adolescent girls' lives draws on photovoice techniques, ethnography, narratives, and other data.

The book contains several "notebooks" and includes photographs, poetry, narratives, and academic prose, all woven together into a rich, embodied exploration of the lived experiences of the girls and of Bach's experience as a woman reflecting on her own girlhood, a teacher, a mother of a daughter, and a graduate student of curriculum. Bach uses feminist theory and concepts to help communicate the truths she constructs about the ways in which the girls resist, accommodate, internalize, reject, and embody the meanings of "girl" generated by school systems and the larger culture. She writes:

> I represent my knowing and my shifting subjectivities of identity as I question my position and disrupt the acts of switching between observer and participant. . . . My notebooks acknowledge present theorists, educational researchers, fiction writers, song writers, activists, poets, and visual artists whose works trouble an already interpreted world and turn the lens upon themselves. My hope has been to mess up the master's house, knowing "the master's tools will never dismantle the master's house" (Lorde, 1984, p. 112).

> warning warning warning
>
> we're in the master's house
>
> but not using the master's tools
>
> making strict observance necessary when you open this book. (Bach, 2007, p. ix)

Bach's collages of images and words communicate a world of uncertainty and strength, a vivid portrait and many intentional gaps. She captures the adolescent silences as well as their speech, weaving together their words and hers, their worlds and hers, so that we may encounter them from our own perspectives.

Article-Length Exemplars

An exemplar of an article-length project that engaged in woven crystallization is López, Eng, Randall-David, and Robinson (2005) who combined photovoice and grounded theory in a participatory action research project that explored breast cancer survivors' perspectives on their quality of life. The article includes one of the photographs taken by a participant, which features a family bible. The picture represented the role of religion in her meaning of quality of life. Although the article reflects primarily a traditional, analytical, grounded theory voice and hence is not as fully crystallized a form as some, it nonetheless describes extensive work with photographs, including an exhibit in which the women presented the photographs to groups of community members. The authors include not merely a photo of participants or a schematic, but a photo that was part of their data and a thus significant exemplar of participants' meaning making. Given the constraints of journals, this combination of forms of analysis and (limited) visual representation effectively showed meaning to its audience rather than only telling.

Another excellent journal-length article that reflects the goals of woven crystallization is an account by Clark/Keefe (2006) that explores the experience of the author and another woman professor who had been first generation college students of working class or poor families and later became academics. She weaves poetry, narrative, block quotations, and an image of a painting to build her autoethnographic, "performance-oriented 'ourstory' that blends academic, personal, biographical, and popular culture discourses" (p. 1180). Her work draws from Magolda's (1999) "mystory" account of a qualitative inquiry seminar that invokes passages of music lyrics and other popular culture discourses, excerpts from scholarly and methodological essays, personal journals, narrative, and analytic prose.

A final example of article-length woven crystallization, Minge (2007) offers "The Stained Body: A Fusion of Embodied Art on Rape and Love," a painfully compelling text that explores body and memory of love and of rape through "embodied art," which she defines as "the process of inquiry that adds depth of emotion, perception, sensory detail, meaning, and creation of meaning to both the lived and the recreated experience through the blending of various art forms" (p. 252). The text weaves poetry, autoethnographic narrative, and painting to illuminate the embodied nature of memory and the body as a site of knowledge production.

In each of these exemplars, the bits and pieces of art and analysis work together in layers to illuminate a topic uniquely reflecting the authors' perspectives. The woven structures, while each different, offered readers a sense of atypical order, inviting them to experience various facets of a project a little bit at a time, in contradictory and complementary ways. Each of these texts satisfies, even as it mystifies and points through its layers of meaning to the lack of a single, coherent core of absolute Truth.

SHARPENING EDGES AND SEPARATING SPACES: PATCHED CRYSTALLIZATION

Authors also may choose to produce crystallized multigenre texts that include a succession of juxtaposed genres, or *patched crystallization,* rather than mixing or weaving small pieces of contrasting genres all together. While linked in one manuscript, the pieces also function semi-autonomously as coherent individual texts, rather like a sampler quilt where each block is pieced together with triangles, squares, and other shapes that together reflect a distinct pattern; side by side, each block is different, yet related to those on either side of it. The challenge authors face here is to make each piece speak on its own *and* in harmony (and/or counter harmony) with its neighboring representations. Researchers will find such an approach neither more nor less difficult than weaving together smaller bits of different genres, but rather as presenting a somewhat different set of challenges to construct. I offer several suggestions for constructing patched multigenre texts.

Orientation

First, be very clear about where you are going in your text by offering your reader an orientation to your text. Even if you do not wish explicitly to offer up such a statement in the text, it should form the guiding force behind the work. Challenging your readers is fine, but going too far can make your text seem unapproachable or less than engaging. Unlike in woven texts, readers of patched texts must wait a longer time between genre shifts, and generally they should not be left wondering what one piece has to do with the next. Unless you have a truly compelling reason not to, I suggest you tip your hand immediately or after only an introductory experience (e.g., a brief narrative, thought-provoking quote, or other opening gambit). This sets a stage and some basic scenery that your audience can then keep in mind as you successively place each new character into the story and develop the action, thus revealing more about the world you create on your stage. Do not be afraid you are giving away your point upfront: As an analogy, consider that only after the characters find the murder victim does the mystery of "whodunit" begin (A. W. Frank, 2004). Orienting your readers with a purpose statement also grants you greater latitude to go a little wild and try something daring in your representations, because your reader can discern confidently that all will come together in the end (i.e., that the detective will correctly identify the murderer, and you will pull all the pieces of your work together into a meaningful whole).

Forge Thematic Connections

Although differences between genres should be sharp, readers should be able to identify clear connections in the content or lesson of each successive piece in a patched text. Many options for highlighting such connections exist: For example, make some of the snippets in your analysis function as elements of narratives in another chapter, or exemplify each of your content categories with a corresponding poem to make clear the resonating meanings across each of the genres. Some disconnect between genres in a patched text may be productive and generative; too much can confuse and disorient. You certainly can play with deliberately misleading readers, but this must be done with great care and never without good reason. In general, enhance the resonance of your pieces with each other by running one or more threads throughout each of your genres. A thread might be attention to expressions of power or of cross-cultural conflict, both of which could be examined analytically as well as incorporated into poetry, narrative, or other artwork.

Minimize Bleeding of Genres

Although not an absolute rule, I recommend that when constructing a patched text that aims to generate truths through multiple retellings, you should strive to make the voices of each piece stylistically distinct from the others. Each piece should have a flavor of its own that dominates despite the commonalties among each of the genres in the text. The strength of patched crystallization lies in the contrasting ways in which truths manifest in disparate genres. Thus, positioning your set of poems next to a series of photographs or a narrative next to a review of theory sharpens awareness of the generic constraints. This strategy may appear to contradict the previous one. I urge you instead to think of them as existing in productive tension and to pursue a balance of connections and distinctions.

Debriefing

Again, while not required, I highly recommend that somewhere—final chapter, appendix, footnotes/endnotes, interludes, interchapters, text boxes,

afterword, or perhaps some intriguing possibility you call into being yourself—
you debrief your readers with your thoughts on some of the ways in which *you*
think your representations fit together. You need not declare an exclusive interpretation or attempt to bind the reader to your authorial intentions; you can
also deconstruct, question, and problematize the individual and collective construction of meanings, adding an additional layer to your text. I commonly
offer explicit connections among the pieces of my work as yet another facet of
the crystal through which readers may encounter the text. I do not see these as
limiting readers' interpretations but as providing more food for thought. The
demands of each piece vary, however, and certainly some pieces will remain
more ephemeral than others.

Patched texts offer the benefit of including multiple genres without having to make them fit closely together, as woven texts require. Readers experience genres one at a time as coherent wholes, even as they link to previous and
subsequent representations within the text.

PATCHED CRYSTALLIZATION EXEMPLARS

Book-Length Exemplars

M. Wolf's (1992) *A Thrice Told Tale* provided inspiration for my own
sharpening of genres for contrast (Ellingson, 2005a). Wolf uses experiences
from fieldwork in Taiwan as a basis for illustrating and problematizing current debates about postmodernism, ethnography, and interpretation. Wolf
divided the book into three main representations. She wrote an account of a
troubled young woman in a Taiwanese village in the form of a fictional narrative. The second account contained a set of fieldnotes from the period during which the incident with the woman occurred that provided perspectives of
villagers and that resonated with a distinctly scientific voice, wherein participants were referred to by number. In the final section, Wolf offered a
scholarly analysis of the incident, published in a mainstream anthropology
journal, that provided an academic dissection of the cultural issues involved
in making an interpretation of the woman's seemingly odd behavior. In
between each of these major segments, Wolf discussed postmodern and feminist concerns with ethnographic representation, including power and co-
optation of others' voices. In the end, the book admirably served the dual
purpose of telling and retelling a story in different voices in order to provide a

complex and compelling consideration of gender, culture, and mysticism, and to demonstrate the constraints and opportunities of ethnographic writing.

In *Communicating in the Clinic,* I divided each genre into a separate chapter, following Wolf's (1992) lead. I wanted to highlight the equally constructed nature of accounts and show how they remain mired in power, so I placed them next to each other in a series, expecting readers to feel a jolt as they moved abruptly from one genre to the next, with no segues. My book consisted of three ethnographic genres—ethnographic narrative, grounded theory analysis, and autoethnography—and a feminist critique (Ellingson, 2005a). I ordered Chapters 2 through 4 intentionally to provide readers with the experience of moving among contrasting styles of writing. I found it far less effective to juxtapose the narrative with the autoethnographic account, or the grounded theory analysis with the feminist critique, because these genres had more stylistic commonalities. If read sequentially, the chapters take readers through a day in the life of the clinic, analyze that daily communication through systematic categorization of communication processes, and then reimmerse readers in story, this time of my personal journey through my fieldwork, data analysis, and writing processes. Then, the next chapter explored power dynamics in both my findings and each of the modes of representations, linking, deconstructing and complexifying all of them, including my role as embodied ethnographer and author of each of the accounts. A conclusion wrapped up my tale with implications for practitioners and administrators in health care, as well as theoretical implications for incorporating Goffman (1959) and the bona fide group perspective (Putnam & Stohl, 1990) into health care research.

Two collections of previously published work that has been recontextualized and reinterpreted also form excellent examples of patched crystallization. Richardson's (1997) *Fields of Play* includes a selection of her published work from the previous decade of scholarship with the articles

> accompanied by "writing-stories" about their production. . . . What I learned about writing methods and about myself I have recently applied to my earlier writings, contextualizing and personalizing them, making it all new for the first time, re-visioning my life and work. The reframing process displaced the boundaries between two genres: "selected writings" and "autobiography." *Fields of Play* repositions them as convergent genres that, when intertwined, create new ways of reading/writing that are more congruent with post structural understandings of the situated nature of knowledge making. (pp. 1, 3)

Richardson's reflections touch on themes of feminism in the academy, the crisis of representation, and the "narrative turn" in social sciences. Readers learn about Richardson's personal life and its intimate connections to her work. The volume contains poetry, narrative, dramatic performance script, social scientific prose, and essay.

Likewise, Ellis's book, *Revisions: Autoethnographic Stories of Life and Work* (in press), presents articles she published during the last two decades, with commentary between them, designed to explore her life and work. She writes:

> I wrap a larger "story of the stories" around segments of my reprinted narratives and the interpretive materials that originally accompanied them. I write new tales into the gaps. I include and react to voices of other scholars and students whose responses and critiques were evoked by my work. . . . To connect the past to my life now, I add current reflections, narrative vignettes, and analyses, which I call meta-autoethnographies, that fast forward these stories to the present. These are occasions in which I revisit my original representation, consider responses, and write an autoethnographic account about autoethnography. . . . My goal is to turn the narrative snapshots I have written in the past into a form more akin to a video—a text in motion—and provide an examination of my work and the lives it represents from a multitude of perspectives, written from my current position. As I reconstruct and revise a piece of my life story, I seek to provide a larger framework that marks and holds the scenes in place, at least for this moment. (Ellis, in press)

Ellis's account brings together many perspectives on representing the self and the other and significant discussion of the ethical and personal issues in writing about intimate others. Taken together, the pieces offer a crystallized account of Ellis's life and of the practice of autoethnography.

Article-Length Exemplars

I located fewer article-length versions of patched crystallization than of woven crystallized accounts, no doubt due in large part to length limitations of journals. One structure embodies the goals of patched crystallization by juxtaposing a narrative presentation with an academic commentary/analysis (e.g., Ellis, 1993). Hirschman (1999) offers an evocative narrative of the fragmented, chaotic, and exhausting experiences of a medical intern. Following the descriptive account, the author offers a compelling argument that the current health communication literature ignores or downplays the specificity of hospitals or other local settings in favor of references to nondescript clinical settings as though they were all the same. Hirschman seeks to advance interpersonal communication within specific health care contexts by encouraging researchers to look closely at the communication in real-life contexts. Another article-length example of patched crystallization is a piece that includes three different ethnographic tales of a soup kitchen (D. L. Miller & Creswell, 1998). In addition to the stories, the authors discuss the process of sense making about and the implications of representing their experiences in the soup kitchen for understanding that setting.

ISSUES IN CONSTRUCTING INTEGRATED CRYSTALLIZATION

Now that we have explored exemplars of woven and patched forms of integrated crystallization, I turn to a discussion of three central issues in constructing multigenre texts: length limitations, pragmatic implications, and ownership of research processes.

Coping With Length Limitations

One of the most frustrating aspects of representing qualitative research is the length restrictions imposed by conventional journals and edited collections. Research report norms developed during the dominance of positivism, where tight quantitative cases could be built in very short manuscripts without sacrificing critical meaning; tables and charts summed up much of the pertinent information. However, in qualitative research, the rich examples, the participants' words, the pictures built of words (or the images captured in photos, or the poems or narratives that evoke a time and place) comprise much of the meaning of the analysis, and these take up "too much" room. Unfortunately, journals seldom bend on these rules (and not only because of stubbornness; they cope with material and financial constraints). I do not advise playing with font size and margins, as editors usually pick up on such space-saving strategies pretty quickly. Since we rarely can escape these limitations, I offer some of my tricks and ones I have picked up from other colleagues over the years.

First, and perhaps most obvious, tighten up the language as much as possible through eliminating any unnecessary words. This has the advantage of not only eliminating excess length but also improving the flow of the writing. Some suggestions: Simple verbs take less room than verb clauses ("spoke" rather than "was speaking"); active voice takes less room than passive ("I collected data," not "the data were collected"); often "that" can be eliminated without sacrificing clarity; vivid verbs eliminate the need to modify verbs with adverbs (e.g., "hollered" is shorter than "stated very loudly"); and of course, some phrases and clauses simply do not add much meaning to your manuscript and can be cut.

Second, do your duty in surveying the field, but no more than that. That is, read widely but then keep your review of literature and related theory selective. The point is to contextualize your exciting new findings, not to rehash everything that came before you in an effort to demonstrate you have done your homework. On a related note, unless you want to write a state-of-the-field or review piece, do not overcite by listing copious numbers of citations after each declarative sentence. I loved doing this when I first began publishing as a graduate student, reasoning (I suppose) that she who cited most won the academic game. That perception is not entirely unfounded, but the practice impedes shortening nonessentials in order to save space for richness. One or two cites provide sufficient coverage for most statements. This same advice applies to the method section; spend your word-count capital on key aspects of data collection and analysis, including establishing your standpoint as author/researcher, and avoid going into lengthy explanations of what ethnography is, how you wrote your fieldnotes, or the exact questions in your interview schedule.

Third, be strategic about details in your findings. In your analytic writing, offer one thick, rich example per theme or category (one quote over 40 words or two lines, depending on journal style) that requires an indented quotation, and make all other examples shorter, selecting key phrases and paraphrasing less important parts to conserve space. With narratives, concentrate on moments, rather than trying to tell a whole story; summarize the backstory in expository prose and then offer an evocative narrative of a moment, or the other way around; begin with a moment and then summarize what happened next. Far better to have a piece of a great story than all of a mediocre story.

Excavating Pragmatic Implications

Regardless of how you structure your multigenre piece, consider the value of making explicit statements of the implications of your work. "There is nothing so practical as a good theory," said Lewin (1951, p. 169). I agree, but also incumbent upon us writers is a duty to show our readers *how* our theoretical/conceptual insights can be utilized outside the ivory tower. I mention this here not only as an issue of enhancing the applicability of research (which I think is a great idea) but specifically as a crystallization issue. One of the best ways to capture readers' interest is to highlight the pragmatic implications of your work for a variety of people, processes, and settings. Such implications may contrast with other genres utilized in crystallized accounts, reinforcing the narrative truth of a story, for example, by demonstrating the story's lessons for others in similar circumstances. For example, Jenks (2005) explored differences between experiences of parents raising children with visual impairments (including herself) and popular press accounts of similar parenting experiences in order to demonstrate how much less tidy lived experiences of parenting children with disabilities tend to be than the "official" accounts. Published accounts reflect the "restitution narrative" form (A. W. Frank, 1995) in which normalcy disrupted by the diagnosis of a child's disability resumes immediately upon parents' adoption of appropriate coping strategies. Jenks's ethnographic work found experiences that resisted easy categorization as either "normal" or somehow uniquely "different," as though parenting a child with disabilities could never be normal, only a difficult enterprise worthy of pity or derision. Instead, Jenks proposes that disability remains both an obdurate reality *and* a socially constructed phenomenon:

> Conceiving disability as a dialectical tension between the physical body and linguistic descriptions of the body offers greater freedom of choice. Coping, then, becomes not an end in itself, or something someone isn't doing correctly, but an active, ongoing, repeated, negotiated behavior. (p. 164)

Hence, Jenks offers a helpful way for parents, teachers, coaches, and other people involved in the lives of children with disabilities to position themselves as they carry out the tasks of daily life with children. The implications of her analysis are clear; we need not choose between a regressive medical model that views disability as merely a manifestation of physical difference, nor feel guilty that we cannot sublimate the very real challenges of parenting a child with disabilities by embracing a social view of disability that presumes all people with difference simply should be valued equally. Jenks stakes some middle ground from which parents and others can both appreciate their coping abilities and point to the need for more social change. Such insights can be woven into analysis and commentary, or they could be placed in appendices if they do not meet the aesthetic goals of your crystallized account.

Own What You Did

One of the most helpful (albeit not foolproof) ways to enhance your account and ward off editorial defensiveness toward creative analytic work in general and crystallization in particular is to be absolutely clear about what you did (and did not) do in producing your manuscript. This includes data collection, analysis, and especially choices made about representation. Terminology and practices vary widely among qualitative methodologists, even within the same discipline (Potter, 1996). For example, in my book on teamwork, I explained how I constructed the "day in the life" account of the interdisciplinary geriatric oncology clinic:

> Obviously, to construct a day, I have taken liberties with chronology, condensing into a single day events that actually happened at different times during my fieldwork. I used the narrative convention of time frame (a day) to provide a sense of plot movement and improve clarity for readers. While faithfully representing the interactions I observed, I altered minor details of an interaction in service of constructing a view of the clinic that reflects the team and the people it serves in an intelligible or comprehensible manner. In addition to the chronology changes, I made two other types of changes. First, I made changes to increase comprehension for readers who are not medically trained. For example, I occasionally inserted explanations that would have been very abbreviated or expressed in jargon in the team members' speech (e.g., spelled out "geriatric depression scale" when the social worker would have said "GDS."). Second, following Institutional Review Board ethical guidelines, I also worked extensively to protect individuals' privacy. . . . To this end, I edited comments between me and team members, changed details of patients' appearance and lives, and created pseudonyms for all staff, patients, and companions. (Ellingson, 2005a, p. 16)

By explaining my process, I help alleviate suspicions that I took an "anything goes," sloppy attitude toward constructing my representation.

While some colleagues may not like or approve of what you did no matter how you explain it, concise, explicit details of your process make it more difficult for them to dismiss it as careless or random. Accounting for your process (even in an appendix or endnote) constitutes an important nod toward methodological rigor. As many have posited, engaging in creative analytic work should be no less rigorous, exacting, and subject to strict standards of peer evaluation (e.g., Denzin, 1997; Denzin & Lincoln, 2005; Ellis, 2004). Moreover, such a roadmap assists others who may seek to follow your lead. One of my persistent criticisms of qualitative researchers is their unwillingness or inability (due to space constraints) to represent the mistakes and misdirections that characterize real research; we neaten it up to sound credible and get published. I do not believe that most qualitative researchers deliberately lie, but we often commit the sin of omission. I find this representational practice particularly problematic when some of the audience for our work—students and those new to our methodologies, in particular—find themselves shocked when in the field or conducting an interview and all goes much less than smoothly than it was "supposed to go." Researchers need models of how to negotiate such uncomfortable circumstances. Some suggestions on issues to own:

- Explain choices you made in composing narratives, poems, or other artistic work; in other words, how did you get from data to text?

- Describe your standpoint vis-à-vis your topic, not just what it is, but (at least some of) *how* it shapes your interactions with your data (e.g., I am a cancer survivor studying clinics so I tend to be more empathetic with patients than health care providers; I am a feminist so I pay a lot of attention to power dynamics).

- Indicate your awareness of and response to ethical considerations about voice, privacy, and responsibility to others. What steps did you take to ensure participant confidentiality? To privilege participants' voices? Consider how your work might be read in ways that *do not* reflect your intentions—for example, what quotes from participants could be taken out of context and used as justification for blaming the victim?—and surround vulnerable voices with preemptory statements that make it more difficult for oppositional forces to excerpt and reinterpret their meaning in regressive ways.

- Detail your analytic procedures (e.g., grounded theory, Charmaz, 2000; systematic introspection, Ellis, 1991; autoethnography, Ellis, 2004). Even if you construct a unique, outside-the-box artistic creation, you should explain your methodology and cite some sources to contextualize your work. Again, this need not interfere with your aesthetic goals; details should be concise and can be placed in an appendix, footnote, or even a separate piece altogether.[3]

The goal is to reveal crystallized projects as embodied, imperfect, insightful constructions rather than immaculate end products.

Woven and patched forms of integrated crystallization represent only early maps of the territory of crystallization. I look forward to encountering the myriad of forms that will undoubtedly develop as more qualitative researchers enlarge traditional boundaries and construct new genres, hybrids, and variations. Using strategies of integrated crystallization, researchers can produce a multigenre text that incorporates a variety of genres and media and reflects multiple epistemologies. These strategies can be used alone or in conjunction with dendritic (or dispersed) crystallization, as detailed in the next chapter.

INTERLUDE

Quilting as Activism

Earlier in the chapter, I described quilting as a metaphor for both the process and the products of crystallization. Quilting also reflects the activist spirit of much multi-method, multigenre work that seeks to improve the lives of people by drawing attention to the complexities of lived experiences, often of oppressed and/or underserved groups. Quilting is a form of social activism practiced by many people and organizations. Articulated by McLaughlin (2004), for example:

> Anabaptist [e.g., Mennonite or Amish] women continue to make quilts as a symbolic and tangible expression of their creativity, community and charity as they work together to put their faith in action. As they stitch together patches that make up a quilt, they are also stitching together the social fabric that expresses their faith and understanding of how that faith is to be lived against the backdrop of the larger culture. They are stitching together the peaceable kingdom of community, creativity, diversity and charity. (p. 151)

Quilts constitute important symbols of culture and family, and they also embody activism in their creation as artwork for display to raise awareness of social and political oppression and to prompt compassionate responses, and as objects to be sold to raise money to support organizations promoting social justice.

I highlight here two organizations of quilters as exemplars of the possibilities for quilting as a form of activism. Quilting parallels the possibilities of crystallization to make a difference in the world. In the same ways that people make quilts to commemorate, to comfort, to warm, to act as symbols, and to function as protection, projects using crystallization are well suited for reaching out to a multitude of people to offer the same.

Perhaps the most famous example is The NAMES Project Foundation, which sponsored the AIDS quilt. The quilt currently contains over 46,000 panels and memorializes more than 90,000 people who have died from AIDS and their loved ones. It has been displayed all across the United States and has been viewed by over 15 million people, raising millions of dollars to provide services for people living with AIDS (www.aidsquilt.org). Initially conceived by gay rights activist Clive Jones in 1985, the AIDS quilt began in 1987 in San Francisco as an effort to document the devastating losses and to ensure that history would remember the names of those lost to the epidemic. The NAMES Project Foundation states that its ongoing objectives include

> To provide a creative means for remembrance and healing, to effectively illustrate the enormity of the AIDS pandemic, to increase awareness of HIV and AIDS throughout the general public, to assist others in providing education on the prevention of HIV infection, and to raise funds for community-based AIDS Service Organizations (ASO's). (www.aidsquilt.org)

The AIDS quilt offers a visual inspiration to action and advocacy, to compassion and cooperation. Moreover, viewing of the quilt has been found to be a successful intervention into the preventative behavior by people at risk for contracting AIDS (Knaus, Pinkleton, & Austin, 2000).

In contrast to the tremendous aesthetic appeal of the AIDS quilt are "ugly quilts" made by volunteers and distributed to people without homes with a completely practical goal of keeping people warm. My Brother's Keeper Quilt Group was begun by Jim and Flo Wheatley in 1985, after a man living on the streets of Manhattan volunteered to help Flo and their ill son as they navigated the subway (www.thesleep ingbagproject.org). Wanting to give something back in recognition of the man's extraordinary kindness in the midst of his own suffering, Flo noticed the bitter cold faced by people without homes, and designed "ugly quilts." She called them ugly quilts for two reasons. First, so that volunteers would not be intimidated by the idea of producing an intricate or beautiful quilt, and instead would feel confident in their ability to follow the simple instructions offered on the Web site. Second, the ugliness of the quilts ensures that they hold no market value, ensuring that people without homes are the beneficiaries and the quilts cannot be sold. The organization estimates they have given out more than 100,000 of these practical, sleeping-bag-like creations made of recycled old drapes, bedspreads, blankets, mattress pads, and donated scrap fabric. The quilters group spawned chapters and associated groups all over the United States and in some other countries. While not aesthetically impressive in a traditional sense, each ugly quilt reflects the caring and efforts of volunteers and has a practical benefit. "Our only purpose is to help the homeless be warm until they can be helped or healed by others in our society" stated their Web site, truly a meaningful purpose (www.thesleepingbagproject.org).

What do these two extraordinary organizations of quilters have to do with practicing crystallization as qualitative researchers? I perceive several parallels. Both involve assembling unremarkable bits and pieces into a meaningful whole that offers a compelling message. Both involve creating work that makes a difference in people's lives, both symbolically and practically. In both quilting and in crystallization, individual stories—of loved ones, of loss, of the making of a quilt—are preserved in the final work, yet the stories come together to present a collective story of suffering, survival, and even triumph that is much larger than any one person. Finally, both illustrate the possibilities for powerful action that arise when people come together with a mission. I hope that these models inspire people to instigate positive social change through their research.

NOTES

1. Some people may find the use of a feminine and feminist metaphor alienating. I concur with Flannery (2001):

> If men [or members of other groups] feel uncomfortable with this metaphor and cannot relate to its association of ideas, perhaps this will give them some sense of what women's relationship to science has felt like for centuries. This metaphor could also highlight the power of metaphors to shape attitudes and to create limits on perceptions. (p. 642)

Metaphors, and language more generally, deeply influence our thinking; to object to a new metaphor is to reveal the power—and negate the myth of neutrality—of traditional, masculine metaphors.

2. Of course, it is possible to strategically represent and (re)analyze a single incident from multiple perspectives, but that should be done explicitly to make a point about methodology or representation; simply repeating exemplars appears sloppy and casts doubt on the richness and variety of your data set.

3. I know that some authors now publish stories without such frameworks, such as Richardson's (1994) "Nine Poems" and Ellis's (1996) "Maternal Connections," but these do not meet the requirements of crystallization in themselves.

SIX

ALL APART

Dendritic Crystallization

━━━◆◆◆◆━━━

*In a snowflake, just an ordinary snowflake, we can find a fasci-
nating story of the spontaneous creation of pattern and form.
From nothing more than the simple act of water condensing into
ice, these amazing crystal structures appear—complex, symmetric,
and in endlessly varying designs.*

—Libbrecht (2003, p. 21)

Ice crystals form in the atmosphere when water vapor transforms directly
into ice. Snowflakes are made of ice crystals that often include dendrites, or
branches. The word *dendrite* comes from the Greek word for tree or treelike,
and physicists and chemists use the term to describe branches of crystals
formed of a myriad of substances, including water. Elaborate crystal branches,
which develop as an ice crystal floats through a cloud (i.e., water vapor),
develop symmetrically around a core crystal, creating the complex and beautiful shapes people commonly think of when they picture snowflakes (Libbrecht,
2003). I borrow the term *dendritic* in order to conceptualize qualitative projects
that continually branch out into patterned but also unpredictable, unique, and
often beautiful forms of representation that reflect multiple epistemologies.
I chose dendritic partly for its resonance with the crystal metaphor that underlies

Richardson's (1994) original concept of crystallization and my development of it, and partly because I appreciate the complementing of a feminine quilting metaphor (discussed in Chapter 5) with a "hard" science term grounded in the physical sciences. Crystallization embodies choice, possibilities, and imagination, moving beyond surface dualities such as hard/soft, feminine/masculine, and art/science—hence, my attraction to deliberately mixing my metaphors to further push the boundaries of the qualitative enterprise.

Despite my passionate advocacy for representing crystallization through multigenre texts, I fully acknowledge the need and desire to reach audiences through traditional academic, professional, and popular outlets that publish single-genre work. Hence, I developed strategies for envisioning crystallization as *dendritic,* an ongoing and dispersed process of making meaning through multiple epistemologies and genres, constituted in a series of separate but related representations based on a data set. I encourage researchers to embrace multiple outlets for fragments of their qualitative projects, a process that retains many of the benefits of integrated crystallized texts and offers other advantages. In this chapter, I provide an overview of the practice of dendritic crystallization and its benefits, discuss strategies for dispersing manuscripts into multiple outlets, and provide an exemplar of an ongoing project involving dendritic crystallization.

DENDRITIC PRACTICES

The process of engaging in dendritic crystallization does not differ radically from producing integrated crystallized texts; researchers undergo the same iterative processes of multimethod, multigenre sense making about their topic. Moreover, the two forms of crystallization are not mutually exclusive; you could publish one or more multigenre texts reflecting integrated crystallization (Ellingson, 2005a) *and* a number of other single-genre articles and chapters, as I produced pieces focusing on aspects of interdisciplinary teamwork and comprehensive geriatric assessment (e.g., Ellingson, 1998, 2002, 2008b, 2008c) that together constitute a dendritic approach.

Like integrated crystallization, dendritic crystallization uses the design processes detailed in Chapter 4. Moreover, researchers can use many of the same principles and techniques for producing multigenre texts discussed in Chapter 5. The difference between integrated and dendritic lies in the more dispersed manner in which researchers publish and share the multiple representations they produce. In addition, a dendritic approach can be productively conceptualized as involving three characteristics: conscious engagement with an ongoing (re)creative process, responsiveness to the research context(s), and development of distinct, often asymmetrical branches. Once again, please think of these characteristics as starting points for your work, not as boundaries.

First, researchers consciously embrace a sense of openness to continual development and evolution of their project as they practice dendritic crystallization. That is, as we gather, analyze, and represent data, we actively seek out possibilities for new directions. Of course, the nonlinear, spiral research structure—moving back and forth among data gathering, analysis, and review of theory and published research—characterizes qualitative research in general (e.g., C. A. B. Warren & Karner, 2005). However, dendritic crystallization involves going beyond looking for connections between your emerging findings and others' research or adding a new theoretical perspective to illuminate unexpected ideas in your data. Rather, it necessitates a mind-set in which researchers *expect* and *invite* radically different ways of knowing to shift their projects.

Second, dendritic processes always are responsive to the contexts of inquiry. Researchers can respond to opportunities, changing relationships, new skills and interests, the needs of participants, and other aspects of their research site or topic. Moreover, the larger sociopolitical context of a project may prompt a popular press representation, a report for a community organization, Web site content, a public presentation, or other communication designed to impact public perception and policy. One of the most powerful aspects of responsiveness is the capacity for different representations, published or otherwise shared separately, to join with each other and with the work of others within and outside the academy to work collectively and make a significant social impact.

Third, although many levels of connection may exist among representations, dendritic crystallization involves the development of distinct and often asymmetrical branches. In other words, pieces of the project must be recognizable as independent from one another and as reflecting—to a greater or lesser degree—contrasting epistemologies. Each project develops branches that offer unique ways of experiencing the world and disperses those pieces of meaning in outlets that reflect the goals of each representation. Many researchers divide their qualitative projects into segments that focus on related research questions, publishing a series of social scientific analyses in different journals; I would not consider projects that produce several separate pieces of the same or very similar genres to embody dendritic crystallization, however. Rather, visual, performing, poetic, or other arts (and/or blends of art and science) would need to form one or more dendrites, complementing the social scientific dendrite.

BENEFITS OF DENDRITIC CRYSTALLIZATION

First, producing multiple texts that utilize a variety of forms of analysis and genres enhances your sense-making processes. As explained in Chapter 5, composing narratives while writing analytic memos stimulates formation of connections, highlights the relationships between individuals and collective stories, illustrates patterns with examples, and influences your thinking and reasoning, enriching each of these practices. Tacking back and forth also reminds you that no form can claim innocence; you author all of them. Hence, the separately published accounts may be complexified and better developed because you worked on your dramatic script while coding your data, for example.

Second, dendritic crystallization enables researchers to satisfy multiple goals. I know I am not alone in my desire to show *and* tell and to explore multiple aspects of my data. One of the simultaneously wonderful and frustrating aspects of qualitative research is the long periods of time absorbed by projects and the voluminous data that we produce. Even after publishing a book and several articles and chapters, I could have written more about interdisciplinary geriatric oncology teamwork. With dendritic crystallization, we have the opportunity to experiment broadly. This approach also avoids the "all your eggs in one basket" approach to publishing a single text that can be too risky a gamble, particularly for students and junior or contingent faculty.

Next, dendritic crystallization can forge a path to reaching multiple audiences. By dividing up your work and publishing your narratives in an ethnography journal, grounded theory analysis in an applied scholarship journal, and a thought piece or practical suggestions in a relevant newsletter or industry-specific newspaper, and also presenting a workshop for your participants and performing in a local theatre, you adapt to your audiences and avoid having your work dismissed out of hand for blaspheming the preferred methodologies and genres of any given outlet. Researchers may also reach lay audiences in the hope of engaging in productive dialogue and activism (see Frey & Carragee's edited collections, 2007a, 2007b). SunWolf's research on communication dynamics and cognition among jurors provides an excellent example. In addition to publishing scholarly research (e.g., SunWolf & Seibold, 1998), she writes for and conducts workshops for attorneys (including public defenders), providing practical knowledge for understanding juror deliberation processes, along with specific strategies for connecting with them (e.g., SunWolf, 2006, 2007). A related benefit is the opportunity to make connections among your audiences by citing, referring to, distributing copies of, or otherwise informing your audience of pieces of your work that they might not gravitate toward if confronted with the piece on its own, without first having encountered your work in their preferred genre.

Finally, dendritic crystallization can help enhance researchers' personal satisfaction in their work. Reinharz (1992) notes that for many feminist researchers, their research embodies a quest to understand, develop, and promote positive change. Inspired by our passions, we engage in multiple methods over the course of long-term research projects. The journey becomes both a personal and professional odyssey toward positively impacting the world. Continual development of a project—such as through dendritic crystallization—may be personally meaningful for many researchers. Notes one group of collaborative researchers: "We would be remiss not to acknowledge the personal fulfillment we have derived through these [activist and research] experiences. Our lives have been enriched as a result of our encounters with [our participants]" (Harter et al., 2007, p. 111). Dendritic crystallization may prove similarly enriching.

DISPERSING CRYSTALLIZED FINDINGS

Each project lends itself to a different approach to dispersing pieces. I offer here some guidelines to help in that process, which will likely develop organically. Strategies include keep the forest and the trees, segment by research question, pragmatism, recognize external constraints, target audiences, make each piece count, practice guerilla scholarship, and bridge dendritic pieces.

Keep the Forest *and* the Trees

As you make decisions about what to include, in what form, for what purposes, keep in mind your project's larger picture. I find this wider purpose difficult to keep in my head when immersed in a study; moving back and forth among the concrete details of narratives, the analytic perspective involved in constructing patterns from the data, and my paradigmatic/ideological goals presents a significant challenge. Yet, that big picture view remains critical to the construction of a crystallized project; each piece adds to the forest of your work. To illustrate, consider several aspects of my big picture for the ethnographic exploration of a dialysis unit: my overall paradigm of social constructionism, my feminist commitments to praxis and critique of power, and my pragmatic goal of the transformation of the medical establishment into a more humane and just environment for employees, patients, and loved ones. Thus, in my dendritic crystallization project on communication and power in a dialysis unit, my paradigmatic focus is on how participants socially constructed (and contested) meaning among the patients, staff, corporate executives, insurance companies, pharmaceutical companies, state and federal regulatory bodies, and other stakeholders; who bears responsibility, for example, when a patient experiences complications of treatment? Ideologically, I focus on the distribution and intersections of power and whose voices, values, and vulnerabilities are marginalized; for example, what are the implications of staff members labeling patients "noncompliant" when they refuse total submission to the brutal dietary and fluid restrictions required of people receiving dialysis? I also include in my reflections attention to my own power as an ethnographer, considering my own privileges and vulnerabilities as an embodied presence in the field and as a writer. My pragmatic goal involves improving the experience of dialysis care for patients by finding ways that they can be empowered to act on their own behalf, and to improve work satisfaction and performance for staff, particularly the paraprofessionals known as "patient care technicians" whose contributions to patient care are marginalized by government and organizational policies. Collectively, these goals constitute a big picture of my project, and I work to ensure that each piece I produce adds to the picture—aesthetically, conceptually, and ethically.

I chose from a near infinite number of possibilities to focus on several key research questions, each of which (to greater and lesser extents) addresses my overall goals for ethnographic research. I highlight the varying experiences of time by patients, staff, and the ethnographer in dialysis (Ellingson, 2006b); disciplinary power in dialysis as it relates to patient compliance/adherence and to paraprofessionals' contributions to knowledge building and care giving; paraprofessionals' understandings of professionalism in health care; the role of extreme routinization of care giving and communication in the dialysis unit

(Ellingson, 2007); and the role of backstage communication among staff in the experience of dialysis care. Each of these questions assumes a social construction of meaning, focusing on power and hierarchy in health communication, and seeks to develop specific recommendations for health care delivery. Whatever your choices in producing a dendritic crystallization of your topic, be sure that each piece contributes toward your goals. You also may have more specific theoretical goals as well that you want to incorporate, although those are less central to my dialysis project.

Segment by Research Question

Perhaps the simplest approach to segmentation involves having one piece per research question. This presumes that your questions can stand alone reasonably well, perhaps with brief explanations of other aspects of your project in your literature review to contextualize each individual inquiry. Focused research questions free you from having to cover a huge topic and instead facilitate crystallization of a narrower one. If one or more related questions are too closely bound to address separately, consider a book or monograph, or attempt to focus the questions more tightly to enable you to explore fully a more narrow slice of your project. Although I always begin my research with one or two broad research questions, more specific ones inevitably arise as I learn more about my ethnographic site and build relationships with participants. If you invest the time in conducting extended participant observation and/or in-depth interviews, you will generate a lot of data with multiple foci. Dividing pieces up to explore in multiple venues provides a wonderful means to do justice to the complexities of your topic. Like incremental theory builders in interpersonal communication, qualitative researchers can also publish in a series, summarizing previous work and then adding the next layer in subsequent publications.

Pragmatism for Researchers

Be pragmatic in making representational decisions; get your work done. One of my doctoral committee members, Dr. Carolyn DiPalma, used to chant to me whenever I came to her with more ideas, problems, and questions about my project: done is good, done is good, DONE IS GOOD! She taught me that great ideas that you never finish writing/producing to share with others remain only that—ideas. Of course, we should strive for excellence, but we should also embrace opportunities to get things done.

In service of the goal of getting things done, be strategic; divide data in ways that fit with opportunities to complete work in a timely manner. I urge you to shape pieces of your work to calls for submissions to edited collections, conference panels, special issues of journals, or other fora. Divide your project according to the foci of courses you teach (or take) and let the reading and preparation for those courses do double-duty. This is not cheating; it is being smart. Many savvy scholars do this automatically and may wonder why I bother to point it out; I mention the strategy here because for a long time I considered this approach something to be ashamed of, something not quite professional, even a bit sleazy. I have heard people speak disparagingly of others who "milk" their dissertations or other data sets. While I do concede the possibility of going to extremes by "retreading" work or making the same basic argument over and over without adding any new insights or content, I find such intellectual laziness relatively rare. Most of us segment our qualitative data sets and adapt portions of our analyses and representations because we spent years and countless hours collecting and conducting them and they are *rich.* We cannot hope to come close to exhausting our data, and so we produce legitimate and often highly valuable scholarship by drawing fresh water from already drilled wells. For example, I published a chapter on power issues in dialysis in response to an invitation to contribute to a collection featuring interpretive health communication research edited by Ellingson (2008a). Throughout my fieldwork and interviews, I reflected continually on the ways in which Foucault's ideas on regulatory power related to the strategies used by the dialysis center administration to control patient care technicians and then strategically invoked by those same technicians to exert control over patients. I explored this "side" issue fully in response to an invitation; without that invitation, I would not have explored that facet of my ethnographic data in the same way.

Recognize External Constraints

Space constraints—usually in terms of page limits, but also pertaining to numbers of photos and figures that can be included in a manuscript, or the length of a film eligible for screening at a conference or film festival—remain a fact of academic life. Breaking up material into subtopics or more focused issues allows you to deal more thoroughly with a specific issue. Page limits particularly constrain narratives, which tend to take up an inordinate amount of room by journal and edited collection standards, particularly when coupled with analysis or reflections. Narrowing your topic, thesis statement, or research question may enable you to more richly explore your topic in a more detailed narrative, or to include more (space-intensive) dialogue. For example, I divided an exploration of the experience of time in the dialysis unit from the larger question of the relationships between frontstage and backstage communication in the dialysis unit, even though time was a crucial element to staff's choices to engage in communication. This decision enabled me to focus not only on analysis of time but also to invite readers into the world of the dialysis unit through narratives that show more than tell.

Target Audiences

Another recommendation for dendritic crystallization is to target outlets that you want to reach, such as method-specific, topic-specific, or discipline-specific journals, and divide your work up according to what would best appeal to these different audiences. For instance, you can publish an artistic, evocative, layered account in *Qualitative Inquiry* to reach an audience of ethnographers and interpretive qualitative researchers from sociology, communication, anthropology, and education; a grounded theory analysis in *Journal of Applied Communication Research* to reach organizational, interpersonal, and group communication scholars; and a content analysis or a case study in *Qualitative Health Research* to qualitative research scholars in nursing, medicine, social work, medical sociology, medical anthropology, health communication, and the like. Scholars should make decisions about outlets for dendritic crystallization according to their professional development needs and desires.

Make Each Piece Count

As addressed above in my comment about "milking" data sets, retreading material only to add to your list of publications leaves a lot to be desired as a justification for dendritic crystallization. Instead, think about how you can maximize the value and contribution of each article, essay, narrative, or other artwork. Make sure that each piece of your dendritic crystallization provides some rich material and unique argument that differs in important ways from any of your other pieces. That does not mean you should not refer to any of the same ideas, literature, methods, or theory in more than one representation, but that you be able to point to and articulate (ideally in a single sentence) the unique contribution of each piece. Moreover, I urge readers to take advantage of the particular opportunities and constraints of each genre, outlet, or medium by choosing wisely which points to make in which form. Trying to accomplish the goal of showing individuals' suffering, while (probably) possible in a traditional scholarly journal article, may be better suited to a performance piece or a series of poems. Tracy's study of communication and emotion provides an excellent example: In a mainstream journal, she published a scholarly analysis of emotional labor of social directors on a cruise ship (Tracy, 2000). This same data yielded a case study included in a volume of organizational cases intended for use by students in organizational communication courses (Tracy, 2006). Then, she authored a script, performed, and acted as a consultant to the director of an ethnodrama, presented as a live performance that offered an embodied representation of the personal and professional rewards and costs of such work for her participants (Tracy, 2003). Each of these forms aptly reflected their content and offered a rich contribution to our knowledge about emotion work.

Practice "Guerilla Scholarship"

Next, pushing the representational envelope reflects a good goal but not the only or even the highest one. Equally important is getting your message out and being subtle (or even sneaky) may be required. If you feel as passionately as I do that your work holds the potential to help people, to promote social justice, to shed light on a complex problem, and/or to significantly influence your discipline, then make sure your important work that most directly serves those goals gets done and published. If that goal requires adapting to a format you do not particularly enjoy, so be it. Pieces count in dendritic crystallization when they count in the world. In order to count, some work may have to accommodate traditional conventions that may not fit comfortably with postmodern, feminist, or narrative sensibilities, but which currently constitute the cost of admission to hallowed disciplinary ground. Explains Rawlins (2007),

> I was still seduced in all my earlier work by the dominating ethos of quantitative social science into aping its trappings, writing style, and subdivisions . . . in order to *pass* as a serious researcher. I call such activity *guerilla scholarship*. It is necessary when certain ways of knowing are stringently enforced to the exclusion and neglect of others. The stated and unstated regimes of certain journals require these kinds of accoutrements. (p. 59)

If subterfuge is required to effect change, then do it. Do not fear that you sell your soul; instead, embrace your righteous guerilla persona and infiltrate mainstream publication outlets. Miller-Day's (2004) book-length qualitative study of communication among grandmothers, mothers, and adult daughters illustrates the possibilities of guerilla scholarship: Miller-Day organized the text in a conventionally structured research report format, but she repeatedly breaks out of the social science box by weaving in rich details of the setting of her interviews, including her own thoughts and emotional responses during her fieldwork, many of which display a keen wit, for example, "I observed three females with expertly applied makeup and crisply ironed designer clothes. My first thought was that this family had won the genetic pool in God's lottery" (p. 55). Moreover, the text includes lyrics from a stage play that contains a dialogue that embodies the contradiction in mother–daughter relationships Miller-Day explores. Segments of dialogue from interviews, fieldnotes, and narratives stand on their own but also are structured into themes, tables, and models, building toward a carefully explicated theory of "necessary convergence." Miller-Day succeeds in conforming sufficiently to traditional qualitative writing and organizational standards in her book, even as she transcends them.

Perhaps my favorite form of "guerilla scholarship" (Rawlins, 2007) is to cite within an article multiple other works that reflect different methods, genres of representation, ideologies, even paradigms. For example, Harter, Norander, and Quinlan (2007) dared to cite their research group's narratives written for a nonprofit agency's Web site (Harter et al., 2005) and a newspaper article (Novak & Harter, 2005) in a scholarly article on public intellectualism and activism published in a mainstream journal. Who knows what unsuspecting reader might follow the trail of cites (one of my treasured pastimes!) straight into a forest of new practices that could broaden her or his horizons. Reference sections fulfill this function, of course, but footnotes, epigraphs, highlighted quotes in an essay or report, and interludes or other interrupting discourses can all be places to invoke the methodological or representational Other and lure the audience into new fields of play (see Richardson, 1997). With the goal of dendritic crystallization, connecting threads among your separate pieces becomes especially vital.

Methods sections also offer good places to highlight connections; when I discuss grounded theory, I sometimes engage in some guerilla scholarship by mentioning other forms of data and how I constructed them at the same time, thus influencing my analysis and writing processes. I urge qualitative scholars to share (or at least hint at) your other work—mention that you also performed your findings when you report how you derived inductive categories; in your performance playbill or flyer, add a note about reports based on the same data. You can also push the envelope through footnotes and the occasional provocative or creative phrase here and there that challenges the standards of acceptability in a publication outlet and thus subversively broaden the horizons of the publication.

Bridge Dendritic Pieces

Having engaged in dendritic crystallization, you also may move beyond guerilla scholarship to actively put your separately published or produced pieces into direct conversation with each other. Such meta-analytical discussion of your work serves a function similar to that of creating a multigenre text through integrated crystallization: that is, simultaneously to enrich and problematize your knowledge claims, as well providing a context in which to explore methodological, epistemological, or theoretical issues that your research illustrates. A wonderful example of such a discussion is Lieblich's (2006) essay that illuminates the processes involved in conducting a qualitative study of women's stories, writing a popular press book, and writing a play:

> Writing the narrative of this process has helped me become newly aware of some methodological, ethical, and political issues entrenched in narrative research. Furthermore, it made me more aware of my position as a researcher, of the participants as people with lives independent of the research, and of our interrelationship with its many layers and faces. (p. 61)

The insights that arose as Lieblich constructed her account added yet another layer to her findings and representations. Suggestions for constructing "conversational" pieces include the following three strategies.

First, you might write an essay that crystallizes your dendritic crystallization, that is, present a case study that describes and provides brief excerpts (or images) of each of your disparate analyses and representations and then explore how they inform, contradict, complement, complexify, and illuminate one another. Just as in multigenre texts, the goal in such a piece is not to claim that you "got it all" or even that you achieved more/better meaning through assembling your disparate analyses and representations, but rather to illustrate how others can benefit from methodological, theoretical, practical, and/or topic-specific lessons that arose from your process of crystallization. For example, in the feminist critique (Chapter 5) of *Communicating in the Clinic,* I explored the limitations of ethnographic and autoethnographic narratives to represent and speak for the other, and my own complicity in the hierarchy of the medical system. You could publish the essay in a journal devoted to qualitative methodology, the commentary section of a mainstream journal in your discipline, or perhaps a special issue of a journal or edited collection on a topic that your research addresses.

"Writing stories" (Richardson, 2000b) offer a second possible format. Such stories reveal and complexify the process of knowledge production by offering views of the behind-the-scenes action, including personal details of researchers' lives and/or messy details of fieldwork, sense making, and writing practices. Rather than claiming that your process story authenticates your other analyses/representations, your story should generate insights about fieldwork, knowledge construction, and the writing life as they play out in a research project that engages in dendritic crystallization. Writing stories, reflection stories, and other accounts of the research process often take the form of confessional tales that emphasize authors'/researchers' humanity and imperfections, their navigation of insider/outsider status and points of view, and their conversion or shift in understanding as they developed relationships with participants over the course of their projects (Van Maanen, 1988).

For example, Harter, Norander, and Quinlan (2007) published an essay in a management journal about the process of producing multiple accounts and promoting social change with Passion Works, a cooperative artist's studio for people with and without developmental disabilities. The authors adopt an academic voice to establish a theoretically rich framework within which they discuss the interconnectedness of their work toward social justice in the form of "locally situated and everyday moments of action" (p. 106) within their communities and their academic scholarship. Adelman and Frey (2001) published a chapter of confessional tales in an edited volume that explored their personal experiences about researching and writing their ethnography of the "fragile community" within an AIDS residence (Adelman & Frey, 1997).

Finally, in her ethnography of village life in Togo, Charlés's (2007) final chapter reveals the process of "constructing an intimate text." Drawing from her academic training, she closely describes deliberating over how to tell her story, including decisions about changing characters' names, leaving out identifying photos (the book has none, except a murky cover shot), and consulting with a valued Togolese colleague throughout her process. She wrestles on the page with the potential effect of her story on all those involved and considers her accountability to readers. In each of these examples, the authors confess their humanity and the personal choices involved in producing accounts. For projects involving dendritic crystallization, such writing stories may provide an important window into a researcher's self as it relates to a project's theoretical, empirical, and ideological goals.

One final strategy for placing your dendritic accounts into conversation with each other involves taking advantage of communication technologies. The Internet offers incredible possibilities for highlighting connections among pieces of your work via Web pages, forming multigenre exhibits. For example, Miller-Day (2005) and colleagues have done this beautifully in "HOMEwork: An Ethnodrama" available on the Web:

> Based on observational data and narratives collected through in-depth interviews with mothers, adolescents, and social service professionals in the community, a stageplay and ethnodrama was developed, produced, and performed for more than 150 policy makers, program developers, community agencies, and community members in Harrisburg, Pennsylvania. Community organizations have requested additional performances for the state legislature and for local social service agency staff. DVD's of the performance were created for dissemination to agencies and organizations with the possibility of a re-staging of the ethnodrama at the Pennsylvania State Capital Building for state legislators. (http://cas.la.psu.edu/research/maternal/homework.html)

The Web site includes a script written by Miller-Day, video clips of the live performance, cites of publications (available for download in PDF format) including reports for foundations and agencies, a conference paper, a public address, and a working paper, and links to other resources. A scholarly article about the project is forthcoming (Miller-Day, in press). As discussed in Chapter 3, opportunities for multigenre video, audio, and graphic work—including pieces bringing together separate publications and performances—also now exist via online journals and on Web sites linked to journals or professional organizations: *Liminalties: A Journal of Performance Studies* offers a great example (http://liminalities.net).

A DENDRITIC EXEMPLAR

My ethnography of a dialysis clinic functions as an illustration of the possibilities of dendritic crystallization. I want to share one version of this project—a realistic view of a project's development and evolution to supplement the deceptively tidy accounts of ethnography that proliferate in the research literature (some of my own included). I begin with my initial goals, and then discuss my data collection processes. I explore the development of my muse map for further analysis and for choosing and developing my representations through dendritic crystallization. I intend this not as a prescription for others' work practices but as a jumping off point, an exemplar for comparison, and a touchstone for inspiration.

At the beginning of the project (see the Interlude at the end of this chapter for a story of how I gained access to my site), I articulated the following three goals for the project in my proposal to both the company in whose clinic I wanted to conduct my fieldwork and to the Human Subjects Board at my university:

- To further develop the concept of embedded teamwork (Ellingson, 2003) into a complex and more nuanced model of professional clinic practice.

- To articulate a theory of the relationship between communication among health care providers and communication between health care providers and their patients. My previous study indicates there are intricate connections between the two, and I want to delineate these connections and develop an explanatory framework.

- To explore patients' perceptions of health care teamwork and of team members' communication with patients. Most research has focused on health care provider–patient communication as a dyadic relationship, rather than investigating that communication in the context of patients who communicate with a series of team members of different disciplines.

After receiving approval, I began my fieldwork. I engaged in participant observation for 2 to 3 hours per session, approximately twice per week, from October 2003 to June 2004, culminating in over 100 hours of observation. I adopted the observer-as-participant role (Lindlof & Taylor, 2002). That is, both staff and patients were aware of my identity as a researcher, and I observed and conversed with patients and staff, while assisting in minor tasks (e.g., lowering patients' recliner position). Most of the staff and patients were aware of far more of my identity than merely my status as a researcher. Staff and patients asked me many questions about my position as a university professor and about my personal life, including my marriage, pets, and leisure activities, and I answered them freely. In addition, because I walk with a limp and multiple surgeries have disfigured my right leg, many staff and some patients asked me questions about my health, and I disclosed my status as a bone cancer survivor (see Ellingson, 1998). My personal disclosures appeared to enhance my rapport with my participants and facilitated the development of trust between us. Moreover, I felt an ethical obligation to reciprocate with personal information when I asked my participants to share their lives with me. However, I avoided discussing with participants the research questions of my study, and explained only that I was interested in documenting mundane communication in the unit (which I often referred to as "what you do all day"). When time permitted, I asked staff members questions in informal interviews. While "on the floor" (i.e., in the treatment room), I took notes and transcribed brief conversations on a palmtop computer; these notes were expanded into fieldnotes.

After my period of fieldwork, I announced my interest in interviewing staff, who were reassured that participation in interviews was voluntary. From June to August 2004, I conducted semistructured interviews with 17 staff members, including the social worker, registered dietitian, nurse manager, head technician, two technician assistants, unit secretary, two registered nurses, and eight patient care technicians. Participants completed a Human Subject Board–approved informed consent form, provided basic demographic data, and were given a $40 gift certificate for participation. Interviews were audio-recorded and transcribed. Next, I solicited patient participation in a Human Subjects Board–approved structured oral questionnaire concerning perceptions of staff communication; I recruited 20 patients and gave each a $20 gift certificate as a thank-you gift. I recorded patient responses, which averaged about 10 minutes; questions and responses were transcribed. Finally, I gathered documents produced by the dialysis company to gain insight into how the organization represented its practices and policies, including a nutritional guide, the patient handbook, and the patient care technician training manual.

I conducted a grounded theory analysis of fieldnotes, interview transcripts, oral questionnaire transcripts, and organizational documents beginning shortly after commencing fieldwork (see Charmaz, 2000; Strauss & Corbin, 1990). Throughout my fieldwork and interviewing, I coded data and produced preliminary analytic memos, continually revising and reflecting upon emergent patterns and questions. During my analysis, I also wrote short narratives and poetic transcription (see Chapter 3 on ethnographic narratives and poetry), presented several conference papers, and gave two talks to the staff at the dialysis unit.

Near the conclusion of my data collection (fieldwork, interviews, and organizational documents), I returned to my stated goals and constructed a more detailed muse map (Madison, 2005). I generated a list that looked roughly like this:

1. How does extreme routinization of health care provision influence (and come to be influenced by) communication? (What are the dominant routines of dialysis care? How do they shape communication? What are the dominant routines of dialysis care?) Genre: Grounded theory analysis. Outlet: mainstream health communication journal.

2. What are the backstage communication processes in dialysis care? And how is backstage communication negotiated in the frontstage of dialysis unit? Genre: Brief research report; update to typology developed in JACR piece [Ellingson, 2003].

3. How is professionalism negotiated through communication by PCTs [patient care technicians] and TAs [technical aides]? What does professionalism mean to paraprofessionals? How is power operating? Genre: Narratives? Critique? Outlet: maybe somewhere open to creative work.

4. People seem to have differing ideas about what time is. "Time and Again," a play on the endless repetition of dialysis, and of differing views of time. Genre: layered account combining grounded theory and vignettes. Outlet: *Journal of Contemporary Ethnography? Symbolic Interaction?*

5. Develop a model of clinical communication, bridge the frontstage and backstage of communication, drawing on data and findings from both the geriatric oncology program that engaged in assessment and treatment planning and the dialysis unit, which engaged in treatment. Genre: theoretical essay, applications? Outlet: *Communication Theory?* Maybe go for a top journal such as *Communication Monographs?* Or should it be in a health care–related journal?

This map emerged through a messy and iterative process, and I have continually adapted it since. Nonetheless, the map provided me with a set of parameters within which to work and provided inspiration.

The routinization piece struck me immediately as a "telling" much more than a "showing" piece, in that I found it impossible (and not terribly interesting) to show endless repetition of behaviors. I wanted to demonstrate that what happens in the dialysis unit is that nothing seems to happen, because the same things happen over and over all day long, with the same patients, week after week. Important insights into health care communication arise from repetitive interactions, and I wanted to explore those in relation to theory and research on communication between providers and patients and on communication among interdisciplinary staff members. The challenge of illustrating absence in evocative narrative intimidated me, but even more, it simply seemed like a poor fit between message and genre. I decided to develop the analysis of routinization with *Health Communication* in mind as a likely outlet.

On the other hand, the ideas about time actually emerged from some brief narratives I had constructed out of my data, all of which touched on how time passed in the unit. I searched the Web for quotes about time and collected several thought-provoking ideas. Then, I collaborated with Dr. Elaine Jenks to develop a panel sponsored by the Disability Caucus of the National Communication Association. Since ESRD/kidney failure qualifies patients for disability support and Medicare (government health insurance coverage), I thought that exploring their experience with this disabling chronic disease might be illuminating, and I proposed an abstract on the topic that eventually morphed into a paper that was rejected at one journal for lacking a sufficient theoretical framework. I transformed that paper by reframing it with Flaherty's (2003) concept of time work, and have resubmitted to another journal.

Meanwhile, as I mentioned earlier, Zoller and Dutta invited me to contribute to their forthcoming edited volume on interpretive approaches to health communication research. I really wanted to focus on power, and I started writing narratives about the complexities of power and resistance in the unit. Unfortunately, at least in the stories I worked on, the complexities proved so great and so enmeshed in larger (difficult to show) discourses of power in health care delivery that I felt unable to represent them meaningfully in self-contained narratives; for each moment in the unit, pages of backstory seemed necessary. Instead, I explored the interconnections between power exercised by the staff over the patients and the ways in which nurses and physicians exercised power over technicians who provided most of the hands-on care to patients, using a first person but otherwise conventional qualitative analytic voice.

My exploration of power led to an interest in professionalism, as defined in the health care professional literature and as paraprofessional staff experienced it while they, as I saw it, were disciplined to conform to professional standards of providing compassionate and high-quality care but denied any of the autonomy, respect, and recognition typically accorded to professionals. I reread my transcripts of interviews with technicians and found their words eloquent. Grounded theory analysis provided a set of coherent themes, but the "snippets" of data used to illustrate them paled in comparison to the transcripts. Of course, fragmentation of participants' voices always forms a weakness of research reports, but it seemed more pronounced in this case. I felt I was doing a poor job representing the voices of these articulate people. So I reviewed my favorite transcript and selected one lovely excerpt of a technician's expression of what it meant to him to do his job well, and I edited it into a poetic transcription. After beginning the process, I reread work on poetic transcripts (see Chapter 3). I then excerpted pieces of transcript from several other technicians to illustrate other themes in the data. Eventually, I constructed a grounded theory/poetic transcription hybrid piece.

While writing *Engaging Crystallization,* I have continued to work on other fragments of my project, primarily the revision of the rejected manuscript on time in dialysis and the theoretical account of frontstage and backstage communication in health care settings, and I anticipate further accounts that will arise as opportunities present themselves. I hope by exposing some of the details of my research process, I aid researchers in forging their own paths.

As a researcher immersed in an ongoing dendritic crystallization of communication in dialysis, I find the process challenging and rewarding. I missed the opportunity to combine genres into a single book-length text, although combining grounded theory and poetic transcription and constructing a layered account both provided satisfying opportunities to bring together disparate pieces of the project. On the other hand, I shed some light on a series of neglected topics and developed some pragmatic suggestions for improving the experience of dialysis care for providers and patients. As with other projects, I have the nagging sensation that potential abounds to do even more with my data and personal experiences, and stopping points must therefore be somewhat arbitrary. However, the dendritic nature of this project, while different from my previous ethnography that produced an integrated crystallized book, nonetheless satisfied and at times even thrilled me. Unsurprisingly, it also raised questions.

BUT IS THIS REALLY CRYSTALLIZATION?

I have pondered whether the dendritic practice of segregating genres of representation into separate publications or production venues really constitutes a valid form of crystallization, or is simply an overly optimistic view of the potential for separate accounts to build (and contest) meaning. How can individual pieces, loosely—if at all—connected in an academic diaspora, collectively challenge notions of knowledge production and claim making? Can dendritic crystallization challenge such notions to the degree possible through multigenre texts that blend or juxtapose different ways of knowing in an immediately recognizable and explicitly contrasting format? These questions strike me as legitimate.

On its own, each single-genre representation only hints at the possibilities of crystallization, of celebrating the richness of findings *and* their partiality, the particularity of a given standpoint *and* the possibility of authentic connection with others across difference, the need for representing voices of marginalized groups *and* the dangers of doing so. But the hint matters. In an increasingly globalized and connected world, scholars, activists, artists/performers, and others can find your vitae or home page on the Web and see the list of publications representing a range of methods and genres. Web sites make multigenre work freely available; photos, documents, and video/audio clips can be downloaded. Databases make limited distribution journals available to wide audiences. Conferences such as the annual International Congress of Qualitative Inquiry at the University of Illinois bring together people from around the world to discuss their qualitative work. I do not believe I merely engage in wishful thinking when I promote dendritic crystallization as a mode of resistance to the art/science dichotomy. Rather, subtle connections and simply the co-existence of multiple genres produced by a researcher or research team testify to the multiplicity and partiality of truth.

CONCLUSION

Dendritic crystallization opens many options for producing multigenre work that is dispersed to a variety of publication outlets. I embrace the notion of crystallization as a journey and an ideal, not simply a standard or destination. Haskins (2003), drawing upon the work of rhetorician Michael Calvin McGee, argues that

> a rhetorician's job, therefore, is to put these discursive fragments together in the hope of bringing fragmented audiences into a community at a particular moment in time, to use the momentum created by this temporary identification to bring about change. (p. 5)

Qualitative researchers can connect fragments of art and social science through multigenre crystallized texts and, in particular moments, through dendritic crystallization in ways that impact the academy and the world beyond. To do this well, we must write and represent well, and I address that topic in the following chapter.

INTERLUDE

Coincidence, Synchronicity, and Putting It Out to the Universe

---

My work always seems not only to adapt to emerging opportunities but to begin from lucky "coincidences." The dialysis project began with a chance meeting. My colleague SunWolf invited me to attend a talk by an alternative medical practitioner in her senior thesis section on communication and hypnosis. Having been interested in complementary and alternative medicine for a long time (Ellingson, 2004), I wanted to go.

As the time dawned nearer, however, my piles of papers to grade grew intimidating, and I considered making an excuse not to go. But in the end, I reluctantly grabbed my keys and headed down to SunWolf's classroom. I arrived early, and I saw SunWolf standing in the front of the room talking with one woman, while another stood quietly nearby. I set my keys down on a student desk and stood uncertainly, not wanting to interrupt their conversation. I smiled at the petite, blond woman who stood off to the side, and she smiled and approached me. "Do you drive a Beetle?" she asked.

Surprised, I nodded. "Yes, I do. How did you know?"

"Your key," she said, gesturing to my large, rectangular remote entry key with its prominent VW logo. "I love my Beetle. I had one of the original ones in the early '70s, and I got one of the new ones as soon as they came out. What color is yours?"

"It's red, the turbo model. And I have these fabulous wheels—the rims look like daisies, white petals with yellow centers." We continued to chat and finally got around to asking what each other did. I explained that I was a professor in the same department as SunWolf and that I studied interdisciplinary communication among health care providers.

My companion's eyes lit up and she said, "Really? Because we could use someone to study that in the company I work for. I am the director of social work for a chain of dialysis centers. My name is Brenda, by the way."

"I'm Laura." We shook hands, and I smiled, my mind racing with the possibilities.

And that was how my project started. You may consider it chance, fate, or even divine intervention. I prefer to think of it as *synchronicity,* Jung's (1973) term for seeming coincidences that result from alignment of "universal forces." Rather than a causal relationship in which a cause leads directly to an effect, synchronicity involves simultaneous cause and effect. Jung argued that such incidents occur with much more frequency than random chance would allow. Synchronous incidents appear random but actually occur when we act in harmony with our true selves and larger purposes. Jung believed that an underlying dynamic connects people through the "collective unconscious," enabling synchronous happenings that simultaneously meet two or more people's needs, such as Brenda's concerns about her company and my interest in finding a local research site. I agree with Jung's principle, but you do not have to embrace his philosophy if it does not resonate for you. Regardless of your beliefs about the source and meaning of coincidences, you can still take advantage of them when they occur. This is not to say that we should sit around waiting for happy accidents, but that we should always be watchful and ready to act when one presents itself.

SEVEN

WRITING ACROSS
THE CONTINUUM

———◆———

The labors and satisfactions of authorship cannot be avoided.

—Geertz (1988, p. 140)

Click, click, click. I used my mouse to navigate my computer desktop and open my e-mail program. Perusing my mailbox, I mentally categorized messages, opening only those that really should not wait until tomorrow.

The clock read 3:30 on a beautiful northern California afternoon, and I was eager to abandon my office for my Friday night ritual of cooking dinner for my pregnant friend Genni and her daughter, bath time, and a few hours of scrapbooking after the kid surrendered to sleep. I still had to stop by the grocery store for some fresh basil, and the knowledge that the traffic would grow exponentially worse every minute after 4 p.m. spurred me along. I dismissed note after note as nonurgent. Abruptly, I noticed a message with a large attachment and gasped. It came from a production editor and contained the PDFs of a journal article that I had accepted for publication in *Qualitative Health Research.* Clicking eagerly, I downloaded and opened the file and stared for a moment at the wonder that is seeing my name on a typeset page.

I don't know if page proofs eventually fade into routine for other researchers, but the joy of seeing my words set in print has not diminished one bit in the 11 years since my first article came out.

I printed the file and dashed down the hall to the network printer to retrieve it, smiling broadly when I held the pages in my hands. Of course, I would have to proofread every line of it, and the editor wanted changes by Tuesday, so I mentally shuffled my priorities to make room in my schedule. But not tonight. Returning to my office, I gathered up my purse, keys, and sunglasses, set the page proofs in my purple and blue Laurel Branch tote bag, and dashed out the door.

After a quick trip to the gourmet market and a not-so-quick trip up the peninsula from San Jose to Palo Alto, I opened the door to Genni's home and called out, "Hello!"

"Hi!" came the friendly response from the back of the house. "MJ, Aunty is here!" I dumped the groceries along with my purse and scrapbooking bag, grabbed my page proofs, and hustled into the family room where MJ, aka Marissa Jane, sat with her mother, surrounded by Lego blocks.

"Wawa!" said my chosen-family niece, jumping up to hug my leg ("Laura" is hard to say when you're 18 months old).

"Hi, Pumpkin." I hugged the beautiful little girl and then her mum. "Oh, guess what?" I cried, dispensing with our usual "how are you" routine.

Genni looked at me expectantly. "What happened?"

Flushed with excitement, I handed her the page proofs of my article. She beamed. "How wonderful!" she said. She started reading, and I watched as her face gradually contorted into a puzzled frown before she finished the abstract. "Uh. Umm, this looks *great!*" she said, recovering rapidly. "I'm so proud of you."

"You don't know what I'm talking about, do you?" I said, my shoulders sagging.

This woman earned an MBA and held a prestigious position as a compensation analyst in a large law firm; needless to say, she is highly intelligent. But she couldn't make sense of my discussion of ethnographic embodiment (Ellingson, 2006a). "Well, no," she replied. "But it *looks* impressive." Genni offered a reassuring smile as MJ waved a bright blue block at me, an invitation to play.

I scanned the pages of my article unhappily, feeling self-conscious about indulging in the exclusive jargon that arises at the intersection of ethnographic methodology, feminist theorizing on embodiment, and health communication research. I felt proud of my proficiency with this language, as though I had earned my right to use it. At the same time, I wondered what good my argument would do if the only people who could makes sense of and apply it were those in my narrow scholarly community.

All language choices come with a cost. Regardless of which genres you engage in a crystallized project, virtually all projects will involve some amount of writing, and many will rely primarily or exclusively on the written word. Language holds no possibility of neutrality; to name and explain is to judge (e.g., Gergen, 1999). The types of judgments we make and the values they reflect are deeply tied to the languages we choose to write in. While academic jargon may seem the most specialized and exclusive, all language reflects particular cultures and groups that simultaneously generate and are influenced by their system of symbols. Narrative language and structures more closely resemble dominant language norms, but those very similarities render it problematic, because readers/listeners largely take for granted the familiar, that is, fish missing the centrality of the water that they swim in.

Moreover, all genres challenge researchers to write well. Many reasons exist for producing inaccessible, unclear, or even bad writing. Much research writing feels passionless; no evidence comes forward to let readers know the author cares about the topic, participants, or society in general. The residues of positivism often lead authors to still their enthusiasm for their topic, lest they be thought of as emotional, naive, or simply breaking the rules of the research report genre. Other minds may ask great questions but not form great sentences. Still others received bad advice on how to sound impressive, authoritative, and credible. Likewise, some narratives fall flat—weak dialogue, lack of plot, shallow characters, trite descriptions—despite good effort, perhaps reflecting therapeutic sense making for the author, but not functioning as successful stories in themselves.

Richardson (2000b) boldly and insightfully revealed a dirty secret of qualitative research: Some of it is mind-numbingly boring. Boredom is in no way inevitable, however. In this chapter, I explain a few key reasons why dull, unclear writing proliferates and explore some recommendations for alleviating this vexing problem. In addition to specific writing strategies, I offer structural, organizational, and creative ways to enrich the telling of qualitative research findings in an engaging manner. I also plant the seeds of insurrection, encouraging readers to enlarge the boundaries of what is acceptable in traditional qualitative publishing outlets by pushing those boundaries in subtle and not-so-subtle ways. I suggest that qualitative researchers, regardless of which genres they embrace and produce, benefit from practicing the craft of writing, and I provide resources for guiding and enhancing that practice. At least some of what I suggest will be fairly obvious to some readers, and many strategies reflect my idiosyncratic preferences. Writing is a personal process that every-one must develop for themselves. Nonetheless, I sketch a map of the writing territory in the hope that the map may provide some encouragement to those setting out once again into familiar areas, some guidance to those venturing into the unfamiliar, or some inspiration to those braving unrecognizable ter-rain. Before discussing those strategies, I first review standards for what counts as good writing on the middle-to-left and the middle-to-right ends of the qualitative continuum.

EVALUATING WRITING AND REPRESENTATION

Traditionally, postpositivist and other analytic scholars have stressed good writing as a technical skill needed to produce clear, concise, and compelling reports. Clarity, accuracy, and persuasion represent typical goals for conven-tional report writing. That is, from the middle to the right side of the qualitative continuum, writing exists primarily as a means to an end, or a way to transfer information effectively. After an overview of a few standards for assessment, I then offer an aesthetics of the conventional research writing genre as an alter-native way of thinking about research reports not only as information transfer, but also as a genre with its own type of beauty.

Middle-to-Right Area of the Continuum

A number of scholars developed standards for assessing the rigor of grounded theory and other systematic forms of qualitative analysis (Hall & Callery, 2001). Assessing the rigor of the analysis cannot be accomplished separately from eval-uating the quality of the representation, that is, the writing that embodies the analysis. Writing is the medium through which the data is recorded and analyzed and the argument or case for the findings is structured, elaborated, and strategi-cally presented to audiences. Hence, to evaluate the rigor of the analysis is to evaluate the written account thereof. Since the written representation so deeply intertwines with its production, it is helpful to consider some of the standards for rigorous qualitative analysis when considering how best to write analysis.

Standards vary but reflect common priorities. Potter (1996, pp. 192–197) provides an excellent discussion of eight different sets of standards for evaluat-ing the quality of qualitative work. Glaser and Strauss (1967) originally offered four standards for assessment of grounded theory reports: *fit* between the findings and the world they purports to represent, *workability* of the findings, *relevance* of the analysis to key problems/issues, and *modifiability* of the grounded theory over time to accommodate change. More broadly, Fitch (1994) established the following standards for qualitative data analysis: (a) researchers should have been deeply involved with the group or topic; (b) at the same time, researchers also must achieve sufficient distance from their participants to gain a broader perspective; (c) claims should be saturated in data; (d) data should be preserved as accessible records; and (e) data and analysis should include consideration of inferences and interpretations, as well as concrete phenomena (p. 36). Charmaz (2005) points out that "increasingly, researchers justify the type, relative depth, and extent of their data collection and analysis on *one* criterion: saturation of categories" (p. 526, original emphasis). She offers four criteria for evaluating grounded theory work, particularly that which aims to promote social justice: *credibility* of the data collection, analysis, and representation processes; *originality* of the analysis and of its significance; *resonance* of the analysis with participants and larger social trends; and *usefulness* of findings for both everyday life and further research (p. 528).

Many qualitative methodologists further recommend member checking as a way to enhance further the quality of analysis and honor participant perspectives, also referred to as recalcitrance or taking findings back to your participants for feedback (e.g., Lindlof & Taylor, 2002; Reinharz, 1992; Tompkins, 1994; C. A. B. Warren & Karner, 2005). Charmaz (2000) also recommends awareness of the constructed nature of knowledge and the influence of researchers' positionalities on the findings we produce. Reflexive consideration of your role in data gathering and analysis enhances "theoretical sensitivity," or "an awareness of the subtleties of meaning of data" (Strauss & Corbin, 1990, p. 41).

Thus, the standards for evaluating the quality of an analysis suggest that we ideally write in ways that maximize the research report as a rhetorically persuasive case that the above (or similar) standards have been met in the production of a meaningful set of findings. I offer aesthetic standards for assessing the rhetoric of research reports.

An Aesthetics of Conventional Qualitative Research Writing

Readers evaluate qualitative analysis by scrutinizing the written report thereof; we cannot assess rigor apart from the language in which authors express it. Research reports represent more than simply a window into a completed analysis, however; ideally, conventionally written research reports should embody an academic/analytic aesthetic. We all have read articles that manage to convey a point but lack elegance, while other research reports delight us with a particularly effective turn of phrase or evocative explanatory metaphor. If we grant that some research writing is terribly boring, it does not follow that the only solution to this problem is to discard the entire genre in favor of narrative and poetic work. Instead, we could reclaim the genre and strive to improve the overall quality of writing in qualitative reports. I propose that we can appreciate the aesthetic appeal of qualitative analysis as a creative genre in much the same way that we appreciate painting, sculpture, or fiction— as a source of imagination, beauty, pleasure, and hope (Dewey, 1934/1980). In this section, I sketch an aesthetic view of qualitative analysis reports, suggesting that in addition to reflecting rigorous analytic processes, social science writing should feature pleasing qualities such as: symmetry, voices, flow, cohesiveness, and eloquence.

Symmetry. The symmetry of good qualitative reports arises as authors explore each of their themes in turn, following a set rhythm. Like the verses of a song or each stanza of a poem, each segment of analysis should parallel the others. Rather than merely repetition, well-structured analysis establishes a pattern that readers come to anticipate and to find satisfaction in having their expectations fulfilled. First, the theme is named, and the names ideally should be of similar length and form of language: all active verbs or metaphors or types of roles, for instance. Then, we receive a definition or explanation of the theme; such definitions serve to delineate the scope of the category, to explain what it includes and excludes. Next, the author explores several examples, linking each in turn to the theme's definition. Analysis should repeat this same rhythm for each theme, establishing a pleasing cadence. Of course, variations of this pattern proliferate; one particularly strong one used by some authors is to begin discussion of each theme or category with an anecdote or more extensive example and then to work through a series of shorter quotes or descriptions to further support the claim, repeating this pattern for each theme. Symmetry of form pleases the eye and the ear.

Voices. In the best research reports, each morsel of participants' words that the author offers fascinates readers. Quotes from transcripts, fieldnotes, or participants' writing provide glimpses into people's language, sense making, and culture and leave us both satisfied and eager to learn more. When judging qualitative analysis as an aesthetic endeavor, we focus on the degree to which the data excerpts are rich, thick, and intriguing. Skillful weaving of the author's and participants' voices highlights the similarities and differences of their experiences and perspectives. Longer quotes do not always highlight participants' experiences better than shorter ones; selection of telling phrases and revealing comments requires an artisan's touch. Moreover, researchers should place the participants' voices in a context of dialogue between the researcher's ideas and the participants' ongoing lives. A. W. Frank (2005), drawing on Bakhtin (1984), suggests that

> the research report must always understand itself not as a final statement of who the research participants are, but as one move in a continuing dialogue through which those participants will continue to form themselves, as they continue to become who they may yet be.... Dialogue begins with the recognition of the others' unfinalizability.... Dialogue depends on perpetual openness to the other's capacity to become someone other than whoever she or he already is. (p. 967)

To render voices richly yet without a sense of finality—that is, with a sense of ongoing possibility and indeterminacy—presents a strong challenge. The strongest qualitative researchers work hard at the craft of writing, constructing both their participants and themselves through strategic selection and arrangement of data excerpts so that a dialogue among them takes place. Such dialogue sparks readers' imagination as it suggests the potential for the world to be constituted differently than it currently is—as all great art does.

Flow. The logical flow of argumentation characterizes well-written reports. We revel in the structured flow of sound analysis, not merely able to comprehend the argument and its justification, but to appreciate the elegance of its execution in the written word. Aesthetically, qualitative reports should move seamlessly from introduction to theory and literature review, through method into results, and from discussion to conclusions, with each piece setting the stage for the next. The method section, for example, should not appear to be a momentary departure from the discussion of the topic at hand but an important, integral element of it. Pleasing research reports offer transitions or other orienting elements that enable readers to move through each stage of the authors' argument in a continuous flow.

Cohesiveness. Reports invigorate when all the pieces come together in the end to form a coherent and useful reading of a place, space, group, person, or process. Like a puzzle where all the pieces fit together to make a single meaningful picture that is larger than any single piece can portray, or a symphony in which each note and each instrument comes together to create an experience far greater than the individual sounds made by each musician, a well-crafted analysis comes together to create an overall understanding of or reading of its object of analysis. This meaning could still contain contradictions or paradox; to be cohesive is not necessarily to be singular in point. But good reports leave readers having grasped an overall purpose or point that is grounded in each part of the report.

Eloquence. Finally, an aesthetics of conventional research writing requires eloquent expression as a standard. Beautiful writing tends to be one of those things that we know when we see it, and we find it difficult to articulate precisely why some authors' word choice fits so beautifully and others merely suffice to explain but do not intrigue or edify. We may grasp immediately the centrality of word choice in narrative, poetic, and other openly creative or artistic forms, but we often do not make explicit the value of polishing the language of more conventionally academic writing. Yet, we should. Theorists speak of certain theorems or equations as *elegant* in their capacity to encapsulate a large amount of information and/or a complex relationship in a simple linguistic and/or numeric statement. Likewise, careful linguistic crafting of a research report can enhance it aesthetically, serving to make it more beautiful while simultaneously furthering its primary goal of effectively communicating meaning about a topic.

I do not exaggerate when I claim to love the beauty of a good qualitative research report, nor do I consider aesthetic value to be merely an added bonus to the rigorous aspects of good qualitative analysis. Rather, I believe we can blur the boundaries between art and reporting even when using conventional research writing forms. Crystallization provides one way to accomplish that blurring, and I extend the expectations for aesthetically pleasing writing to those segments of a crystallized text (or series of texts) that take the form of analytic reporting as well as those rendered through artistic genres.

Evaluating Creative Analytic Writing

Although many scholars rightly question the imperative to provide criteria for assessment (e.g., Clough, 2000), others point to the need to hold "alternative" or creative analytic work to high standards and avoid the "anything goes" mentality to which detractors often point when they characterize narrative and artistic work in the social sciences (Ellis, 2004). Reasonable consensus seems to exist, however, that such standards cannot mimic those of traditional positivism or even postpositivism. Lather (1993) proposes a *validity of transgression* that resists static, empiricist notions of assessing the quality of scientific research and replaces them with attention to the ways in which research can be understood as embodying ironic, neo-pragmatic, rhizomatic, and/or voluptuous validity. Lather (1991) also proposed *catalytic validity* as one way of conceiving of the value of qualitative work, that is, the extent to which the research process (including providing feedback on findings, co-constructing accounts, participating in interviews or focus groups, etc.) provides a catalyst for participants to act on their own behalf to make positive changes for themselves and others.

Richardson (2000b, p. 937) proposed the following standards for assessing creative analytic representations, whether written or in another medium: *substantive contribution* of the work to the understanding of a phenomenon, *aesthetic merit* of the work as a piece of art, *reflexivity* of the author regarding her/his role in the work and an awareness of the epistemological implications of the account, emotional and intellectual *impact* of the work on the audience, and an *expression of a reality* within the work as one that resonates with verisimilitude—a credible, embodied account. Other sets of standards on evaluating the worth of projects include those proposed in a special forum section of an issue of *Qualitative Inquiry* focused on assessment of "alternative modes of qualitative and ethnographic research," in which Richardson (2000a), Denzin (2000), Bochner (2000), Ellis (2000), and Clough (2000) offer criteria for conceptualizing the value of creative social science work. For example, Bochner offered these criteria for assessing narratives: abundant, concrete detail; structurally complex narratives; evidence of authors' emotional credibility, vulnerability, and honesty; narrative expression of two selves, that is, a life course reimagined or transformed by crisis; evidence of a high degree of ethical self-consciousness; and "a story that moves me, my heart and belly as well as my head" (Bochner, 2000, pp. 270–271).

You can apply any or all of these standards to the artistic portions of crystallized texts. Although no single standard for evaluating quality of creative analytic work exists, crystallized texts benefit most when they include richly evocative artistic work. Your goals for crystallization may be artistic, theoretical, methodological, ideological, and/or practical, all of which require an engaged reader who can be motivated to think and act by your artistry and analysis. Even after you improve your skills in writing (and/or painting, performing, sculpting, etc.), you will need to advocate for your work within and beyond the academy.

IMPROVING YOUR PROCESS

How we write bears as much consideration as *what* we write. Crystallization involves multiple processes of meaning making, most of which involve various types of writing—notes, outlines, brainstorming, reflections, journals, plans, and task lists, as much as representation of results. Writing is a method of inquiry, not just a way of "mopping up" at the end of a project (Richardson, 1994, 2000b). Hence, before looking at some mechanics of writing, I offer suggestions about rethinking your ontology, or way of being in the world, as a writer and the mindset and practices that accompany that way of being. I suggest that qualitative researchers reclaim our identities, honor our styles, improve our focus, and read voraciously.

Claim your identity as a writer. I urge you to think of yourself as a (real) writer and reject the social bifurcation of scholarly or professional writing from "creative" writing. Scholarly writing can be just as creative as a fictional novel or poem born of a nonscholar's imagination. Even if you write about statistical analysis, you write via language and hence create meaning through symbols, which constitutes artwork. I find that embracing an identity as a writer (i.e., not just a scholar or researcher) helps both to prioritize writing time and to relish the process of writing. Once we claim the identity of a writer, we free ourselves to utilize the many tools and techniques of the trade (see the discussion of writing resources at the end of the chapter).

Honor your work style. Once you affirm yourself as writer, carefully observe yourself to determine your writing style and then honor that style. Every writing book I have ever read suggests carving out daily writing time, and that recommendation works well for some people. But it simply does not work for me, nor for at least some others (see Charmaz, 2007). I am a binge writer and realizing that has helped me to build flexibility into my schedule rather than the reserved blocks of time that seem to help many others. Now when I catch a wave while writing, I ride it until it breaks. I do not catch one every day, but when I do, I can get a tremendous amount done by postponing other obligations and continuing to write. Of course, some commitments cannot be delayed, but others can, especially since I began prioritizing flexibility over rigid defense of certain blocks of time. Consider the number of times you took an unscheduled break from your writing to help a colleague or your child; I bet your schedule could accommodate an occasional last minute call to reschedule a meeting so you can keep riding your writing wave. I periodically reschedule lunches, dinners, and meetings with peers in order to continue working when the words are flowing; most people understand. The point is not that others should emulate my work style but that you should figure out what works best for you and then advocate for your right to work that way as much as possible.

Improve your focus with some sort of practice. I realize this sounds sort of woo-woo, new age-ish, or perhaps just crazy. Nonetheless, I suggest you keep a journal, pray, practice mediation, or in some way take care of yourself spiritually/emotionally and release stress (LeShan, 1974; Parachin, 1999). I keep a daily journal as a warm-up for writing and a way to get nagging stuff out of my head. I also pray and do a sort of moving meditation as well.[1] Other people I know do Tai Chi, take a daily walk with their dog, or enjoy long baths. Being a mentally healthier person makes you a better writer, and regular self-care practices aid in that goal. On a related note—and I hate it when people tell me this but I am going to say it anyway—engage in some form of regular, moderate exercise. You do not have to become a gym rat; walking works well. I love water aerobics classes and riding a recumbent trike on local bike trails; other friends like yoga, Pilates, dancing (hip-hop, line, or swing), or gardening. Exercise helps decrease stress, increases energy, and stimulates creative thinking, all of which lead to better and easier writing. Exercise makes a huge difference for everyone I know who practices it.

Read, read, read. This last one is fairly self-explanatory, although do treat yourself to Stephen King's (2000) eloquent and entertaining ramble on why writers need to read everything they can get their hands on. I will add that I do not think it matters in the least what you read so long as you do so. I have learned a lot from badly written books that provide excellent examples of what *not* to do. I also enjoy reading trashy novels and mysteries while working out on treadmills and stair-stepping machines, and I believe that these too enhance my writing because they draw me into the worlds that they create and make me reluctant to stop reading. I raced through the latest *Harry Potter* book too. *People* magazine works for some people; all those pictures stimulate your brain. A good story is a good story. I certainly am not advocating that researchers not read the latest and classic works within their own and related disciplines, but perhaps you will feel better about indulging in beach books and treadmill trash if I reassure you that they will indeed make you a better writer. For an excellent guide on "reading like a writer," see Prose (2006).

WRITING WELL

While acknowledging the risks of reifying qualitative methods as being either art or science, I have nonetheless divided this section on improving writing (and the suggested responses to criticisms of crystallization in Chapter 8) into two sections. The vast and varied middle ground of qualitative work provides virtually unlimited options for blending aspects of art and science. While I heartily endorse blending, I nonetheless find good heuristic value in grouping the middle-to-right and the middle-to-left areas of the continuum for this discussion of writing, because the broad domains tend to make different demands on the author and on readers. Exceptions abound, but guidelines also prove remarkably applicable across wide swatches of the qualitative continuum, and work that blends science and art can benefit from suggestions for both styles of writing (see Figure 1.1, pp. 8–9). The division into social science and creative analytic writing here serves merely to organize my recommendations; I hope readers will embrace my suggestions in any way they find useful, regardless of what generic label they may choose for their work. Moreover, many of these ideas are adaptable and can serve as touchstones for scholar-artists creating works in media other than written work.

Strategies for Improving Social Science Writing

We all can improve our social scientific writing, and a number of scholars provide sound recommendations for how to do so (see Caulley, 2008; Charmaz, 2007; Madison, 2005; Richardson, 2000b; Richardson & St. Pierre, 2005). Most qualitative methods textbooks include sections on effective writing as well (e.g., Berg, 2007; Lindlof & Taylor, 2002; Morse & Field, 1995). I highlight here several techniques that I find particularly useful.

First, be conscious of the direct and indirect ways in which you show up in your work. Use first person so you can own your actions: *I* collected the data, *I* conducted analyses, *I* sought Institutional Review Board approval, and so on. First-person voice usually provides the most concise and precise way of describing research processes, findings, and implications. In addition to being present as an authorial "I," let readers know who you are in your project. Describing your standpoint can be done in the introduction, method section, or in a footnote if the outlet does not approve or if such an explanation might distract from the aesthetic goals of your story or other representation. For example, I positioned myself as an embodied presence in my fieldwork in a grounded theory analysis:

> It bears mentioning that I walk with a pronounced limp due to reconstructive surgeries for bone cancer in my right leg, and patients and companions often asked about it. I answered all questions about my personal health history and status as a researcher but avoided discussing what I was studying, except to say that I "wanted to understand how patients and team members communicated with each other." While I did not announce my identity as a cancer survivor to every patient, I did reveal it when asked about my limp and leg brace because I believe it would have been unethical to deceive patients and their companions about my survivor status. Patients and companions often said that they were glad that I had some idea of what they were experiencing, and that it was comforting to talk with a survivor. (Ellingson, 2003, p. 115)

In this excerpt, I inform readers of one way in which my embodied presence influenced my interactions in the clinic. I located this subtle reminder of my presence in an endnote; I also wrote an essay on the topic (Ellingson, 1998). Many options exist for incorporating the self in ways that make your work interesting to your readers and make yourself more fully humanized. Of course, some readers will dismiss authors for having admitted to "biases"— see Chapter 8 for strategies on defending your work from criticism. However, many scholars interested in improving the health care system actually have thanked me for situating myself and letting them see from where I spoke. Such positioning has the potential to strengthen our accounts significantly because doing so provides another layer to our analyses, enriching the account by grounding it clearly in our particular perspective.

An obvious strategy that bears repeating is to effect clarity. Show your draft to someone whose opinion you respect but who is not an expert in your subfield; ask her or him to read it and tell you what they do not understand.

Then take the feedback seriously as you rewrite. Some clarity enhancing techniques are to:

- Write as precisely as possible.

- Anticipate and preempt other interpretations through explicit explanations.

- Define the theoretical or methodological jargon you use.

- Consider breaking long sentences into two separate sentences.

- Go through your manuscript and search for passive construction, eliminating as many as possible by rewording them into active voice. However, be cautious not to hold this rule as a holy grail; accounts benefit from some sentence structure variety, and sometimes active voice only makes a sentence seem contrived.

- Use meaningful levels of headings; enough for skim-ability, not so many that the subdividing gets in the way of the coherence of your manuscript.

- Be careful about using verb tenses that slow your writing down, particularly verbs ending in "-ing," as they tended to involve bulkier predicates; for example, "she was working today" is clumsier than "she worked today."

- Read your work out loud and see where you stumble or run out of breath; use this as a guide to where your writing needs to be smoother.

Finally, clear writing also comes from good analysis; beware of *analytic interruptus* (Lofland, 1970). Take pains to engage in careful and conscientious memo-writing processes to be sure you developed a typology of clearly defined themes that overlap as little as possible and that are supported by a wealth of examples; well-developed analysis makes it easier to explain yourself to readers. Stay centered on your research question or statement of purpose as you develop your points; a clear focus and overall point bring all these ideas together into a meaningful analysis.

Enriching findings by using all your senses provides another strategy for concisely conveying meaning. As other qualitative methodologists have suggested, researchers could pay more careful attention to all of their senses as they conduct research and include relevant details in the "thick description" of their qualitative findings in order to clearly portray participants' worlds (Conquergood, 1991; Geertz, 1973). Haraway (1988) posits that Western science privileges optical knowing as the dominant epistemology, that is, seeing is believing. However, I also smelled, tasted, touched, and heard the clinics I studied. For example, hunger, fatigue, and allergy attacks made me impatient and less attentive during some periods of observation. I wrote too about the chill of the air conditioner, the smell of the photocopier ink, the taste of pizza in the break room, and the dizzying cacophony of voices as 10 or more health care professionals worked in a small area in the backstage of a clinic. This strategy of drawing on all your senses to record data is obviously relevant to fieldwork, but researchers should use all of their senses regardless of methodology. Thus, a researcher distributing surveys on physician–patient communication in a public clinic might note the details of temperature, smell, and appearance of the waiting room, for example. The researcher's sensory experience may provide clues about the organizational context in which patients receive care.

Next, a caution on a minor but distressingly common offense: Avoid overusing rhetorical questions in your manuscript. What do you think when you read a question in a report or essay? Is it thought provoking or distracting? Can you use too many and overwhelm your reader? Do you ever wonder why the author doesn't just come out and make the point at hand? Would you like me to stop asking you questions yet? Get the idea? An occasional provocative question can be effective as a way to vary sentence structure, draw a reader into a dialogue, and provide a flourish to your prose. Too many rhetorical questions, on the other hand, annoy readers and also may sound like powerless speech (Wood, 2008), making the author seem less credible.

A final suggestion involves taking care with metaphoric language. In order to make sense of data and construct patterns and concepts, we draw upon labels and descriptors, which often take the form of metaphors. Strive to use creative and fresh and memorable metaphors and figurative speech (Charmaz, 2007; Richardson, 2000b). Fitting metaphors communicate a great deal; trite, overused ones obscure meaning and bore readers. Moreover, be careful about invoking unconscious metaphors in your analysis, particularly those that arise from discourse in the subject area. For example, in the dialysis clinic, staff used the metaphor of "pitching in" to explain the importance of helping other staff members in order to keep the unit running smoothly (Ellingson, 2007). This metaphor evokes images of tossing coins into a communal pot to benefit everyone, each person giving of their own resources to meet the needs of the group or a given member of the group at a specific time. When I adopted the metaphor myself in my analysis of this practice as part of the routine of dialysis care, I

considered carefully what evocations this metaphor would have for people outside the context of dialysis.

Strategies for Improving Creative/Narrative Writing

Many authors have written in recent years about autoethnography and
other narrative and performative genres within the social sciences (e.g., Denzin,
1997; Ellis, 2004). Since these involve the production of literary genres,
authors now strive to become better writers in what are, for many researchers,
genres in which they received no formal training. Literary writing proves difficult to teach, as anyone who has taken or taught a creative writing class
knows. I will first discuss several specific strategies I have found instrumental,
then offer several works that I find helpful as guides to writing.

What's the point? Legendary Hollywood powerbroker Samuel Goldwyn said,
"If you want to send a message, use Western Union," implying that films
should not be expected to bear the burden of communicating a particular lesson, moral, or specific meaning to audiences. Movies and other creative work
generally do not propose to give explicit messages, but they nonetheless communicate vital lessons or morals about humanity. You need not address deep
and abiding truths in creative analytic work that forms part of a crystallized
text, although autoethnography and performances often do. Subtle truths about
the human condition or the mundanity of daily life deserve exploration as
much as tragedies, joys, and painful conundrums. The work should express
some point, lesson, or truth; readers should come away from the text having
learned from the author. I remain surprised by the number of autoethnographic
narratives (usually presented as conference papers) whose purpose or meaning
(apart from therapeutic value for the author) eluded me. Keep in mind that the
moral of the story may develop or shift in the process of creating the work; you
need not begin creating your text with a specific lesson in mind as long as you
end up with one—some of the best points develop unexpectedly.

Beside the point. At the same time, the important message being communicated should take a back seat to the artistry of the story or performance itself.
Enticing the audience reflects a legitimate goal in a time when many question
the relevance of academia to the world (A. W. Frank, 2004). In an episode
of the television drama *West Wing,* actor Laura Dern, portraying the newly
designated U.S. Poet Laureate Tabitha Fortis, said to the White House

Communications Director: "You think I think that an artist's job is to speak the truth. An artist's job is to captivate you for however long we've asked for your attention. If we stumble into truth, we got lucky" (Sorkin, 2002). Captivating an audience presents a tremendous challenge to even the best writers, but no worthier goal exists. We learn best from those books and stories that we cannot put down and those films that we stare at unblinkingly, our hearts pounding as the characters race toward the final, inevitable climax. Immersed in worlds created for us and with us by excellent writers and film makers, we cannot help but learn about life's big lessons along the way. No story that captivates fails to offer significant truths; concentrate in your artwork on creating art inspired by your data, and truths will emerge.

Verisimilitude. Seek truthfulness, not The Truth. Like many of you, I initially trained as a social scientist, albeit a feminist one, and I often feel resistant to editing details to make a better story when that causes small deviations from my conception of "what really happened." The exercise at the end of Chapter 2 demonstrates how much more *true to* an experience a narrative can be than a transcript, yet I found it challenging to serve the story over incidental facts. Mishler's (1991) critique of accuracy as a naive standard for evaluating transcription aids in understanding the issue. He argues that moving from oral to written speech involves not accurate dictation but translation. Just as ideas moving from one language to another may make it impossible to express many ideas literally, writing down oral speech renders it a different entity altogether. We do not hear speech the same way we read it; we make allowances and select bits and pieces when we listen that jar us if encountered in writing. Retaining the *actual* dialogue in written form does not convey the *truth* of what happened in the (oral) moment. Also, writers inevitably must condense experiences that took place over long periods of time. For example, I accomplished condensation of action in my ethnographic narrative of the geriatric oncology clinic in part by rearranging incidents that happened over the course of 2 years into a single day. This constructed account rang true to my experiences and provided a fitting portrayal of the staff, patients, and patients' companions in the clinic. Not slavishly adhering to the literal sequence of events improved the story vastly and enabled readers to enter into the world of the clinic in a much more engaging manner, and hence to experience their world more (truth)fully in all its complexities.

Working genres. Take advantage of the best each genre has to offer. One of the strengths of crystallization centers on the capacity to invoke multiple genres so that each piece fits its function with its ideal form. Film enables stunning visual accounts, so maximize color, shots, and angles of vision. Poetry requires linguistic distillation of ideas down to essential bits made all the richer by their brevity. Narratives provide plot and characters, journeys, and time-passage. Photos freeze moments, and collages offer melding of textures. Regardless of which form of creative analytic work you engage in, use it to your utmost advantage.

Purposefully engage in "writing as a method of inquiry." Richardson (1994, 2000b) echoes many famous writers of literature when she advises that we begin writing and see where our ideas go. Resist the urge to plan every single detail in advance and allow the page to lead you. Crystallization benefits from this process, at least initially. I find it helpful to open up a separate file to do this, as I feel more open to possibilities on the blank page than when constrained by what I already wrote. Writing to find out what we have to say excites and occasionally unnerves, often generating fresh ideas and perspectives. Although you can return to this strategy at any point for inspiration and problem solving, I do not advise researchers to proceed through their entire project without a plan, following only where your writing leads. Some design and mapping provides focus, guidance, and coherence (see Chapter 4).

Selectivity. Remember that you cannot tell the whole story of your topic, or even the majority of it. Each scene you shoot or picture you paint functions as a synecdoche for some aspect of the place, group, or topic you explore. I witnessed hundreds of interactions, documented most of them, analyzed many of them, and wrote stories and poems about a mere handful of them. Trying to pack it all in leads to a "list-y" sort of writing: "this happened and this happened, then this happened. . . ." Avoid dry, choppy writing (and frustration) by selecting moments rather than epics.

Think with your body. Draw on all your senses. Rather than describe what the room looked like, describe the hot, moist air or the scent of stale coffee or the squishy feel of the shag carpet under your participants' feet. Describe the spicy sauce or the deep chocolate dessert (read a few restaurant reviews to see how dishes come alive). Moreover, I encourage you to think of writing itself as an embodied practice:

> Come to [your topic] not with your mind and ideas, but with your whole
> body—your heart and gut and arms. . . . What people don't realize is that

> writing is physical. It doesn't have to do with thought alone. It has to do with
> sight, smell, taste, feeling, with everything being alive and activated. . . . You
> are physically engaged with the pen, and your hand, connected to your arm,
> is pouring out the record of your senses. (Goldberg, 1986, pp. 37, 50)

When we resist the Cartesian mind/body split and embrace writing as
something we enact with our whole bodies, not just our heads, we more easily recall sensuous details and construct more visceral prose.

Pain and/or passion make good writing. Dramatic experiences tend to inspire
the creation of good art. Here's a story:

A colleague invited me to speak to a graduate qualitative methods class
that had read one of my essays that discusses my status as a cancer survivor
(Ellingson, 1998). After describing a few aspects of my ethnographic self in an
oncology (cancer) clinic, I took questions from the students for a while. One
guy in the back of the room shifted restlessly in his chair, his face wearing a
faintly irritated look. When I called on him, he challenged: "But what if we
don't have something like that to write about? You're lucky enough to have
cancer experiences to write about, but I don't."

I smiled. "That's a good question, and I will answer it. But first I have to
point out that this is probably the only place I've been where it is considered an
advantage to have survived fifteen surgeries, thirteen months of chemotherapy,
years of physical therapy, and all the complications that go along with that. I
feel very blessed to be alive, but I wouldn't say that having cancer was lucky.

"Now, to answer your question more directly, those of us who have lived
through painful personal, familial, or community crises do have plenty to write
about that is deeply engaging, or at least has the potential to be. You're right—
much, if not most, great writing deals with suffering and loss; these things drive
us to write. Pain needs expression, and creating beauty out of pain redeems it,
heals us, and shows the world our perspectives." I think of some of the incredible art surrounding AIDS, the Holocaust, and Hurricane Katrina; making art is
what humanity does when confronted with suffering. "But that doesn't mean
that you have nothing to say if you haven't yet had any really horrible experiences. Or if you have but you don't want to write about those times.

"Write about your passions," I told him and the rest of the class. "Write
about whatever you get excited about—baseball, nature, great books, food,
travel, politics, music. What do you love? Whatever it is, write about it. What
makes you furious? Write about that."

After the class ended, I looked up one of my favorite quotes on writing that helps to explain the unique perspective that each of us brings to our writing because of our individual passions, preferences, and peculiarities. Pulitzer Prize–winning author Annie Dillard (1989) wrote:

> Why do you never find anything written about that idiosyncratic thought you advert to, about your fascination with something no one else understands? Because it is up to you. There is something you find interesting, for a reason hard to explain. It is hard to explain because you have never read it on any page; there you begin. You were made and set here to give voice to this, your own astonishment.[2] (¶ 2)

I feel passionate about reforming the health care system—what are you passionate about? To decide how to channel your passions and give voice to your astonishments, see the discussion on wondering (Chapter 4, pp. 74–77). Of course, you can also write about topics that aren't your passions and/or that you have not already experienced (see the discussion of outsider perspectives, Chapter 4, pp. 77–78).

BAG OF TRICKS

The following ideas work for me, regardless of the type of writing in which I am engaged, including writing of analytic memos or other types of note taking and sense making that precede final representations. I developed a number of my own strategies that almost embarrass me in their simplicity and idiosyncrasy, but I share them in the hope that they will make others' writing processes smoother:

• I create what I call a "stuff" file for each of my ongoing writing projects (e.g., this chapter file was called "Ch 7 write," and I made a "Ch 7 stuff" file too). In it, I put excerpts of my manuscript that I cut from the text. Experts advise writers to "kill your darlings" (e.g., King, 2000), but I like to put mine in cold storage instead. Placing words in another file makes it infinitely easier for me to cut because I know I can always go back and get excerpts later. I almost never retrieve material, but the knowledge that I can if I want to somehow frees me from the often unwise impulse to preserve all that I have written.

- To avoid writing paralysis, I practice an iterative approach to the writing, in much the same way I engage in ongoing data analysis over the course of a long project. I build in layers: start with an outline, put in quotes and paraphrases from relevant articles, copy and paste brief excerpts from other manuscripts, for example, a description of participants or a quote about theory. Then I write a paragraph or two, freely skipping from section to section to add a few lines or as much as a couple pages. I continue in this mode of construction until I have at least half of a draft. Then, I begin at the introduction and fill in the body of the text, noting in brackets places where I leave gaps that I must return to fill. I repeat this process until I finish the manuscript.

- When I feel stuck about how to rework a section of a manuscript, I copy the section and paste it in a separate document so I can play with it. After I rework it, I paste it back in the main document and delete the original portion of the text. Something about focusing in on the single segment apart from the remainder of the piece frees me to think outside the box; physically moving the segment makes it more approachable.

- When I just cannot seem to get any writing done, I move to another physical location. Das (2007) pointed out that when you think you have writer's block it may instead be understood as "location staleness. You cannot write because you are in a location of poor energy" (¶ 12). Although initially skeptical, I now devotedly follow this advice with great success, often working at a coffee shop, my school office, and at home in a single day. If such movement is not practical for you, you could try moving from your home office to the dining room table, or from your school office to library or conference room.

For more ideas on writing practices, see the list of writing resources at the end of this chapter. The list by no means exhausts the possibilities, but rather offers a sample of the guides to which I continually turn for inspiration.

CONCLUSION

Writing well provides an invigorating challenge for qualitative researchers. Crystallization furthers the challenge to working in two or more distinct genres, each of which necessitates different aesthetic and substantive choices.

Researchers may benefit from focusing not only on improving the quality of their writing itself but also on implementing or revising their daily rituals and practices that form crucial components of the writing life. This chapter ends with an interlude concerning how we write about difference and an overview of writing resources. The next chapter describes lessons learned about crystallization and then provides suggested strategies for responding to criticism of crystallization from gatekeepers representing both the artistic/interpretive and the realist/social science ends of the continuum.

INTERLUDE

Representing Difference

Of course, there are all sorts of differences between people. But only some differences matter.

—Jenks (2005, p. 153)

As disfigurements go, mine is not that bad. Most of the time, pants or a long skirt cover my misshapen leg and enable me to pass within the parameters of normal, although my limp gives me away when I am tired or in pain, and I often move awkwardly up and down stairs. My impaired condition makes me sensitive to how people respond to my differences and affords me a hint of what those living with far more pronounced and/or stigmatized differences cope with every day. Crystallization enables complex and nuanced representations but cannot let us off the hook of responsibility for invoking standards of normality and difference. As we make endless decisions about how to describe the differences among ourselves and others, we inevitably point to "a difference that makes a difference" (Bateson, 1979, p. 76) through a narrative detail, analytic description, or conceptual argument. Qualitative researchers need to think seriously about how we construct differences in our writing and other representations. Consider this story:

A bored-looking woman of Asian heritage approaches me as I hurry through the food court at the Westshore Mall. "Try our teriyaki chicken!" she demands with a smile, holding out the tray of samples speared with toothpicks.

"No thanks," I mutter to her and then again to the man by the Cajun fast food counter who tries to get me to taste their Bourbon chicken. Intent on my errand to drop off a print to be matted and framed before heading to the university, I walk as quickly as I can down the wide corridors of the mall, my khaki shorts swishing softly with each step. I am almost to the frame shop when I see a woman coming toward me stop, look at my leg with disgust etched clearly in her face, elbow her friend and then point directly at me. Despite the fact that this is only a more obvious version of the staring that happens several times a day when I expose my misshapen leg by wearing shorts in public, I am stunned. Her friend glances at me and then looks away quickly. I stand still as they pass, humiliation forming a hard knot in my stomach and fury pounding in my chest. Many years have passed since cancer disfigured and impaired my right leg, and still, on a bad day, a thoughtless person can reduce me to tears by reminding me without words that I do not fit in. I want to cry, but mostly I want to shout at the woman that I am not an object, that *I see her seeing me*. Instead, I wipe the tears away with the back of my hand and walk tiredly to the frame shop.

The social impulse is to label people who deviate from ideal norms as "different." In the story above, the woman in the mall clearly construed me as different. But as Minow (1990) argues, the experience of being "different" is possible only in relationship to others. Nothing inherently different exists in an individual until someone holds her/him up to a socially agreed-upon norm which s/he does not meet. Thus, my scarred and impaired leg only differs in relationship to a socially constructed idea of what a healthy female leg should look like. Minow argues that society puts people into categories in order to include and exclude members of particular groups from political, social, and economic spheres. No politically neutral labeling exists; my "difference" significantly impacts others' judgments of me. Consider another story:

The sky is a crystal clear blue and the morning sun warms my skin as I take a seat on the end of a bench at the Disney Port Orleans Resort bus stop. My spouse Glenn stands next to me as we wait with the crowd for a bus to take us to the MGM theme park for the day. I adjust my leg brace and remove a pain pill from my purse that I swallow with a swig of spring water from the bottle Glenn is carrying; it is going to be a long day of walking. A woman with a preschooler sits down on the other end of the bench, and the little boy immediately wriggles free of his mother's grasp to stand on the pavement. Pointing at the Mickey Mouse on his T-shirt, the child smiles happily, looking to his mother for agreement. She nods, and he turns and walks over to me. I tense, but offer the child a friendly smile.

"Hi!" I say brightly.

"Hi!" he says. His little brown eyes widen as he looks at my leg. Confused, he points to my leg brace and looks to his mother. "What's that?"

I groan inwardly, having been through this scene before. The mother usually either pulls the child away roughly, hushing him or her in embarrassment because "we don't talk about things like that," or she loudly proclaims that "the lady is veeeeery sick"— both of which leave me feeling ashamed and wishing I hadn't worn shorts, despite the intense Florida heat. This woman does neither. Instead, she turns to me with a warm smile, then addresses her son. "Well, it's like a big Band-Aid," she says simply.

The boy appears to consider the explanation, then looks to me questioningly. Relieved and grateful to this woman for finding a kind way to explain, I nod in confirmation. "Yes," I say. "It's like a big, blue Band-Aid." Satisfied, the boy nods and goes off in search of greater adventure, his mother trailing after him. Glenn gently squeezes my shoulder with his hand, and for a moment before the bus arrives, I pretend that it is always this simple to communicate difference.

This woman appeared to have attempted to word her explanation in way that deemphasized difference by establishing a connection between my brace and a concrete point of comparison within the young child's experience (i.e., Band-Aids). As qualitative research writers, we confront representational dilemmas more complex than simply pointing out difference with disgust or framing difference with childlike simplicity. However, these examples demonstrate the power of our capacity for framing difference. Perhaps the most important issue concerns acknowledging our complicity with and/or resistance to cultural categories of difference. Minow (1990) details five unstated assumptions of the social construction of difference that point to the need for us to recognize our active role in constructing difference in our representations.

> First, we often assume that "differences" are intrinsic, rather than viewing them as expressions of comparisons between people on the basis of particular traits.... Second, we typically adopt an unstated point of reference when assessing others. It is from the point of reference of this norm that we determine who is different and who is normal.... Third, we treat the person doing the seeing or judging as without perspective, rather than as inevitably seeing and judging from a particular situated perspective.... Fourth, we assume that the perspectives of those being judged are irrelevant or are already taken into account through the perspective of the judge.... Finally, there is an assumption that the existing social and political arrangements are natural and neutral. (pp. 50–52)

When engaging in crystallization, we must consciously think about how our participants and ourselves judge difference. Drawing on each of Minow's unstated assumptions, I offer suggestions for reflecting on how to represent difference consciously, ethically, and productively in crystallized texts.

- Emphasize the relationality of difference. That is, resist the urge to label or describe some people as belonging to less powerful categories while leaving others with the privilege of remaining unmarked. Thus, rather than labeling only the poor, also describe affluence; instead of pointing out only those who resist heteronormativity as part of the LGBTQ community, mark the presence of heterosexual expression. By describing concrete others to whom those who are "different" can be compared, we avoid simply reinforcing the taken-for-grantedness of obscured norms.

- Make any standards you invoke explicit; do not leave unstated norms as implied ideals compared to which you find others lacking. Take responsibility for judgments by clarifying your criteria, whether they come from biomedical perspectives, a particular critical perspective (e.g., feminism), ethical principles, educational standards, or other sources.

- Next, describe the standpoints from which you make your judgments of the people and worlds that you represent. Elaborate on not only your demographic characteristics, but also your experiences in the field, theoretical or methodological alliances, and relevant beliefs and values so that readers understand that you (and others) construct difference not from an all-knowing view but from a specific sociopolitical location.

- Focus on the perspective of those being judged different, not just those with the privilege to render authoritative judgments of others: Pay attention to the ways in which the members of the group you represent understand, label, and describe themselves and their reasons for their perceptual and linguistic choices.

- Delve into the history of laws, regulations, and systems of categories that reinforce difference to show how, when, why, and by whom they were socially constructed. Emphasize that existing arrangements are neither natural nor inevitable, but the consequence of specific events and decisions that privilege some at the expense of others.

Crystallization holds the potential for rendering complex portraits of commonality and difference, but invoking multiple genres does not guarantee nuanced and provocative representations of social categories. I urge researchers to take seriously the implications of labeling ourselves and others, and to reflect upon who stands to benefit when others are judged to be different. Ideally, crystallized accounts should problematize both specific categories of difference that are central to a research project (e.g., people with disabilities) and the processes by which such categories come to be socially constructed. Moreover, we should reflect upon our own participation in ongoing discourses of difference within the representations we construct.

WRITING RESOURCES

A sample of my favorites:

Cameron, J. (2002). *The artist's way: A spiritual path to higher creativity.* New York: Tarcher. (Original work published 1992).

Cameron's book provides a guided journey to reclaim your creativity as a spiritual practice. She provides a number of great writing and reflection exercises and inspirational ideas, whether or not you decide to follow her "12 steps" toward "creative recovery." Following Cameron's advice, I begin each writing session or work day by writing "morning pages," stream of consciousness writing that cavorts around the page, spewing junk that builds up in my mind. For some reason, this frees one's mind up and makes writing flow much better. People have asked me why or how this works, and I have no idea. Cameron says that you don't have to understand something to use it, and I agree.

Goldberg, N. (1986). *Writing down the bones: Freeing the writer within.* Boston: Shambhala.

Drawing upon principles of Zen Buddhist practice, Goldberg provides a series of brief, thought-provoking essays, many of which include great writing exercises. In addition, she offers practical advice and motivating ideas about writing. I particularly like her emphasis on the need to engage with others in talk, laughter, friendship, and in writing communities to foster our writing skills and identity.

King, S. (2000). *On writing.* New York: Scribner.

Part memoir, part "how to" manual, and a darn good read. I don't even like Stephen King's novels, but the account of his journey to become a writer fascinates me. Many of his suggestions on constructing vivid stories also ring true. For example, he unleashes a diatribe against the overuse of adverbs as a lazy way to write that slows down the story without adding clarity.

Lamott, A. (1995). *Bird by bird: Some instructions on writing and life.* New York: Anchor Books.

By far the most helpful and funniest book on writing out there. Two of my favorite writing tools come from Anne Lamott. One is to picture the story I am trying to tell through a "one-inch picture frame" and then write only what I can see through that limited perspective; she calls this a "short assignment." This technique helps tremendously with that feeling of being overwhelmed by the enormity of a manuscript. The other is to tell myself that I only have to write a "shitty draft" of the article, which can be revised later; this helps circumvent the stifling effects of perfectionism. Lamott points out that writers pass harsh judgments on their writing, often obsessively editing as they write. She advises that we give ourselves permission to just get ideas down on paper that we can fix up later. On bad days, I actually type "shitty draft" on the first page of my manuscript or of the blank computer file I struggle to fill.

NOTES

1. See the Benson-Henry Institute for Mind Body Medicine on the relaxation response, a state in which you generate beneficial beta waves in your brain; this state is possible to attain both through meditation and from repetitive movement (such as walking or biking): http://www.mbmi.org/basics/whatis_rresponse_elicitation.asp.

2. I urge readers to read Dillard's remarkable essay, "Write Till You Drop," originally published in *The New York Times*. It never fails to inspire me. Available for free download at http://www.nytimes.com/books/99/03/28/specials/dillard-drop.html.

≍ EIGHT ≍

PUBLISHING AND PROMOTING CRYSTALLIZATION

———◆◆◆———

There are no stories out there waiting to be told and no certain truths waiting to be recorded; there are only stories yet to be constructed.

—Denzin (1997, p. 267)

Some of the stories yet to be constructed may be productively, elegantly, and even courageously performed through a crystallized text or series of texts. Although not a panacea for all that ails the field of qualitative methodology nor a one-size-fits-all format for every project, crystallization provides a path toward constructing richly descriptive, useful, and artful representations of qualitative research. When we release the urge to discover definitive, singular Truth and surrender the need for certainty, we may discover the joys of "delicious ambiguity" (Radner, 1989), intervene into the "taken for grantedness" of daily life (Gergen, 1994), and become a pebble of innovation whose splash sends out ripples that impact the breadth of the qualitative research pond. In this chapter, I consider several lessons I have learned from crystallization, discuss crystallization's utility in social justice research, and offer suggestions for responding to common misunderstandings of and criticisms to crystallized texts.

LESSONS OF CRYSTALLIZATION

Both the processes and the products of crystallization reinforce the constructed and partial nature of all knowledge and of all modes of knowledge production. I understand crystallization as an emergent framework; hence I have opted not to present any static conclusions. Instead, I offer several lessons that arise again and again as I practice crystallization and read the work of others whose goals reflect the principles I promote.

Lesson One: The pervasive effects of dichotomous thinking continue to limit our ability to make sense of data and to represent it in meaningful ways (Ellingson & Ellis, 2008). Continuums offer multiplicity and the benefit of more than one correct answer. Challenging the art/science and the story/report dichotomies through crystallized texts opens up the field to more possibilities by embodying a range of representation. Regardless of where you locate yourself on the methodological continuum, I urge you to resist "us/them" mentality in judging others' work and the field of qualitative methods; few people fit the "anything goes, touchy-feely" caricature of autoethnographers/artists, and equally as few truly believe in the myth of value-neutral, completely objective research. I recognize that we accept serious risks in emphasizing methodological and epistemological commonalties over material differences (see Ellingson & Ellis, 2008), but I prefer those risks over those incurred when we paint the "other side" as distorted straw persons (see K. I. Miller, 2000). Much of that distortion arises from the perceived need to establish two polarities. Ideally, crystallized texts should reinforce a continuum of possibilities and dispel dichotomous views by representing multiple ways of knowing the world.

Lesson Two: The question must determine the method(s). Avoid methodolatry (Chamberlain, 2000), or reifying and privileging methodological concerns at the expense of other important considerations and seeking only to apply a favored method regardless of the question posed or the opportunities presented. Instead, utilize methods of data collection, analysis, and representation that enable you to most fully address the questions you pose. Like any other approach, crystallization should be implemented in ways that respond to the nature of the questions being asked, not done for its own sake or out of a desire merely to be considered innovative.

Lesson Three: "It's just more data." I say this to my students all the time and they roll their eyes at me. But I knew this in my gut all along, my research experience now bears it out, and many of my colleagues concur. To say, "it's just more data," means that you respond to any unexpected deviations from your research plan with curiosity rather than with shame and frustration. The wonder of social construction is that the entire journey "counts," not just the good parts (Mishler, 1986). We can learn from what seem at first like harmful missteps and mistakes if we think of them as providing yet more data to consider for our study, instead of considering them failures that inherently compromise our research. Thus, awkward interviews, embarrassing fieldwork incidents, shifts of topic focus, and dropped balls of administrative details, all reveal more about our participants, their worlds, and ourselves as researchers. For example, I was mortified by being publicly scolded by a physician while conducting participant observation, but upon reflection the incident revealed a lot about the culture of medicine. Once you finish fretting over what you perceive as an undesirable research experience, carefully document the details of what happened and your feelings about it, then add the account to the rest of your data. When engaging in crystallization, use some of those uncomfortable moments to deepen your analysis, construct reflexive writing stories (Richardson, 2000b), shed light on your participants' world, and/or complexify any stories or analyses that appear too tidy (and therefore unrealistic).

Lesson Four: Qualitative researchers are embodied, unique selves (Coffey, 1999; Ellingson, 2006a). Many researchers pay lip service to recognizing and articulating the standpoints from which we write, but we must go further than that. Too many times we provide obligatory statements about our identities as researchers, but we do not go the next step toward exploring the impact of who we are on *how* we research and *what* we produce. While most qualitative researchers eschew objectivity, we nonetheless produce accounts that often only minimally reflect an awareness of our unique selves as they impact our work. Crystallization necessitates a deep degree of reflexivity because it invokes the researcher's self on so many different levels as it constructs and deconstructs meaning.

CALL TO ACTION: EMPLOYING CRYSTALLIZATION TO PROMOTE SOCIAL JUSTICE

Much of the practice of ethnography and other qualitative methods remains rooted in the passion for protesting injustice that characterized the Chicago School, many members of which explored marginalized groups in urban settings (e.g., C. A. B. Warren & Karner, 2000). Conquergood (1995) argued that the goal of applied research is always political, potentially revolutionary, and never neutral:

> We must choose between research that is "engaged" or "complicit." By engaged I mean clear-eyed, self-critical awareness that research does not proceed in epistemological purity or moral innocence: There is no immaculate perception. . . . The scholarly commitment of the engaged intellectual is to praxis. . . . By praxis I mean a combination of analytical rigor, participatory practice, critical reflection, and political struggle. (p. 85)

I concur with Conquergood: researchers cannot remain uninvolved—to refuse to advocate or assist is to reinforce power relations, not to remain impartial. Conquergood's (1994) study of youth gangs in Chicago constitutes an outstanding example of applied communication research that promotes social justice by rejecting standard characterizations of gang members in favor of more nuanced, compassionate accounts constructed through extensive, hands-on involvement with participants. Calls to socially engaged work proliferated across the social sciences during the last decade. For example, the third edition of the *Sage Handbook of Qualitative Methods* (Denzin & Lincoln, 2005) focuses on strategies for promoting social justice and accomplishing political work through qualitative research; see also the forum on social justice research in *Communication Studies* (Frey, Pearce, Pollock, Artz, & Murphy, 1996; Makau, 1996; Wood, 1996), and the special issue of *Journal of Applied Communication Research* with articles on conducting participatory and applied research for social justice (Artz, 1998; Crabtree, 1998; Frey, 1998; Hartnett, 1998; Pearce, 1998; Ryan, Carragee, & Schwerner, 1998; Varallo, Ray, & Ellis, 1998).

I encourage readers to think of their work as always already political in its practices and implications and to use crystallization to highlight the material and ideological consequences of representation of others. Moreover, we must engage in dialogue with the worlds outside of the academy in order to effect social change. When we bring our ideas to the general public, we act as public intellectuals who

> are more than just righteous in their stance; they embody and enact moral leadership. They are not afraid to speak out; rather, they thrive as "rabble-rousers" grounded in ethical pillars. . . . When the intellectual speaks to a "public," ideas are not just heard but debated, discussed, and passed on in recursive societal dialogue. (Papa & Singhal, 2007, pp. 126–127)

When we speak out, we move beyond the important work of knowledge creation and theory building to apply our scholarly resources to benefit people in concrete ways. This requires us to engage as much in listening as in speaking.

Moreover, we must expand our definition of what counts as a "public" with which to engage with our work.

> By embracing a framework of multiple publics—local and national, enduring and temporary—we can better recognize and affirm the meaningful work that scholars do for local, particular communities . . . [and] we call for greater institutional and material recognition of these multiple forms of public intellectual work. (Brouwer & Squires, 2003, p. 212)

Getting credit for our "nonscholarly" work and the representations we produce as part of the crystallization process bears serious material consequences for hiring, tenure, promotion, and allocation of resources. Of course, we all can afford to volunteer time in our communities, but significant engagements with the public need to be central to our academic mission. Crystallization (particularly dendritic forms) offers an ideal mechanism for accomplishing the goal of public engagement because of its emphasis on producing a range of representations suitable for a variety of stakeholder audiences, both within and outside the academy. We will not find engaged research easy. We need courage to speak out.

> At a time when our civil liberties are being destroyed and public institutions and goods all over the globe are under assault by the forces of a rapacious global capitalism, there is a sense of concrete urgency that demands not only the most militant forms of political opposition on the part of academics, but new modes of resistance and collective struggle buttressed by rigorous intellectual work, social responsibility, and political courage. (Giroux, 2004, p. 77)

As a faculty member at a Jesuit university, I receive considerable encouragement and support from my institution to act "in solidarity" with the needs of oppressed peoples, making public engagement an obvious choice for me. However, many other researchers at a wide range of institutions find creative ways to garner publications from engaged research through strategic placement and promotion of work. I encourage all faculty to move courageously in this direction toward engagement and away from complicity.

I now turn to a discussion of strategies for disseminating our engaged, multigenre work within academic outlets.

GETTING THE WORD OUT: PURSUING PUBLICATION

Some editors will welcome your crystallized work with open arms. I remain grateful for and humbled by the support I have received from my editors and impressed by the open-mindedness of some other editors who have embraced innovative work. However, in my experience, articles, chapters, books, performances, multimedia presentations, and other texts that utilize strategies that reflect the goals of crystallization do not find welcome by all, or even the majority, of colleagues. Despite professed support, I often find colleagues in the form of peer reviewers, journal and edited volume editors, departmental/college faculty evaluation committee members, and the like to be highly critical of such work on its face. Tellingly, their critiques often fail to mention the *form* or perceived incompatible elements of the piece at all, and instead provide streams of nitpicky complaints about the most minute elements of the manuscript. Alternatively, I receive the two-line review that basically states that the paper constitutes an abomination and must be rejected (and presumably burned, I infer). These critics seem uncomfortable but without being willing and/or able to express why.

Over time, layered accounts (Ronai, 1995) have become fairly common, but even then, they find publication primarily in such strong qualitative methods-focused (rather than discipline- or topic-focused) journals as *Qualitative Inquiry, Journal of Contemporary Ethnography, Ethnography,* and *Symbolic Interaction.* Even those outlets who welcome layered accounts and other interpretive work may have specific expectations for evocative prose, coherent argumentation, use of particular theoretical perspectives, and/or other sacred mores. Yet, many of us wish to speak to and with communities of scholars, practitioners, and theorists in health care, education, human services, government, community organizations, activist groups, business, and other groups who cannot be realistically reached via a small number of journals focused on interpretive scholarship. I believe that very few, if any, scholars act simply with petty territorialism, seeking to punish those who trespass against established conventions. But more than a few of them are rendered uneasy, threatened, and defensive by work that pushes the boundaries, which crystallized texts often do.

While I have faced such defensiveness from all along the qualitative continuum, they primarily fall into two "camps": (some) postpositivists who think that artistic works compromise the validity of accompanying inductive analysis and (some) artsy folks who think that those who practice qualitative analysis needlessly hold onto—or worse, are duped by—irrelevant, patriarchal, and/or passé conventions of science. These criticisms reflect two levels of perceived incommensurability: (1) philosophical objections to logical and epistemological inconsistencies in the work (i.e., objections to putting art and science (together), and (2) symbolic approaches that focus on the lack of consistent symbol sets and common vocabularies across "systems of explanation" (K. I. Miller, 2000, p. 63; i.e., objections that the work makes no sense, is not explained meaningfully). In the interest of providing practical assistance to those who want to engage in and publish works of crystallization, I provide a few general suggestions for preparing and "selling" your crystallized work, and then offer some suggested responses to common criticisms.

One fairly obvious tactic is to engage exclusively in dendritic crystallization, as discussed in Chapter 6. By strategically dividing up your work into segments that each adhere to a single genre, you can target specific publication outlets and meet their individual expectations in each of your pieces, without compromising your ability to work in other genres for other outlets. Dendritic crystallization is not less valuable or easier than crystallization that yields multigenre texts, nor is it mutually exclusive with it. Moreover, opportunities to practice guerilla scholarship enable practitioners of crystallization to plant seeds in other gardens (Rawlins, 2007).

Second, for any work of crystallization, I highly suggest preemptive inclusion of strategic explanatory and/or justifying statements within manuscripts and/or cover letters in order to ward off editorial defensiveness, when possible. Of course, authors should avoid being defensive themselves and avoid accusing editors, even subtly, of being close minded. Think more along the lines of offering some persuasive statements about the value of your boundary-spanning, innovative, cutting-edge work that challenges limitations of existing approaches to your topic, and the like. Express your certainty (even if you don't feel it) that the editor will appreciate your fresh perspective and creative way of representing your research.

Third, be extra careful to avoid giving editors and reviewers a simple reason or excuse to reject your work, that is, do not be sloppy. Be incredibly neat in your formatting, do a thorough reference check to ensure that all in-text citations have corresponding references and all references are cited in your text, be sure every one of your references adheres to the preferred style of the journal (e.g., APA, MLA), proofread or get someone to do it for you, and look out for ambiguous statements that might evoke criticism by unintentionally overclaiming a finding or implying a measurement not warranted by your data. Professionalism dictates such careful manuscript preparation anyway, but manuscripts that push the boundaries cannot afford even minor mistakes that might tempt reviewers to dismiss them out of hand. Many will dismiss the work anyway, but that is no reason to make it easy for them.

JUSTIFYING YOUR WORK

For those who have not already learned of the rigidity of many research publication conventions through personal experience, let me assure you that they persist. For those of you coping with social and scholarly rejections, let me offer both hope and empathy (see this chapter's interlude) and some ways to respond to some of the most common concerns I encounter, first from the methodological middle-right, then from the middle-left. I structured this discussion with paired criticisms and suggested responses. I welcome readers to adapt these ideas in whatever way proves useful in seeking publication, or simply as ideas to keep in the back of your mind as you practice crystallization.

Criticisms From the Methodological Right
(Including IRB/Human Subjects Boards)

Criticism: You can do that "artsy stuff" *only* after you establish the social scientific rigor of your method and contributions of your findings. For example, Morse, a highly accomplished researcher and leader in the field of qualitative methods (e.g., Morse & Field, 1995; Morse & Richards, 2002) and editor of *Qualitative Health Research* (http://qhr.sagepub.com), cautions that "alternative" forms of representation must not replace or even precede more conventional accounts of qualitative research analyses:

> The research results disseminated in an arts-based form must follow careful qualitative work conducted as we have done for decades. The play or the artwork cannot, and must not, be the first or the only results emanating from a qualitative project. The refereed article first produced then provides the criterion to evaluate the message of the adequacy of the alternative arts-based "publication" used to provide supplemental or alternative dissemination of the findings. Thus, the alternative representation of the research is not an end in itself, but, rather, an essential and significant additional means for dissemination, accessing a different audience. (Morse, 2004, p. 887)

Response: I deeply respect Morse, and I concur with her view that artistic work is not the same as social scientific analysis. However, I disagree with her (and others') mandate that creative analytic work cannot be "first" or "only" products of a qualitative project. I engage in this discussion about our difference of opinion in the interest of creating better rationales for what we do and why. Readers should keep in mind that productive differences of opinion about methodological issues abound within the community of qualitative researchers, and that continuing dialogue enriches the field. I encourage authors to do both more conventional and creative analytic work too, but contend that one mode need not necessarily precede or require another. We can engage in rigorous data analysis processes that we then express in creative genres, or produce narrative work that then leads to systematic analyses. Moreover, researchers can enact multiple modes of sense making concurrently. While artistic representations cannot fully capture the meaning of any phenomenon, neither can conventional reports. The tendency to romanticize traditional qualitative analysis as the primary and hence only authoritative account obscures its limitations as an inherently partial account embedded in relations of power. Qualitative (or quantitative) reports require readers' faith that the authors conducted rigorous analysis and that they have offered a fair, thorough, and nuanced analysis of their data. Invocation of the report genre does not automatically ensure such rigor, anymore than adopting an artistic genre precludes or casts doubt on it. The rhetorical advantage of the report genre manifests in its explicit discussion of procedures, which enhances perceptions of accountability. Authors should be trustworthy to the highest standards of excellence in any genre. One compromise involves offering methodological details in a method section, appendix, epilogue, or elsewhere in artistic representations to allay concerns about the rigor of analytic procedures (see discussion of options in dendritic crystallization, Chapter 6).

Criticism: Your work is hopelessly subjective.

Response: Owning your standpoint involves risk: "To admit one's passions is to see through a glass darkly" (Gergen, 1999, p. 76). For those concerned with my lack of objectivity, I routinely offer two responses. First, I paraphrase Gergen's (1999) views on the subjectivity/objectivity dichotomy using my own pithy rejoinder: *Objectivity is merely a rhetorical accomplishment.* I often elaborate that people attempt to persuade others through argumentation that they achieved objectivity, but that does not make it so.[1] Second, I suggest that interrogating my subjectivity through continual reflection on my role in data collection, analysis, and representation offers far more rigor than *pretending* my subjectivity does not exist or has been somehow eliminated from the process of my research (see Harding's 1993 discussion of "strong objectivity").

Criticism: You simply cannot do that; everyone knows you cannot combine creative work with analysis and expect to get it published by a reputable journal.

Response: Language and meaning are not static, and neither are research methods and conventions. We do not say "thee" and "thou" any more. Thirty years ago we could not publish a paper that used first-person voice; now APA [or insert your disciplinary standard] considers it appropriate language—most journals allow it, and many even require it. Likewise, methodological evolution continues, and crystallization offers one innovative way to represent qualitative research findings. A few great journals that publish this type of boundary-spanning work include *Qualitative Inquiry, Cultural Studies<=>Critical Methodologies, Journal of Contemporary Ethnography,* and *Ethnography.*

Criticism: Your findings are not generalizable because you only studied one person, group, or setting, or a nonrepresentative sample.

Response: Crystallization does not involve claims of generalization. Instead, my findings offer rich descriptions, theoretical insights, and pragmatic implications for practitioners in the types of settings I studied. While of course health care teams [or restaurants or group homes or whatever you study] vary, they also have a lot in common and hence can benefit from my research. One benefit of my crystallized account lies in the utility of being able to reach multiple audiences instead of only academics. Let me give you an example of my work's implications for practitioners. . . .

Criticism: Your findings are not valid because those stories (poems, photos, etc.) reflect individuals and are not representative of the corpus of your data.

Response: The term validity is a contested term that holds different meanings for researchers depending upon where researchers situate themselves on the methodological continuum (Potter, 1996). Since I do not claim to measure anything, I do not need a representative sample in order for my creative work to offer rich descriptions that embody the meanings in my data. Instead, I selected illustrative, evocative, moving exemplars to build my case. A long tradition of inductive analysis exists in qualitative methods, and my work reflects this approach (e.g., Lindlof & Taylor, 2002).

Criticism: Your methods are not reliable or replicable.

Response: As a social constructionist I do not believe that any qualitative research can be reliable or replicable; all meaning is intersubjective (i.e., co-created in the moment), and hence it is not only inevitable but *beneficial* that each researcher will generate somewhat different findings when studying the "same" place or group (e.g., Gergen, 1999). Rather than reliability, I focus on reflexivity: careful consideration of the individual point of view (i.e., positionality) of the researcher as it relates to data analysis, knowledge construction, and representation (e.g., Fine et al., 2000; Lindlof & Taylor, 2002).

Criticism: Your presentation is not ethical because you did not secure permission to present participants' voices as a performance [or other creative representation].

Response: My work conforms to ethical standards for research. The informed consent procedures included a reference to any report or public presentation of the data, and my [insert genre or medium] is a form of public presentation. I made appropriate changes to protect the identities of my participants through the use of pseudonyms and changes to other identifying characteristics. Moreover, my creative account actually fulfils the ethical imperative of giving voice to marginalized groups with its foregrounding of my participants' voices in ways that demonstrate their strength and resiliency [or other positive characteristics] (Conquergood, 1995; Madison, 2005; Nielsen, 1990).

Criticism: Your manuscript does not follow appropriate APA (or other) style.

Response: Those style conventions got in the way of my artistic/representational goals for this work. However, I would be happy to include an overview, appendix, reference list, postscript, or other addendum to my work that would fulfill the purpose of providing appropriately formatted documentation of sources, procedures, and methods, and to address any other editorial concerns you might have.

Criticism: Your book wouldn't fit in our list, since our audience doesn't read work of that type.

Response: I understand that my work appears atypical. However, most readers embrace or at least are open to considering work that pushes the envelope of accepted practices, provided it fits their area of focus and is well done.

Let me explain to you how my work meets the goals of your series articulated in your call for submissions and how my work complements your current list of publications. . . .

Criticism: You are trying to do too much; you include everything but the kitchen sink in your manuscript!

Response: The manuscript reflects a careful balance of coverage. Of course, breadth and depth always trade off in any representation. While I do include multiple forms of representation, I also narrowed the scope of my inquiry accordingly, enabling me to fully explore a more tightly defined topic area. A concrete example of how I limited my range of inquiry is that early in my project with the IOPOA team, I considered many aspects of interdisciplinary communication in several settings. Yet, in my book, I focused specifically on the interdisciplinary team members' collaborative communication in the backstage of the clinic. The appearance of several contrasting genres may increase the perception of length; in reality, my manuscript falls within the normal topical parameters for this outlet.

Criticism: You shouldn't do that kind of work; people will think you are one of those crazy, navel-gazing storytellers who are hurting our discipline, compromising our department's reputation on campus, and/or ruining academics' credibility with the public.

Response: Smile tolerantly and quote Bochner (1997): "We know we're onto something, when we're told, 'You mustn't think that way'" (p. 425). People tend to fear and find fault with things they do not understand. Try to transform the confrontation into a teachable moment by explaining some of the basic tenets of crystallization and/or the interpretive turn in the social sciences (e.g., Denzin & Lincoln, 2005). If your mentor or a senior colleague offers this caution "in your best interest," then also consider having a few examples of more mainstream work you can use for show and tell to demonstrate your ability to adapt to a variety of audiences. One skill I learned from my work with crystallization is the ability to move from one methodological speech community to another in order to survive (e.g., get your dissertation approved, get hired, earn tenure), thrive (secure a book contract, publish in a prestigious journal), and meet goals with multiple audiences (e.g., influence practitioners). I consider it arrogant and elitist—albeit tempting—to continue to address only those who already agree with you; being able to write in multiple genres that span the qualitative continuum can only serve you in enacting positive change both within and outside of the academy. I also find it helpful to quote Richardson (2000b):

> Students will not lose the language of science when they learn to write in other [artistic] ways, any more than students who learn a second language lose their first. . . . There is no single way—much less one "right" way—of staging a text. (p. 936)

In sum, practitioners from the middle-to-right of the continuum tend to object to the failure of crystallized texts to conform to traditional formats, goals, and stylistic norms. Your goal must be to explain how you meet the spirit of such norms in an alternative manner, and/or how you embody other—equally rigorous and important—standards for quality work.

Criticisms From the Methodological Left

Criticism: You have turned a story told into a story analyzed; you break apart a story instead of thinking *with* a story (see A. W. Frank, 1995).

Response: Thinking about and with stories are not mutually exclusive practices; we can do both. Crystallization does not invalidate or cancel out the contributions of one form of analysis with those of another. Multiple genres and forms of analysis complement each other within a social constructionist framework that positions all representations as equally mired in power and limited by the indeterminacy of language (see Holstein & Gubrium, 2008). Analysis is a form of story too; it constitutes an academic narrative (Gergen, 1994). Moreover, good reasons exist for analyzing stories, such as identifying patterns and critiquing implicit cultural norms (see Charmaz, 2000, 2006), just as we have good reasons to use narrative or poetic genres to communicate some truths (e.g., Ellis, 2004).

Criticism: You uphold or submit to patriarchal conventions by including analysis that manifests the disembodied voice of academe, the "god trick" (Haraway, 1988).

Response: No form, genre, or method is inherently patriarchal or incompatible with feminist, critical race, or other perspectives. Moreover, theory or method is "not inherently healing, liberatory, or revolutionary. It fulfils this function only when we ask that it do so and direct our theorizing towards this end" (hooks, 1994, p. 61). Neither are stories or other artistic representations inherently subversive, liberatory, or reflecting of noncanonical truths.

While stories may be more open to multiple interpretations, they do not escape their authorship; we make no fewer power-laden decisions in the construction of a video, poem, or performance than we do in writing a social scientific report; no innocent position exists from which to analyze and represent in any genre (Wolf, 1996). Awareness of my own involvement with research and writing and active reflexive consideration of my own role in meaning making is vital to all of my work, including rigorous qualitative analysis. Allow me to explain how I included consideration of my standpoint in my sense making processes. . . .

Criticism: You ruin the flow of the film, narrative, essay [insert other genre or medium] with your academic/analytic prose.

Response: This piece is not intended to be a seamless text. The qualitative analysis functions as part of a layered structure (Ronai, 1995), and it fits exquisitely well with the work's purpose, which is to [insert purpose—e.g., to reveal the subtle manifestations of power in health care organizations]. It is unproductive to criticize a hammer for being a poor screwdriver; likewise, criticizing a layered account for not being a short story or a narrative film for including explicit discussion of theory rejects the value of honoring each genre on its own terms, including hybrid genres. By combining more than one genre—and hence more than one epistemology—in my representation, I reveal the constructed nature of all accounts. In doing so, I challenge my audience to resist simplistic understandings of the topic and problematize the nature of knowledge construction.

Criticism: Your incorporation of social scientific analysis demonstrates that you are naive, a modernist, a latent positivist, or (my personal favorites) a "hopelessly second wave feminist" or one who "surrenders her authority to science."[2] You clearly do not understand postmodernism, poststructuralism, narrative theory, feminist theorizing about epistemology and methodology, or [insert other perspective].

Response: My work reflects neither naiveté nor lack of comprehension of postmodernity [or other perspective] and related aspects of the interpretive turn. In fact, my work reflects what Richardson (2000b) calls creative analytic practices; it is both creative in its representation *and* analytic in the meanings it embodies. By juxtaposing social science with artistic representations, I complexify and demystify both as socially constructed representations; each is partial, situated, and bears both strengths and weaknesses grounded in their respective genres. I don't accept the neutrality of analyses any more than I think of stories or art as anything other than emanating from a particular standpoint and historical moment. Reinscribing caricatures of all social scientists as slavishly naive positivists is inaccurate and unproductive (K. I. Miller, 2000). We need to move beyond dichotomous views of qualitative researchers as either artists or scientists and embrace a continuum of methods where art and science can blend in an infinite number of ways (Ellingson & Ellis, 2008; Ellis & Ellingson, 2000).

Criticism: Good stories *are* theories; it is not necessary to include other, social scientific articulations of analysis and/or theory. In fact, relying on theory undermines the effectiveness of your artistic representation.

Response: I certainly agree that good stories can be theories (Ellis & Bochner, 2000), but that does not invalidate crystallization as an effective strategy for illuminating some topics and processes. In fact, we can think of theories as stories of how the world works. Artwork gives us much to feel, think, and appreciate; in crystallization, we think, feel, and critique on other levels as well. You do not have to give up theory to embrace stories, nor vice versa. It all depends upon your representational and analytic goals. Different questions—about research topics, methodological processes, or the researcher (and the researcher–participant relationship)—require different strategies for answering. Some of us pose questions more satisfactorily answered with the inclusion of more formal articulations of theory. Let me explain to you why I chose to include this particular theory and how it illuminates my topic. . . .

Criticism: Your mentor, advisor, or editor says of your work of crystallization, "You are trying to do too much; you include everything but the kitchen sink in there!"

Response: [same as above criticism from the middle-right]

Criticism: An editor says (or you fear s/he will say), "Your book wouldn't fit in our list, since our audience doesn't read work like *that.* "

Response: Actually, my work fits well with your list's focus on [insert topic area]. My crystallization framework improves my ability to illuminate the complexity of that topic. People doing interpretive work tend to be extraordinarily broad-minded; they won't dismiss well-written grounded theory [or other form of inductive analysis] out of hand, especially since it is enhanced with other artistic genres. This postmodern form of triangulation allows researchers to view the topic through multiple lenses, enriching understanding and reinforcing the partial and constructed nature of all knowledge claims.

ENCLOSING WILD POWER:
A CONCLUSION/INVITATION

> The writer knows her field—what has been done, what could be done, the limits—the way a tennis player knows the court. And like that expert, she, too, plays the edges. That is where the exhilaration is. . . . Now gingerly, can she enlarge it, can she nudge the bounds? And enclose what wild power?
>
> —Annie Dillard (1989, ¶ 6)

Thinking of crystallization as embodying *wild power* provides an energizing trope for our work. Crystallization skirts the edges of academic publishing conventions, drawing power from art, science, and endless combinations of artful science and scientific artwork. I offer crystallization as an emergent framework that promises tremendous opportunity to promote positive change in the world through qualitative research. One area of productive change centers on the growth and development of crystallization itself. I eagerly anticipate that readers adopting and adapting the principles contained in this book will use their imagination to expand the boundaries not only of qualitative research but of my current conceptualization of crystallization as a framework. I welcome constructive feedback and explanations of how you made crystallization your own. I hope to sustain dialogue and widen the community that plays along multiple edges of academic norms. If you would like to share your thoughts and experiences, please contact me at lellingson@scu.edu.

INTERLUDE

When Your Work Is Rejected

"I'd like an Earl Grey tea, please," I said to the burly guy at the bakery counter. "For here."

"OK," he replied. "Anything else?" He gave me a winning smile and nodded to the display on his left, inviting me to splurge on one of the dozens of butter-and-sugar-laden goodies that lined the glass case.

I groaned inwardly. "No, thank you."

After doctoring my tea with copious amounts of low-fat milk and a little Splenda, I surveyed the seating area and chose a table with an electrical outlet at its base. I set up my Mac laptop with its lovely lavender "Macskin" cover; arranged the small pile of photocopied, underlined, and annotated articles; placed my tea to the left of my computer; and sighed. My trip to the bakery constituted a last ditch effort to get some uninterrupted writing time, something I rarely seemed to manage in my office.

A tension headache loomed on the horizon. Slogging through spring quarter at the university always exhausted me, but this time I was teaching two sections of qualitative methods, which meant loads of grading and individual appointments with students. Meanwhile, I had a publisher interested in a proposal who wanted sample chapters ASAP, two overdue manuscript reviews for journals, a revise and resubmit decision I had sat on for 5 months, and a bad case of spring fever. *Get a grip,* I told myself. *Get some work done.*

Taking a deep breath, I plunged into my analysis of aunts in extended family networks, pausing only to look up information in the articles or to sip my tea. I worked steadily for over an hour, then paused to sigh again. Deciding I deserved a minibreak, I opened my e-mail program, grateful for the bakery's free Wi-Fi Internet connection.

My mailbox screen popped open and I saw it immediately—a decision on my latest journal submission. Trembling, hoping, fearing, I double-clicked the message and read:

Dear Dr. Ellingson:

Re: Manuscript # 2007–0084 entitled "The Poetics of Professionalism among Dialysis Technicians"

Thank you for submitting the above manuscript. I have received the reviewers' comments (please see below) and regret that your article has not been accepted for publication.

Thank you for your support of [journal].

Sincerely yours . . .

Much to my horror, tears welled in my eyes and began flowing down my cheeks. A sob burst from my throat, and I grabbed two beige, recycled paper napkins and held them against my face. I struggled to remain silent, mortified by my reaction. The lunchtime crowd swarmed around my table. *StopitstopitSTOPIT!!!* I chanted to myself. *Breathe deeply.* I tried, but it was just too much to keep inside. I assumed people were staring by now, but reminding myself of that fact didn't help to stem the tide. I continued crying, grateful at least for the loud hum of conversation that partially obscured my napkin-muffled wailing. After a while, I realized I was sweating copiously; the legs of my khaki shorts felt damp and my thighs stuck to the cheap vinyl seat. Miserable, I took a sip of my now-cold tea.

When the tears stopped, I chanted the standard litany to myself, hoping against hope that it would provide comfort.

> I've been rejected before; it's no big deal.
>
> Everyone gets rejected.
>
> Carolyn Ellis's first book was rejected more than 30 times before it found a publisher.
>
> I am still a good researcher.
>
> I have rich data and conducted a sound analysis.
>
> I am a good writer.
>
> The piece can be revised and sent elsewhere; there are plenty of other journal-fish in the academic sea.
>
> And that editor is probably an evil, close-minded, patriarchal, power-hording scumbag anyway.

But it still hurt—especially since I actually respect that editor a great deal and know that s/he bears no resemblance to my bitter description. This I know: Rejection will *always* hurt, and it always embarrasses me.

I debated with myself whether to include this narrative in the book. On one hand, I staunchly maintain that my reaction is nothing of which I should be ashamed. In fact, sharing it may provide comfort to others coping with inevitable rejection and perhaps serve as a reminder to those prone to writing nasty, unconstructive, petty, arrogant reviews that *they hurt real people* when they do that. On the other hand, I hate sounding weak and weepy; it seems so unprofessional and unproductive (not to mention it reinforces stereotypes of women as overly emotional). The anonymous reviewer system resembles democracy, in my mind: It is the worse possible system, except for everything else out there. And I can even admit (most of the time) that some of my rejections were well deserved; my work generally improves after getting feedback from reviewers and editors. But rejection still hurts, and I encourage you to acknowledge the pain and to find nurturing, nondestructive ways to comfort yourself when the inevitable happens.

NOTES

1. Gergen (1999) wrote,

> If rhetoric is the art of persuasion, then the study of rhetoric is the illumination of power in action. . . . More dangerous are those who seem only to be reporting the facts—the world as it is outside anyone's particular prejudice. . . . The language of objective reality is essentially used as a means of generating hierarchies of inclusion and exclusion. . . . Objectivity cannot refer to a relationship between the mind and the world; rather, as the rhetorical analyst proposes, objectivity is achieved by speaking (or writing) in particular ways. (pp. 73–74)

2. These are actual examples of comments made to me about my work by other academic professionals.

REFERENCES

Abu-Lughod, J. L. (1993). *Writing women's worlds: Bedouin stories.* Berkeley: University of California Press.

Adelman, M., & Frey, L. (1997). *The fragile community: Living together with AIDS.* Mahwah, NJ: Lawrence Erlbaum.

Adelman, M. B., & Frey, L. R. (2001). Untold tales from the field: Living the autoethnographic life in an AIDS residence. In S. L. Herndon & G. K. Kreps (Eds.), *Qualitative research: Applications in organizational life* (pp. 205–226). Cresskill, NJ: Hampton Press.

Adelman, M., & Shultz, P. (Producers). (1991). *The pilgrim must embark: Living in community* [film]. Annandale, VA: Speech Communication Association's Applied Communication Series.

Adler, R. B., & Towne, N. (2005). *Looking out, looking in: Interpersonal communication* (11th ed.). Fort Worth, TX: Harcourt Brace.

Allen, D. (2002). *Getting things done: The art of stress-free productivity.* New York: Penguin.

Alvesson, M., & Sköldberg, K. (2000). *Reflexive methodology.* Thousand Oaks, CA: Sage.

Anderson, L. (2006). Analytic autoethnography. *Journal of Contemporary Ethnography, 35,* 373–395.

Anfara, V. A., Jr., & Mertz, N. T. (Eds.). (2006). *Theoretical frameworks in qualitative research.* Thousand Oaks, CA: Sage.

Angrosino, M. V. (1998). *Opportunity house: Ethnographic stories of mental retardation.* Walnut Creek, CA: AltaMira Press.

Apker, J. (2001). Role development in the managed care era: A case of hospital-based nursing. *Journal of Applied Communication Research, 29,* 117–136.

Artz, L. (1998). African-Americans and higher education: An exigence in need of applied communication. *Journal of Applied Communication Research, 26,* 210–231.

Athens, L. (2006). Who is better than whom? Two tales from melting pot boils over. *Qualitative Inquiry, 12,* 1101–1116.

Atkinson, P. (1997). Narrative turn in a blind alley? *Qualitative Health Research, 7,* 325–344.

Atkinson, P. (2006). Rescuing autoethnography. *Journal of Contemporary Ethnography, 35,* 400–404.

Atkinson, P., Coffey, A., Delamont, S., Lofland, J., & Lofland, L. (Eds.). (2001). *The handbook of ethnography.* Thousand Oaks, CA: Sage.

Austin, D. A. (1996). Kaleidoscope: The same and different. In C. Ellis & A. P. Bochner (Eds.), *Composing ethnography* (pp. 206–230). Walnut Creek, CA: AltaMira Press.

Babrow, A., & Mattson, M. (2003). Theorizing about health communication. In T. L. Thompson, A. M. Dorsey, K. I. Miller, & R. Parrott (Eds.), *The handbook of health communication* (pp. 35–62). Mahwah, NJ: Lawrence Erlbaum.

Bach, H. (2007). *A visual narrative concerning curriculum, girls, photography etc.* Walnut Creek, CA: Left Coast Press.

Baker, T. A., & Wang, C. C. (2006). Photovoice: Use of a participatory action research method to explore the chronic pain experience in older adults. *Qualitative Health Research, 16,* 1440–1449.

Bakhtin, M. (1984). *Problems of Dostoevsky's poetics* (C. Emerson, Ed. & Trans.). Minneapolis: University of Minnesota Press.

Banks, A., & Banks, S. P. (1998). *Fiction and social research: By ice or fire.* Walnut Creek, CA: AltaMira Press.

Banks, S. P. (2000). Five holiday letters: A fiction. *Qualitative Inquiry, 6,* 392–405.

Barker, J. R., Melville, C. W., & Pacanowsky, M. E. (1993). Self-directed teams at Xel: Changes in communication practices during a program of cultural transformation. *Journal of Applied Communication Research, 21,* 297–312.

Bateson, G. (1979). *Mind and nature: A necessary unity.* Toronto, Canada: Bantam Books.

Behar, R. (1996). *The vulnerable observer: Anthropology that breaks your heart.* Boston: Beacon Press.

Belenky, M. F., Clinchy, B. M., Golberger, N. R., & Tarule, J. M. (1986). *Women's ways of knowing: The development of self, voice, and mind.* New York: Basic Books.

Benjamin, W. (1968). Theses on the philosophy of history. In H. Arendt (Ed.), *Illuminations* (pp. 253–264). New York: Schocken.

Berg, B. L. (2007). *Qualitative research methods for the social sciences* (6th ed). Boston: Pearson.

Berger, L., & Ellis, C. (2002). Composing autoethnographic stories. In M. V. Angrosino (Ed.), *Doing cultural anthropology: Projects for ethnographic data collection* (pp. 151–166). Prospect Heights, IL: Waveland Press.

Berger, P., & Luckmann, T. (1966). *The social construction of reality.* Garden City, NY: Doubleday.

Bertram, S., Kurland, M., Lydick, E., Locke, R., & Yawn, B. P. (2001). The patient's perspective of irritable bowel syndrome. *The Journal of Family Practice, 50,* 521–525.

Bochner, A. P. (1997). It's about time: Narrative and the divided self. *Qualitative Inquiry, 3,* 418–438.

Bochner, A. P. (2000). Criteria against ourselves. *Qualitative Inquiry, 6,* 266–272.

Borkan, J. (1999). Immersion/crystallization. In B. F. Crabtree & W. L. Miller (Eds.), *Doing qualitative research* (pp. 179–194). Thousand Oaks, CA: Sage.

Braithwaite, C. A. (1997). Sa'ah naagháí bik'eh hózhóón: An ethnography of Navajo educational communication practices. *Communication Education, 46,* 219–233.

Breed, W. (1972). Five components of a basic suicide syndrome. *Life Threatening Behavior, 3,* 3–18.

Brooks, L. J., & Bowker, G. (2002). Playing at work: Understanding the future of work practices at the institute for the future. *Information, Communication, and Society, 5,* 109–136.

Brouwer, D. C., & Squires, C. R. (2003). Public intellectuals, public life, and the university. *Argumentation and Advocacy, 39,* 201–213.

Burke, K. (1973). *The philosophy of literary form: Studies in symbolic action.* Berkeley: University of California.

Butler, J. (1990). Performative acts and gender constitution: An essay in phenomenology and feminist theory. In S. E. Case (Ed.), *Performing feminisms: Feminist critical theory and theatre* (pp. 270–282). Baltimore, MD: Johns Hopkins University Press.

Butler, J. (1997). Performative acts and gender constitution: An essay in phenomenology and feminist theory. In K. Conboy, N. Medina, & S. Stanbury (Eds.), *Writing on the body: Female embodiment and feminist theory* (pp. 401–417). New York: Columbia University Press.

Buzzanell, P. M., & Ellingson, L. L. (2005). Contesting narratives of maternity in the workplace. In L. M. Harter, P. Japp, & C. Beck (Eds.), *Narratives, health, and healing: Communication theory, research, and practice* (pp. 277–294). Mahwah, NJ: Lawrence Erlbaum.

Cameron, J. (2002). *The artist's way: A spiritual path to higher creativity.* New York: Tarcher. (Original work published 1992)

Campbell, K. K., & Jamieson, K. H. (1995). Form and genre in rhetorical criticism: An introduction. In C. R. Burgchardt (Ed.), *Readings in rhetorical criticism* (pp. 394–403). State College, PA: Strata Publishing.

Carlson, E. D., Engebretson, J., & Chamberlain, R. M. (2006). Photovoice as a social process of critical consciousness. *Qualitative Health Research, 16,* 836–852.

Carr, J. M. (2003). Poetic expressions of vigilance. *Qualitative Health Research, 13,* 1324–1331.

Caulley, D. N. (2008). Making qualitative research reports less boring: The techniques of writing creative nonfiction. *Qualitative Inquiry, 14,* 424–449.

Chamberlain, K. (2000). Methodolatry and qualitative health research. *Journal of Health Psychology, 5,* 285–296.

Chapman Sanger, P. (2003). Living and writing feminist ethnographies: Threads in a quilt stitched from the heart. In R. P. Clair (Ed.), *Expressions of ethnography: Novel approaches to qualitative methods* (pp. 29–44). Albany: State University of New York Press.

Charlés, L. L. (2007). *Intimate colonialism: Head, heart, and body in West African development work.* Walnut Creek, CA: Left Coast Press.

Charmaz, K. (2000). Grounded theory: Objectivist and constructivist methods. In N. K. Denzin & Y. S. Lincoln (Eds.), *Handbook of qualitative research* (2nd ed., pp. 509–535). Thousand Oaks, CA: Sage.

Charmaz, K. (2005). Grounded theory in the 21st century: A qualitative method for advancing social justice research. In N. K. Denzin & Y. S. Lincoln (Eds.), *Handbook of qualitative research* (3rd ed., pp. 507–535). Thousand Oaks, CA: Sage.

Charmaz, K. (2006). *Constructing grounded theory: A practical guide through qualitative analysis.* Thousand Oaks, CA: Sage.

Charmaz, K. (2007). What's good writing in feminist research? What can feminist researchers learn about good writing? In S. N. Hesse-Biber (Ed.), *Handbook of feminist research: Theory and praxis* (pp. 443–458). Thousand Oaks, CA: Sage.

Charon, R. (2006). *Narrative medicine: Honoring the stories of illness.* New York: Oxford University Press.

Chawla, D. (2006). The bangle seller of Meena Bazaar. *Qualitative Inquiry, 12,* 1135–1138.

Clair, R. P. (2003). The changing story of ethnography. In R. P. Clair (Ed.), *Expressions of ethnography: Novel approaches to qualitative methods* (pp. 3–26). Albany: State University of New York Press.

Clarke, A. (2005). *Situational analysis: Grounded theory after the postmodern turn.* Thousand Oaks, CA: Sage.

Clark/Keefe, K. (2006). Degrees of separation. *Qualitative Inquiry, 12,* 1180–1197.

Clough, P. T. (2000). Comments on setting criteria for experimental writing. *Qualitative Inquiry, 6,* 278–291.

Coffey, A. (1999). *The ethnographic self: Fieldwork and the representation of identity.* London: Sage.

Conquergood, D. (1991). Rethinking ethnography: Towards a critical cultural politics. *Communication Monographs, 38,* 179–194.

Conquergood, D. (1994). Homeboys and hoods: Gang communication and cultural space. In L. R. Frey (Ed.), *Group communication in context: Studies of natural groups* (pp. 23–55). Hillsdale, NJ: Lawrence Erlbaum.

Conquergood, D. (1995). Between rigor and relevance: Rethinking applied communication. In K. N. Cissna (Ed.), *Applied communication in the 21st century* (pp. 79–96). Mahwah, NJ: Lawrence Erlbaum.

Cook, J. A., & Fonow, M. M. (1990). Knowledge and women's interests: Issues of epistemology and methodology in feminist sociological research. In J. M. Nielsen (Ed.), *Feminist research methods: Exemplary readings in social sciences* (pp. 69–92). Boulder, CO: Westview.

Cooper, J. E., Brandon, P. R., & Lindberg, M. A. (1998). Evaluators' use of peer debriefing: Three impressionist tales. *Qualitative Inquiry, 2,* 265–279.

Crabtree, R. D. (1998). Mutual empowerment in cross-cultural participatory development and service learning: Lessons in communication and social justice from projects in El Salvador and Nicaragua. *Journal of Applied Communication Research, 26,* 182–209.

Creswell, J. W., & Clark, V. L. P. (2006). *Designing and conducting mixed methods research.* Thousand Oaks, CA: Sage.

Croft, S. E. (1999). Creating locales through storytelling: An ethnography of a group home for men with mental retardation. *Western Journal of Communication, 63,* 329–347.

Das, S. (2007, February 12). *Writer's block.* Retrieved September 1, 2007, from http://scumis.scu.edu/~srdas/

Davis, A. (1990). *Women, culture, and politics.* New York: Vintage.

Deetz, S. (2001). Conceptual foundations. In F. M. Jablin & L. L. Putnam (Eds.), *The new handbook of organizational communication: Advances in theory, research, and methods* (pp. 3–17). Thousand Oaks, CA: Sage.

Defenbaugh, N. (in press). "Under erasure": The absent "ill" body in doctor-patient dialogue. *Qualitative Inquiry.*

Denzin, N. K. (1997). *Interpretive ethnography: Ethnographic practices for the 21st century.* Thousand Oaks, CA: Sage.

Denzin, N. K. (2000). Aesthetics and the practices of qualitative inquiry. *Qualitative Inquiry, 6,* 256–265.

Denzin, N. K., & Giardina, M. D. (2007). *Ethical futures in qualitative research.* Walnut Creek, CA: Left Coast Press.

Denzin, N. K., & Lincoln, Y. S. (2000). Introduction: The discipline and practice of qualitative research. In N. K. Denzin & Y. S. Lincoln (Eds.), *Handbook of qualitative research* (2nd ed., pp. 1–28). Thousand Oaks, CA: Sage.

Denzin, N. K., & Lincoln, Y. S. (2005). Introduction: The discipline and practice of qualitative research. In N. K. Denzin & Y. S. Lincoln (Eds.), *Handbook of qualitative research* (3rd ed., pp. 1–32). Thousand Oaks, CA: Sage.

DeSantis, A. D. (2002). Smoke screen: An ethnographic study of a cigar shop's collective rationalization. *Health Communication, 14,* 167–198.

Dewey, J. (1980). *Art as experience.* New York: Perigree. (Original work published 1934)

Diamond, T. (1995). *Making gray gold: Narratives of nursing home care.* Chicago: University of Chicago Press.

Dillard, A. (1989, May 28). Write till you drop. *New York Times.* Retrieved May 20, 2007, from http://www.nytimes.com/books/99/03/28/specials/dillard-drop.html

Diversi, M. (1998). Glimpses of street life: Representing lived experience through short stories. *Qualitative Inquiry, 4,* 131–147.

Dossa, P. A. (1999). (Re)imagining again lives: Ethnographic narratives of Muslim women in diaspora. *Journal of Cross-Cultural Gerontology, 14,* 245–272.

Drew, R. (2001). *Karaoke nights: An ethnographic rhapsody.* Walnut Creek, CA: AltaMira Press.

Drew, S. K., Mills, M., & Gassaway, B. M. (2007). *Dirty work: The social construction of taint.* Waco, TX: Baylor University Press.

Dudley, M. J. (2003). Voice, visibility, and transparency: Participatory video as an empowerment tool for Colombian domestic workers. In S. A. White (Ed.), *Video power: Images that transform and empower* (pp. 286–308). Thousand Oaks, CA: Sage.

Duneier, M. (1999). *Sidewalk.* New York: Farrar, Straus and Giroux.

du Pre, A. (2005). *Communicating about health: Current issues and perspectives* (2nd ed.). New York: McGraw-Hill.

Edley, P. P. (2000). Discursive essentializing in a woman-owned business: Gendered stereotypes and strategic subordination. *Management Communication Quarterly, 14,* 271–306.

Ellingson, L. L. (1998). "Then you know how I feel": Empathy, identification, and reflexivity in fieldwork. *Qualitative Inquiry, 4,* 492–514.

Ellingson, L. L. (1999, November). *Voices in my head: Living with the stigmas of impairment and disfigurement.* Paper presented at the meeting of the National Communication Association, Chicago.

Ellingson, L. L. (2002). The roles of companions in the geriatric oncology patient–interdisciplinary health care provider interaction. *Journal of Aging Studies, 16,* 361–382.

Ellingson, L. L. (2003). Interdisciplinary health care teamwork in the clinic backstage. *Journal of Applied Communication Research, 31,* 93–117.

Ellingson, L. L. (2004). Women cancer survivors: Making meaning of chronic illness and alternative medical practices. In P. M. Buzzanell, H. Sterk, & L. Turner (Eds.), *Gender in applied communication contexts* (pp. 79–98). Thousand Oaks, CA: Sage.

Ellingson, L. L. (2005a). *Communicating in the clinic: Negotiating frontstage and backstage teamwork.* Cresskill, NJ: Hampton Press.

Ellingson, L. L. (2005b, November). *Ritual, repetition, and difference: Perceptions of time in a dialysis unit.* Paper presented at the conference of the National Communication Association, Boston.

Ellingson, L. L. (2006a). Embodied knowledge: Writing researchers' bodies into qualitative health research. *Qualitative Health Research, 16,* 298–310.

Ellingson, L. L. (2006b, November). *The performance of professional identity among dialysis technicians: Narratives, technology, and disciplinary discourses.* Paper presented at the conference of the National Communication Association, San Antonio, TX.

Ellingson, L. L. (2007). The performance of dialysis care: Routinization and adaptation on the floor. *Health Communication, 22,* 103–114.

Ellingson, L. L. (2008a). Changing realities and entrenched norms in dialysis: A case study of power, knowledge, and communication in health care delivery. In H. M. Zoller & M. J. Dutta (Eds.), *Emerging perspectives in health communication: Meaning, culture, and power* (pp. 293–312). New York: Routledge.

Ellingson, L. L. (2008b). Communication within the comprehensive geriatric assessment. In K. Wright & S. Moore (Eds.), *Applied health communication: A sourcebook* (pp. 229–254). Cresskill, NJ: Hampton Press.

Ellingson, L. L. (2008c). Patients' inclusion of spirituality within the comprehensive geriatric assessment process. In M. Wills, (Ed.), *Spirituality and health communication* (pp. 67–85). Cresskill, NJ: Hampton Press.

Ellingson, L. L. (in press-a). Embodied knowledge. In L. M. Given (Ed.), *The SAGE encyclopedia of qualitative research methods.* Thousand Oaks, CA: Sage.

Ellingson, L. L. (in press-b). Ethnography in applied communication research. In L. R. Frey & K. Cissna (Eds.), *The handbook of applied communication research.* Mahwah, NJ: Lawrence Erlbaum.

Ellingson, L. L., & Ellis, C. (2008). Autoethnography as constructionist project. In J. A. Holstein & J. F. Gubrium (Eds.), *Handbook of constructionist research* (pp. 445–465). New York: Guilford.

Ellingson, L. L., & Sotirin, P. (2006). Exploring young adults' perspectives on communication with aunts. *Journal of Social and Personal Relationships, 23,* 499–517.

Ellis, C. (1991). Sociological introspection and emotional experience. *Symbolic Interaction, 14,* 23–50.

Ellis, C. (1993). "There are survivors": Telling a story of sudden death. *The Sociological Quarterly, 34,* 711–730.

Ellis, C. (1996). Maternal connections. In C. Ellis & A. Bochner (Eds.), *Composing ethnography* (pp. 240–243). Walnut Creek, CA: AltaMira Press.

Ellis, C. (2000). Creating criteria: An ethnographic short story. *Qualitative Inquiry, 6,* 273–277.

Ellis, C. (2004). *The ethnographic I: A methodological novel about autoethnography.* Walnut Creek, CA: AltaMira Press.

Ellis, C. (in press). *Revisions: Autoethnographic Stories of Life and Work.* Walnut Creek, CA: Left Coast Press.

Ellis, C., & Bochner, A. P. (2000). Autoethnography, personal narrative, reflexivity: Researcher as subject. In N. K. Denzin & Y. S. Lincoln (Eds.), *Handbook of qualitative research* (2nd ed., pp. 733–768). Thousand Oaks, CA: Sage.

Ellis, C., & Bochner, A. P. (2006). Analyzing analytic autoethnography: An autoposy. *Journal of Contemporary Ethnography, 35,* 429–449.

Ellis, C., & Ellingson, L. L. (2000). Qualitative methods. In E. F. Borgatta & R. J. V. Montgomery (Eds.), *Encyclopedia of sociology* (2nd ed., Vol. 4, pp. 2287–2296). New York: Macmillan Library Reference.

Epstein, B. (1997). Postmodernism and the left. *New Politics, 6*(2 new series), Whole No. 22. Retrieved August 20, 2007, from http://www.wpunj.edu/~newpol/issue22/epstei22.htm

Farrell, A., & Geist-Martin, P. (2005). Communicating social health: Perceptions of wellness at work. *Management Communication Quarterly, 18,* 543–592.

Faulkner, S. L. (2007). Concern with craft: Using ars poetica as criteria for reading research poetry. *Qualitative Inquiry, 13,* 218–234.

Ferguson, K. E. (1984). *The feminist case against bureaucracy.* Philadelphia: Temple University Press.

Ferguson, K. E. (1993). *The man question: Visions of subjectivity in feminist theory.* Berkeley: University of California Press.

Fine, M. (1994). Working the hyphens: Reinventing self and other in qualitative research. In N. K. Denzin & Y. S. Lincoln (Eds.), *Handbook of qualitative research* (pp. 70–82). Thousand Oaks, CA: Sage.

Fine, M., Weis, L., Weseen, S., & Wong, L. (2000). For whom? Qualitative research, representation, and social responsibilities. In N. K. Denzin & Y. S. Lincoln (Eds.), *Handbook of qualitative research* (2nd ed., pp. 107–132). Thousand Oaks, CA: Sage.

Finlay, L. (2002). "Outing" the researcher: The provenance, process, and practice of reflexivity. *Qualitative Health Research, 12,* 531–545.

Fisher, J. A. (2007). "Ready-to-recruit" or "ready-to-consent" populations? Informed consent and the limits of subject autonomy. *Qualitative Inquiry, 13,* 875–894.

Fisher, W. R. (1980). Genre: Concepts and application in rhetorical criticism. *Western Journal of Speech Communication, 44,* 288–299.

Fiske, J. (1993). *Power plays, power works.* London: Verso.

Fitch, K. L. (1994). Criteria for evidence in qualitative research. *Western Journal of Communication, 58,* 32–38.

Flaherty, M. G. (2003). Time work: Customizing temporal experience. *Social Psychology Quarterly, 66,* 17–33.

Flannery, M. C. (2001). Quilting: A feminist metaphor for scientific inquiry. *Qualitative Inquiry, 7,* 628–645.

Foucault, M. (1977). *Discipline and punish: The birth of the prison.* New York: Vintage.

Foucault, M. (1979). My body, this paper, this fire. *Oxford Literary Review 4,* 9–28.

Foucault, M. (1980). *Power/knowledge: Selected interviews and other writings, 1972–1977* (C. Gordon, Ed.; C. Gordon, L. Marshall, J. Mepham, & K. Soper, Trans.). New York: Pantheon Books.

Fox, C. H., Brooks, A., Zayas, L. E., McClellan, W., & Murray, B. (2006). Primary care physicians' knowledge and practice patterns in the treatment of chronic kidney disease: An upstate New York practice-based research network (UNYNET) study. *Journal of the American Board of Family Medicine, 19,* 54–61.

Fox, K. V. (1996). Silent voices: A subversive reading of child sexual abuse. In C. Ellis & A. P. Bochner (Eds.), *Composing ethnography: Alternative forms of qualitative writing* (pp. 330–356). Walnut Creek, CA: AltaMira Press.

Frank, A. W. (1995). *The wounded storyteller: Body, illness, and ethics.* Chicago: University of Chicago Press.

Frank, A. W. (2002). Foreword. In R. Gray & C. Shinding, *Standing ovation: Performing social science research about cancer* (pp. vii–x). Walnut Creek, CA: AltaMira Press.

Frank, A. W. (2004). After methods, the story: From incongruity to truth in qualitative research. *Qualitative Health Research, 14,* 430–440.

Frank, A. W. (2005). What is dialogical research, and why should we do it? *Qualitative Health Research, 15,* 964–974.

Frank, K. (2000). The management of hunger: Using fiction in writing anthropology. *Qualitative Inquiry, 6,* 474–488.

Fraser, N. (1990–1991). Rethinking the public sphere: A contribution to the critique of actually existing democracy. *Social Text, 25/26,* 178–182.

Freire, P. (2000). *Pedagogy of the oppressed.* New York: Continuum. [Original work published 1970]

Freire, P. (2002). *Education for critical consciousness.* New York: Continuum. [Original work published 1973]

Frey, L. R. (1998). Communication and social justice research: Truth, justice, and the applied communication way. *Journal of Applied Communication Research, 26,* 155–164.

Frey, L. R., & Carragee, K. M. (2007a). *Communication activism. Vol. 1: Communication for social change.* Cresskill, NJ: Hampton Press.

Frey, L. R., & Carragee, K. M. (2007b). *Communication activism. Vol. 2: Media and performance activism.* Cresskill, NJ: Hampton Press.

Frey, L. R., Pearce, W. B., Pollock, M. A., Artz, L., & Murphy, B. A. O. (1996). Looking for justice in all the wrong places: On a communication approach to social justice. *Communication Studies, 47,* 110–127.

Furman, R. (2006). Poetic forms and structures in qualitative health research. *Qualitative Health Research, 16,* 560–566.

Galloway, T. (2006). Just the funny bits. *Liminalities: A Journal of Performance Studies, 2.3.* Retrieved July 20, 2007, from http://liminalities.net/archives.htm

Geertz. C. (1973). *The interpretation of cultures.* New York: Basic Books.

Geertz, C. (1988). *Works and lives: The anthropologist as author.* Palo Alto, CA: Stanford University Press.

Geist-Martin, P., Carnett, S., & Slauta, K. (2008). Dialectics of doubt and accomplishment: Re-counting what counts in cultural immersion and adaptation. In L. A. Samovar, R. E. Porter, & E. R. McDaniel (Eds.), *Intercultural communication: A reader* (pp. 401–412). Belmont, CA: Wadsworth.

Gergen, K. J. (1994). *Realities and relationships: Soundings in social construction.* Cambridge, MA: Harvard University Press.

Gergen, K. J. (1999). *An invitation to social construction.* Thousand Oaks, CA: Sage.

Gerla, J. P. (1995). An uncommon friendship: Ethnographic fiction around finance equity in Texas. *Qualitative Inquiry, 1,* 168–188.

Gillespie, S. R. (2001). The politics of breathing: Asthmatic Medicaid patients under managed care. *Journal of Applied Communication Research, 29,* 97–116.

Giroux, H. A. (2004). Cultural studies, public pedagogy, and the responsibility of intellectuals. *Communication and Critical/Cultural Studies, 1,* 59–79.

Glaser, B., & Strauss, B. (1967). *The discovery of grounded theory: Strategies for qualitative research.* Chicago: Aldine.

Glesne, C. (1997). That rare feeling: Re-presenting research through poetic transcription. *Qualitative Inquiry, 3,* 202–221.

Goffman, E. (1959). *The presentation of self in everyday life.* Garden City, NY: Doubleday.

Goldberg, N. (1986). *Writing down the bones: Freeing the writer within.* Boston: Shambhala.

González, M. C. (1998). Painting the white face red: Intercultural contact presented through poetic ethnography. In. J. Martin, T. Nakayama, & L. Flores (Eds.), *Readings in cultural contexts* (pp. 485–495). Mountain View, CA: Mayfield.

Goodall, H. L. (2000). *Writing the new ethnography.* Walnut Creek, CA: AltaMira Press.

Gray, R., & Sinding, C. (2002). *Standing ovation: Performing social science research about cancer.* Walnut Creek, CA: AltaMira Press.

Guba, E. C., & Lincoln, Y. S. (1989). *Fourth generation evaluation.* London: Sage.

Guidi, P. (2003). Guatemalan Mayan women and participatory visual media. In S. White (Ed.), *Video power: Images that transform and empower* (pp. 252–270). Thousand Oaks, CA: Sage.

Hacking, I. (1999). *The social construction of what?* Cambridge, MA: Harvard University Press.

Hall, W. A., & Callery, P. (2001). Enhancing the rigor of grounded theory: Incorporating reflexivity and relationality. *Qualitative Health Research, 11,* 257–272.

Haraway, D. (1988). Situated knowledges: The science question in feminism and the privilege of partial perspective. *Feminist Studies, 14,* 575–599.

Harding, S. (1987). Introduction: Is there a feminist method? In S. Harding (Ed.), *Feminism and methodology* (pp. 1–14). Bloomington: Indiana University Press.

Harding, S. (1991). *Whose science? Whose knowledge? Thinking from women's lives.* Ithaca, NY: Cornell University Press.

Harding, S. (1993). Rethinking standpoint epistemology: What is "strong objectivity"? In L. Alcoff & E. Potter (Eds.), *Feminist epistemologies* (pp. 49–82). New York: Routledge.

Harris, S. R. (2006). Social construction and social inequality: An introduction to a special issue of *JCE. Journal of Contemporary Ethnography, 35,* 223–235.

Harter, L. M., Japp, P. M., & Beck, C. (Eds.). (2005). *Narratives, health, and healing: Communication theory, research, and practice.* Mahwah, NJ: Lawrence Erlbaum.

Harter, L. M., Norander, S., & Quinlan, M. M. (2007). Imaginative renderings in the service of renewal and reconstruction. *Management Communication Quarterly, 21,* 105–117.

Harter, L. M., Norander, S., & Young, S. (2005). *Cultivating connections between self and other.* Retrieved July 20, 2007, from http://www.passionworks.org/articles/collaborative-art.php

Harter, L. M., Scott, J., Novak, D., Leeman, M., & Morris, J. (2006). Freedom through flight: Performing a counter-narrative of disability. *Journal of Applied Communication Research, 34,* 3–29.

Hartnett, S. (1998). Lincoln and Douglas meet the abolitionist David Walker as prisoners debate slavery: Empowering education, applied communication, and social justice. *Journal of Applied Communication Research, 26,* 232–253.

Hartnett, S. J. (2003). *Incarceration nation: Investigative prison poems of hope and terror.* Walnut Creek, CA: AltaMira Press.

Hartsock, N. C. M. (1998). *The feminist standpoint revisited and other essays.* Boulder, CO: Westview Press.

Haskins, E. V. (2003). Embracing the superficial: Michael Calvin McGee, rhetoric, and the postmodern condition. *American Journal of Communication, 6*(4). Retrieved September 20, 2007, from http://www.acjournal.org/holdings/vol6/iss4/mcmcgee/haskins.htm

Hay, L., & Seeger, P. (1958). If I had a hammer [Recorded by P. Seeger]. On *if I had a hammer: Songs of hope and struggle* [CD]. Washington, DC: Smithsonian Folkways.

Hesse-Biber, S. N. (Ed.). (2007). *Handbook of feminist research: Theory and praxis.* Thousand Oaks, CA: Sage.

Hesse-Biber, S. N., & Brooks, A. (2007). Core feminist insights and strategies on authority, representations, truths, reflexivity, and ethics across the research process. In S. N. Hesse-Biber (Ed.), *Handbook of feminist research: Theory and praxis* (pp. 419–424). Thousand Oaks, CA: Sage.

Hirschmann, K. (1999). Blood, vomit, and communication: The days and nights of an intern on call. *Health Communication, 11*, 35–57.

Hochschild, A. R. (1983). *The managed heart.* Berkeley: University of California Press.

Holstein, J. A., & Gubrium, J. F. (2008). *Handbook of constructionist research.* New York: Guilford.

hooks, b. (1994). *Teaching to transgress: Education as the practice of freedom.* New York: Routledge.

Howard, L. A., & Geist, P. (1995). Ideological positioning in organizational change: The dialectic of control in a merging organization. *Communication Monographs, 62*, 110–131.

Hunter, A., Lusardi, P., Zuker, D., Jacelon, C., & Chandler, G. (2002). Making meaning: The creative component in qualitative research. *Qualitative Health Research, 12*, 388–398.

Irigaray, L. (1985). *This sex which is not one* (C. Porter & C. Burke, Trans.). Ithaca, NY: Cornell University Press.

Jago, B. (2006). A primary act of imagination: An autoethnography of father-absence. *Qualitative Inquiry, 12*, 398–426.

James, W. (1907). *Pragmatism, a new name for some old ways of thinking: Popular lectures on philosophy.* New York: Longmans, Green.

Jamieson, K. H., & Campbell, K. K. (1982). Rhetorical hybrids: Fusions of generic elements. *Quarterly Journal of Speech, 68*, 146–157.

Janesick, V. J. (2000). The choreography of qualitative research design: Minuets, improvisations, and crystallization. In N. K. Denzin & Y. S. Lincoln (Eds.), *Handbook of qualitative research* (2nd ed., pp. 379–399). Thousand Oaks, CA: Sage.

Janesick, V. J. (2003). *Stretching exercises for qualitative researchers.* Thousand Oaks, CA: Sage.

Jenks, E. B. (2005). Explaining disability: Parents' stories of raising children with visual impairments in a sighted world. *Journal of Contemporary Ethnography, 34*, 143–170.

Jung, C. G. (1973). *Synchronicity: An acausal connecting principle* (R. F. C. Hull, Trans.). Princeton, NJ: Princeton University Press.

Kemmis, S., & McTaggart, R. (2005). Participatory action research: Communicative action and the public sphere. In N. K. Denzin & Y. S. Lincoln (Eds.), *Handbook of qualitative research* (3rd ed., pp. 559–604). Thousand Oaks, CA: Sage.

Kiesinger, C. (2002). My father's shoes: The therapeutic value of narrative reframing. In A. Bochner & C. Ellis (Eds.), *Ethnographically speaking: Autoethnography, literature, and aesthetics* (pp. 95–114). Walnut Creek, CA: AltaMira Press.

King, S. (2000). *On writing.* New York: Scribner.

Knaus, C. S., Pinkleton, B. E., & Austin, E. W. (2000). The ability of the AIDS Quilt to motivate information seeking, personal discussion, and preventative behavior as a health communication intervention. *Health Communication, 12,* 301–316.

Kontos, P. C., & Naglie, G. (2007). Expressions of personhood in Alzheimer's disease: An evaluation of research-based theatre as a pedagogical tool. *Qualitative Health Research, 17,* 799–811.

Kramarae, C., & Treichler, P. A. (1985). *A feminist dictionary.* London: Rivers Oram Press/Pandora List.

Krieger, S. (1991). *Social science and the self: Personal essays on an art form.* Brunswick, NJ: Rutgers University Press.

Kwok, C., & Sullivan, G. (2007). Health seeking behaviours among Chinese-Australian women: Implications for health promotion programmes. *Health, 11,* 401–415.

Lammers, J. C., & Krikorian, D. H. (1997). Theoretical extension and operationalization of the bona fide group construct with an application to surgical teams. *Journal of Applied Communication Research, 25,* 17–38.

Lamott, A. (1995). *Bird by bird: Some instructions on writing and life.* New York: Anchor Books.

Larsen, E. A. (2006). A vicious oval. *Journal of Contemporary Ethnography, 35,* 119–147.

Lather, P. (1991). *Getting smart: Feminist research and pedagogy with/in the postmodern.* New York: Routledge.

Lather, P. (1993). Fertile obsession: Validity after poststructuralism. *Sociological Quarterly, 34,* 673–693.

Lather, P., & Smithies, C. (1997). *Troubling the angels: Women living with HIV/AIDS.* Boulder, CO: Westview Press.

Lee, K. V. (2006). A fugue about grief. *Qualitative Inquiry, 12,* 1154–1159.

Lesch, C. L. (1994). Observing theory in practice: Sustaining consciousness in a coven. In L. R. Frey (Ed.), *Group communication in context: Studies of natural groups* (pp. 57–82). Hillsdale, NJ: Lawrence Erlbaum.

LeShan, L. (1974). *How to meditate: A guide to self-discovery.* Boston: Little, Brown.

Lewin, K. (1951). *Field theory in social science: Selected theoretical papers.* New York: Harper & Row.

Libbrecht, K. G. (2003). *The snowflake: Winter's secret beauty.* New York: Voyageur Press.

Lieblich, A. (2006). Vicissitudes: A study, a book, a play: Lessons from the work of a narrative scholar. *Qualitative Inquiry, 12,* 60–80.

Lindemann, K. (2007). A tough sell: Stigma as souvenir in the contested performances of San Francisco's homeless *Street Sheet* vendors. *Text and Performance Quarterly, 27,* 41–57.

Lindemann, K. (2008). "I can't be standing up out there": Communicative performances of (dis)ability in wheelchair rugby. *Text and Performance Quarterly, 28,* 98–115.

Lindlof, T. R., & Taylor, B. C. (2002). *Qualitative communication research methods* (2nd ed.). Thousand Oaks, CA: Sage.

Lofland, J. (1970). Interactionist imagery and analytic interruptus. In T. Shibutani (Ed.), *Human nature and collective behavior: Papers in honor of Herbert Blumer* (pp. 35–45). New Brunswick, NJ: Transaction Books.

López, E., Eng, E., Randall-David, E., & Robinson, N. (2005). Quality of life concerns of African American breast cancer survivors within rural North Carolina: Blending the techniques of photovoice and grounded theory. *Qualitative Health Research, 15,* 99–115.

Lykes, M. B., & Coquillon, E. (2007). Participatory and action research and feminisms: Towards transformative praxis. In S. Hesse-Biber (Ed.), *Handbook of feminist research: Theory and praxis* (pp. 297–326). Thousand Oaks, CA: Sage.

Macbeth, D. (2001). On "reflexivity" in qualitative research: Two readings and a third. *Qualitative Inquiry, 7,* 35–68.

Madison, D. S. (2005). *Critical ethnography: Method, ethics, and performance.* Thousand Oaks, CA: Sage.

Magnet, S. (2006). Protesting privilege: An autoethnographic look at whiteness. *Qualitative Inquiry, 12,* 736–749.

Magolda, P. M. (1999). Mystories about alternative discourses in a qualitative inquiry seminar. *Qualitative Inquiry, 5,* 208–243.

Makau, J. M. (1996). Notes on communication education and social justice. *Communication Studies, 47,* 135–141.

Markham, A. N. (2005). "Go ugly early": Fragmented narrative and bricolage as interpretive method. *Qualitative Inquiry, 11,* 813–839.

McAllister, C. L., Wilson, P. C., Green, B. L., & Baldwin, J. L. (2005). "Come and take a walk": Listening to early head start parents on school-readiness as a matter of child, family, and community health. *American Journal of Public Health, 95,* 617–625.

McIntosh, P. (1988). *White privilege and male privilege: A personal account of coming to see correspondences through work in women's studies* (Working Paper No. 189). Needham, MA: Wellesley College.

McLaughlin, E. W. (2004). Quiltmaking as living metaphor: A study of the African AIDS Quilt as a visual parable of the peaceable kingdom. *Journal of Communication and Religion, 27,* 141–168.

Meyer, M. (2004). From transgression to transformation: Negotiating the opportunities and tensions of engaged pedagogy in the feminist organizational communication classroom. In P. M. Buzzanell, H. Sterk, & L. H. Turner (Eds.), *Gender in applied communication contexts* (pp. 195–213). Thousand Oaks, CA: Sage.

Meyer, M., & O'Hara, L. S. (2004). When they know who we are: The national women's music festival comes to Ball State University. In P. M. Buzzanell, H. Sterk, & L. H. Turner (Eds.), *Gender in applied communication contexts* (pp. 3–23). Thousand Oaks, CA: Sage.

Mienczakowski, J. (1996). An ethnographic act: The construction of consensual theatre. In C. Ellis & A. P. Bochner (Eds.), *Composing ethnography: Alternative forms of qualitative writing* (pp. 244–264). Walnut Creek, CA: AltaMira Press.

Mienczakowski, J. (2001). Ethnodrama: Performed research: Limitations and potential. In P. Atkinson, A. Coffey, S. Delamont, J. Lofland, & L. Lofland (Eds.), *Handbook of ethnography* (pp. 468–476). Thousand Oaks, CA: Sage.

Mies, M. (1983). Towards a methodology for feminist research. In G. Bowles & R. D. Klein (Eds.), *Theories of women's studies* (pp. 117–138). London: Routledge.

Miller, D. L., Creswell, J. W., & Olander, L. S. (1998). Writing and retelling multiple ethnographic tales of a soup kitchen for the homeless. *Qualitative Inquiry, 4,* 469–491.

Miller, K. I. (2000). Common ground from the post-positivist perspective: From "straw-person" argument to collaborative coexistence. In S. R. Corman & M. S. Poole (Eds.), *Perspectives on organizational communication: Finding common ground* (pp. 47–67). New York: Guilford Press.

Miller, M. (1995). An intergenerational case study of suicidal tradition and mother-daughter communication. *Journal of Applied Communication Research, 23,* 247–270.

Miller, M. Z., Geist-Martin, P., & Beatty, K. C. (2005). Wholeness in a breaking world: Narratives as sustenance for peace. In L. M. Harter, P. M. Japp, & C. S. Beck (Eds.), *Narratives, health, and healing: Communication theory, research, and practice* (pp. 295–316). Mahwah, NJ: Lawrence Erlbaum.

Miller, W. L., & Crabtree, B. F. (1999). Clinical research: A multimethod typology and qualitative roadmap. In B. F. Crabtree & W. L. Miller (Eds.), *Doing qualitative research* (pp. 3–30). Thousand Oaks, CA: Sage.

Miller-Day, M. (2005). *HOMEwork: An ethnodrama.* Retrieved June 20, 2007 from http://cas.la.psu.edu/research/maternal/homework.html

Miller-Day, M. (in press). Performance matters. *Qualitative Inquiry.*

Miller-Day, M., & Dodd, A. H. (2004). Toward a descriptive model of parent–offspring communication about alcohol and other drugs. *Journal of Social and Personal Relationships, 21,* 69–91.

Minge, J. M. (2007). The stained body: A fusion of embodied art on rape and love. *Journal of Contemporary Ethnography, 36,* 252–280.

Minow, M. (1990). *Making all the difference: Inclusion, exclusion and the American law.* Ithaca, NY: Cornell University Press.

Mishler, E. G. (1986). *Research interviewing: Context and narrative.* Cambridge, MA: Harvard University Press.

Mishler, E. G. (1991). Representing discourse: The rhetoric of transcription. *Journal of Narrative and Life History, 1,* 255–280.

Montemurro, B. (2005). Add men, don't stir. *Journal of Contemporary Ethnography, 34,* 6–35.

Morgan, J. M., & Krone, K. J. (2001). Bending the rules of "professional" display: Emotional improvisation in caregiver performance. *Journal of Applied Communication Research, 29,* 317–340.

Morse, J. M. (2004). Alternative modes of representation: There are no shortcuts. *Qualitative Health Research, 14,* 887–888.

Morse, J. M. (2005). What is qualitative research? *Qualitative Health Research, 15,* 859–860.

Morse, J. M. (2006). The politics of evidence. *Qualitative Health Research, 16,* 395–404.

Morse, J. M., & Field, P. A. (1995). *Qualitative research methods for health professionals* (2nd ed.). Thousand Oaks, CA: Sage.

Morse, J. M., & Richards, L. (2002). *Read-me first for a user's guide to qualitative methods.* Thousand Oaks, CA: Sage.

Murphy, A. G. (2001). The fight attendant dilemma: An analysis of communication and sensemaking during in-flight emergencies. *Journal of Applied Communication Research, 29,* 30–53.

Nakayama, T. K., & Krizek, R. L. (1995). Whiteness: A strategic rhetoric. *Quarterly Journal of Speech, 81,* 291–309.

Nielsen, J. M. (1990). Introduction. In J. M. Nielsen (Ed.), *Feminist research methods: Exemplary readings in the social sciences* (pp. 1–34). Boulder, CO: Westview.

Neufeld, C. (1999). Speakerly women and scribal men. *Oral Tradition, 14,* 420–429.

Novak, D. R., & Harter, L. M. (2005, June 14–18). Blues fest showcase world's best. *StreetWise,* pp. 1–2.

Novek, E. M. (1995). West Urbania: An ethnographic study of communication practices in inner-city youth culture. *Communication Studies, 46,* 169–186.

Nowell, B. L., Berkowitz, S. L., Deacon, Z., & Foster-Fishman, P. (2006). Revealing the cues within community places: Stories of identity, history, and possibility. *American Journal of Community Psychology, 37,* 29–46.

Ong, W. (1982). *Orality and literacy: The technologizing of the world.* New York: Metheun.

Owen, W. F. (1984). Interpretive themes in relational communication. *Quarterly Journal of Speech, 70,* 274–287.

Papa, M. J., & Singhal, A. (2007). Intellectuals searching for publics: Who is out there? *Management Communication Quarterly, 21,* 126–136.

Parachin, J. W. (1999). *Engaged spirituality.* St. Louis, MO: Chalice Press.

Parry, D. C. (2004). Understanding women's lived experiences with infertility: Five short stories. *Qualitative Inquiry, 10,* 909–922.

Parry, D. C. (2006). Women's lived experiences with pregnancy and midwifery in a medicalized and fetocentric context: Six short stories. *Qualitative Inquiry, 12,* 459–471.

Pearce, W. B. (1998). On putting social justice in the discipline of communication and putting enriched concepts of communication in social justice research and practice. *Journal of Applied Communication Research, 26,* 272–278.

Perry, L. A. M., & Geist, P. (1997). *Courage of conviction: Women's words, women's wisdom.* Mountain View, CA: Mayfield.

Polaschek, N. (2003). Negotiated care: A model for nursing work in the renal setting. *Journal of Advanced Nursing, 42,* 355–363.

Potter, W. J. (1996). *An analysis of thinking and research about qualitative methods.* Mahwah, NJ: Lawrence Erlbaum.

Preissle, J. (2007). Feminist research ethics. In S. N. Hesse-Biber (Ed.), *Handbook of feminist research: Theory and praxis* (pp. 515–532). Thousand Oaks, CA: Sage.

Prendergast, M. (2007). Thinking narrative (on the Vancouver Island ferry): A hybrid poem. *Qualitative Inquiry, 13,* 743.

Prose, F. (2006). *Reading like a writer: A guide for people who love books and for those who want to write them.* New York: HarperCollins.

Putnam, L. L., & Stohl, C. (1990). Bona fide groups: A reconceptualization of groups in context. *Communication Studies, 41,* 248–265.

Radner, G. (1989). *It's always something.* New York: Simon & Schuster.

Rambo, C. (2005). Impressions of Grandmother: An autoethnographic portrait. *Journal of Contemporary Ethnography, 34,* 560–585.

Rambo, C. (2007). Handing IRB an unloaded gun. *Qualitative Inquiry, 13,* 353–416.

Rawlins, W. K. (2007). Living scholarship: A field report. *Communication Methods and Measures, 1,* 55–63.

Reinharz, S. (1992). *Feminist methods in social research.* New York: Oxford University Press.

Richardson, L. (1992a). The consequences of poetic representation: Writing the other, rewriting the self. In C. Ellis & M. G. Flaherty (Eds.), *Investigating subjectivity: Research on lived experience* (pp. 125–140). Thousand Oaks, CA: Sage.

Richardson, L. (1992b). The poetic representation of lives: Writing a postmodern sociology. *Studies in Symbolic Interaction, 13,* 19–29.

Richardson, L. (1993). Poetics, dramatics, and transgressive validity: The case of the skipped line. *Sociological Quarterly, 35,* 695–710.

Richardson, L. (1994). Writing: A method of inquiry. In N. K. Denzin & Y. S. Lincoln (Eds.), *Handbook of qualitative research* (pp. 516–529). Thousand Oaks, CA: Sage.

Richardson, L. (1997). *Fields of play: Constructing an academic life.* New Brunswick, NJ: Rutgers University Press.

Richardson, L. (2000a). Special focus: Assessing alternative modes of qualitative and ethnographic research: How do we judge? Who judges? *Qualitative Inquiry, 6,* 251–252.

Richardson, L. (2000b). Writing: A method of inquiry. In N. K. Denzin & Y. S. Lincoln (Eds.), *Handbook of qualitative research* (2nd ed., pp. 923–943). Thousand Oaks, CA: Sage.

Richardson, L. (2007). *Last writes: A daybook for a dying friend.* Walnut Creek, CA: Left Coast Press.

Richardson, L., & Lockridge, E. (2004). *Travels with Ernest: Crossing the ethnographic-literary divide.* Walnut Creek, CA: AltaMira Press.

Richardson, L., & St. Pierre, E. A. (2005). Writing: A method of inquiry. In N. Denzin & Y. Lincoln (Eds.), *Handbook of qualitative inquiry* (3rd ed., pp. 959–978). Thousand Oaks, CA: Sage.

Rinehart, R. (1998). Fictional methods in ethnography: Believability, specks of glass, and Chekhov. *Qualitative Inquiry, 4,* 200–225.

Ronai, C. (1995). Multiple reflections on childhood sex abuse: An argument for a layered account. *Journal of Contemporary Ethnography, 23,* 395–426.

Ronai, C. R. (1999). The next night sous rature: Wrestling with Derrida's mimesis. *Qualitative Inquiry, 5,* 114–129.

Roof, J. (2007). Authority and representation in feminist research. In S. N. Hesse-Biber (Ed.), *Handbook of feminist research: Theory and praxis* (pp. 425–442). Thousand Oaks, CA: Sage.

Rose, G. (1999). Women and everyday spaces. In J. Price & M. Shildrick (Eds.), *Feminist theory and the body: A reader* (pp. 359–370). New York: Routledge.

Ross, J. L., & Geist, P. (1997). Elation and devastation: Women's journeys through pregnancy and miscarriage. In L. A. M. Perry & P. Geist (Eds.), *Courage of conviction: Women's words, women's wisdom* (pp. 167–184). Mountain View, CA: Mayfield.

Ryan, C., Carragee, K. M., & Schwerner, C. (1998). Media, movements, and the quest for social justice. *Journal of Applied Communication Research, 26,* 165–181.

Saarnivaara, M. (2003). Art as inquiry: The autopsy of an [art] experience. *Qualitative Inquiry, 9,* 580–602.

Sacks, J. L., & Nelson, J. P. (2007). A theory of nonphysical suffering and trust in hospice patients. *Qualitative Health Research, 17,* 675–689.

Sandelowski, M. (1994). The proof is in the pottery: Toward a poetic for qualitative inquiry. In J. Morse (Ed.), *Critical issues in qualitative research* (pp. 46–63). Thousand Oaks, CA: Sage.

Sandelowski, M., Trimble, F., Woodard, E. K., & Barroso, J. (2006). From synthesis to script: Transforming qualitative research findings for use in practice. *Qualitative Health Research, 16,* 1350–1370.

Sandgren, A., Thulesius, H., Fridlund, B., & Petersson, K. (2006). Striving for emotional survival in palliative cancer nursing. *Qualitative Health Research, 16,* 79–96.

Santoro, P. (2004). *Lenses.* Retrieved July 20, 2007, from http://www.videoart.net/home/Artists/VideoPage.cfm?Artist_ID=1286&ArtWork_ID=1872&Player_ID=4

Scott, J. W. (1991). The evidence of experience. *Critical Inquiry, 17,* 773–797.

Secklin, P. L. (2001). Multiple fractures in time: Reflections on a car crash. *Journal of Loss and Trauma, 6,* 323–333.

Sedgwick, E. K. (1990). *Epistemology of the closet.* Berkeley: University of California Press.

Shaw, M., & Adelman, M. (Directors). (2001). *Beyond consumption: Retail at the edge* [film]. (Available from Mara Adelman, Dept. of Communication, Seattle University, 900 Broadway, Seattle, WA 98122)

Shear, M. (1986). Media watch: Celebrating women's words. *New Directions for Women, 15,* 6.

Siegel, T., & Conquergood, D. (Producers). (1985). *Between two worlds: The Hmong Shaman in America* [film]. Chicago: Siegel Productions.

Siegel, T., & Conquergood, D. (Producers). (1990). *The heart broken in half* [film]. Chicago: Siegel Productions.

Simmonds, F. N. (1999). My body, myself: How does a black woman do sociology? In J. Price & M. Shildrick (Eds.), *Feminist theory and the body: A reader* (pp. 50–63). New York: Routledge.

Singhal, A., Harter, L. M., Chitnis, K., & Sharma, D. (2007). Participatory photography as theory, method and praxis: Analyzing an entertainment-education project in India. *Critical Arts, 21,* 212–227.

Singhal, A., & Rattine-Flaherty, E. (2006). Pencils and photos as tools of communicative research and praxis: Analyzing Minga Perú's quest for social justice in the Amazon. *The International Communication Gazette, 68,* 313–330.

Sorkin, A. (2002, March 27). The U. S. Poet Laureate [Television series episode]. In C. Misiano (Director), *The West Wing.* New York: National Broadcasting Company.

Sotirin, P., & Ellingson, L. L. (2006). The "other" woman in family life: Aunt/niece/nephew communication. In K. Floyd & M. Morman (Eds.), *Widening the family circle: New research on family communication* (pp. 81–99). Thousand Oaks, CA: Sage.

Sotirin, P., & Ellingson, L. L. (2007). Rearticulating the aunt: Feminist alternatives of family, care, kinship, and agency in popular performances of aunting. *Cultural Studies <=> Critical Methodologies, 7,* 442–459.

Spitzack, C., & Carter, K. (1989). Research of women's communication: The politics of theory and method. In K. Carter & C. Spitzack (Eds.), *Doing research on women's communication: The politics of theory and method* (pp. 11–39). Norwood, NJ: Ablex.

Spivak, G. C. (1988). Can the subaltern speak? In C. Nelson & L. Grossberg (Eds.), *Marxism and the interpretation of culture* (pp. 271–313). Urbana: University of Illinois Press.

Spry, T. (1997). Skins: A daughter's (re)construction of cancer. *Text and Performance Quarterly, 17,* 361–365.

Spry, T. (2001). Performing autoethnography: An embodied methodological praxis. *Qualitative Inquiry, 7,* 706–732.

Stack, C. (1974). *All our kin.* New York: BasicBooks.

Stack, C. (1997). *Call to home: African Americans reclaim the rural South.* New York: Perseus.

Strauss, A., & Corbin, J. (1990). *Basics of qualitative research: Grounded theory procedures and techniques.* Thousand Oaks, CA: Sage.

Strauss, A., & Corbin, J. (1998). *Basics of qualitative research: Techniques and procedures for developing grounded theory* (2nd ed.). Thousand Oaks, CA: Sage.

Stronach, I., Garratt, D., Pearce, C., & Piper, H. (2007). Reflexivity, the picturing of selves, the forging of method. *Qualitative Inquiry, 13,* 179–203.

SunWolf. (2006, June). Juror stress: New challenges to juror competency. *The Champion, 30*(5), 10–15.

SunWolf. (2007). *Practical jury dynamics2.* New York: LexisNexis.

Sunwolf & Seibold, D. R. (1998). Jurors' intuitive rules for deliberation: A structurational approach to communication in jury decision making. *Communication Monographs, 64,* 282–307.

Suzuki, S. (1973). *Zen mind, beginner's mind.* New York: Weatherhill.

Teram, E., Schachter, C. L., & Stalker, C. A. (2005). The case for integrating grounded theory in participatory action research: Empowering clients to inform professional practice. *Qualitative Health Research, 15,* 1129–1140.

Thomson, R. G. (1997). *Extraordinary bodies: Figuring physical disability in American culture and literature.* New York: Columbia University Press.

Thorp, L. (2006). *Pull of the earth: Participatory ethnography in the school garden.* Walnut Creek: AltaMira Press.

Tillmann-Healy, L. (2001). *Between gay and straight: Understanding friendship across sexual orientation.* Walnut Creek, CA: AltaMira Press.

Tompkins, P. K. (1994). Principles of rigor for assessing evidence in "qualitative" communication research. *Western Journal of Communication, 58,* 44–50.

Townsley, N. C., & Geist, P. (2000). The discursive enactment of hegemony: Sexual harassment and academic organizing. *Western Journal of Communication, 64,* 190–217.

Tracy, S. J. (2000). Becoming a character for commerce: Emotion labor, self subordination and discursive construction of identity in a total institution. *Management Communication Quarterly, 14,* 90–128.

Tracy, S. J. (2002). When questioning turns to face threat: An interactional sensitivity in 911 call-taking. *Western Journal of Communication, 66,* 129–157.

Tracy, S. J. (2003, February 7–9). *Navigating the Cruise—A trigger script ethnodrama.* Tempe: Arizona State University, Empty Space Theater, The Hugh Downs School of Human Communication.

Tracy, S. J. (2004a). The construction of correctional officers: Layers of emotionality behind bars. *Qualitative Inquiry, 10,* 509–533.

Tracy, S. J. (2004b). Dialectic, contradiction, or double bind? Analyzing and theorizing employee reactions to organizational tension. *Journal of Applied Communication Research, 2,* 119–146.

Tracy, S. J. (2006). Navigating the limits of a smile: Emotion labor and concertive control on a cruise ship. In J. Keyton & P. Shockley-Zalabak (Eds.), *Case studies for organizational communication: Understanding communication processes,*

(2nd ed., pp. 394–407). Los Angeles: Roxbury Publishing [reprinted from first edition, 2003, p. 374–388].

Tracy, S. J., & Trethewey, A. (2005). Fracturing the real-self ←→ fake-self dichotomy: Moving toward "crystallized" organizational discourses and identities. *Communication Theory, 15,* 168–195.

Trujillo, N. (2004). *In search of Naunny's grave: Age, class, gender and ethnicity in an American family.* Walnut Creek, CA: AltaMira Press.

Underwood, C., & Jabre, B. (2003). Arab women speak out: Strategies for self-empowerment. In S. White (Ed.), *Video power: Images that transform and empower* (pp. 235–251). Thousand Oaks, CA: Sage.

Van Maanen, J. (1988). *Tales of the field.* Chicago: University of Chicago Press.

Varallo, S. M., Ray, E. B., & Ellis, B. H. (1998). Speaking of incest: The research interview as social justice. *Journal of Applied Communication Research, 26,* 254–271.

Veatch, R. M. (1995). Abandoning informed consent. *Hastings Center Report, 25*(2), 5–12.

Walker, D., & Curry, E. (2007). Narrative as communication activism: Research relationships in social justice projects. In L. Frey & K. Carragee (Eds.), *Communication activism* (pp. 345–370). Cresskill, NJ: Hampton Press.

Walkerdine, V. (1990). *Schoolgirl fictions.* London: Verso.

Wang, C., & Burris, M. (1994). Empowerment through photo novella: Portraits of participation. *Health Education Quarterly, 21,* 171–186.

Wang, C. C. (1999). Photovoice: A participatory action research strategy applied to women's health. *Journal of Women's Health, 8,* 185–192.

Warren, C. A. B., & Karner, T. X. (2005). *Discovering qualitative methods: Field research, interviews, and analysis.* Los Angeles: Roxbury.

Warren, J. T. (2001). Doing whiteness: On the performative dimensions of race in the classroom. *Communication Education, 50,* 91–108.

Warren, K. (1994). *Ecological feminism.* New York: Routledge.

Wear, D. (1997). *Privilege in the medical academy: A feminist examines gender, race, and power.* New York: Teachers College Press.

Wheeler, S. (2006). *The making of Sandrah's thesis.* Retrieved November 30, 2007, from http://www.youtube.com/watch?v=F16X_AoVd9I

White, S. A. (2003). Introduction: Video power. In S. A. White (Ed.), *Participatory video: Images that transform and empower* (pp. 17–30). Thousand Oaks, CA: Sage.

Williams, M. (1994). A reconceptualization of protest rhetoric: Women's quilts as rhetorical forms. *Women's Studies in Communication, 17,* 20–44.

Willis, P. (2002). Poetry and poetics in phenomenological research. *Indo-Pacific Journal of Phenomenology, 3*(1), 1–19.

Wilson, H. S., Hutchinson, S. A., & Holzemer, W. L. (2002). Reconciling incompatibilities: A grounded theory of HIV medication adherence and symptom management. *Qualitative Health Research, 12,* 1309–1322.

Wolf, D. L. (1996). Situating feminist dilemmas in fieldwork. In D. L. Wolf (Ed.), *Feminist dilemmas in fieldwork* (pp. 1–55), Boulder, CO: Westview Press.

Wolf, M. (1992). *A thrice told tale: Feminism, postmodernism, and ethnographic responsibility.* Stanford, CA: Stanford University Press.

Wood, J. T. (1996). Social justice research: Alive and well in the field of Communication. *Communication Studies, 47,* 128–134.

Wood, J. T. (2008). *Gendered lives: Communication, gender, and culture* (8th ed.). Belmont, CA: Wadsworth.

Wright, K. (1997). Shared ideology in Alcoholics Anonymous: A grounded theory approach. *Journal of Health Communication, 2,* 83–99.

Zimmerman, A. L., & Geist-Martin, P. (2006). The hybrid identities of gender queer: Claiming neither/nor, both/and. In L. A. Samovar, R. E. Porter, & E. R. McDaniel (Eds.), *Intercultural communication: A reader* (pp. 76–82). Belmont, CA: Wadsworth.

Zoller, H. M. (2003). Health on the line: Identity and disciplinary control in employee occupational health and safety discourse. *Journal of Applied Communication Research, 31,* 118–139.

INDEX

ABOUT THE AUTHOR

Laura L. Ellingson, PhD, is associate professor of communication at Santa Clara University. Her research focuses on feminist theory and gender studies, qualitative methodology, and communication in health care organizations, including interdisciplinary communication, teamwork, and provider–patient communication. She is the author of *Communicating in the Clinic: Negotiating Frontstage and Backstage Teamwork* (2005) and has published articles in *Health Communication, Journal of Aging Studies, Journal of Applied Communication Research, Qualitative Health Research, Women's Studies in Communication,* and *Journal of Social and Personal Relationships.* Currently, she is conducting an ethnography of communication in a dialysis clinic and a qualitative study with Dr. Patty Sotirin (Michigan Technological University) of communication between aunts and their nieces/nephews.